CATTERY DESIGN
The Essential Guide
to Creating Your Perfect Cattery
DAVID KEY

Cattery Design - The Essential Guide to Creating Your Perfect Cattery
by David Key

ISBN: 0-9538002-1-0

First edition May 2006 by David Key

Publisher: David Key

David & Kay Key
Kennel & Cattery Design
PO Box 146, Chipping Norton
Oxfordshire OX7 6WA, UK
+44 (0)1608 646454
www.catterydesign.com
www.kenneldesign.com

Whilst every care has been exercised in compiling the information shown in this book, the author does not accept any liability due to reliance placed on the information given.

Printed and bound by:

Cambridge University Press
University Printing House
Shaftesbury Road
Cambridge CB2 2BS
United Kingdom

Photographs:

Front cover photograph Jupiter Images
Book cat and cattery photographs David & Kay Key
Cat stock images by Istockphoto and Bigstockphoto
Contributing photographers where shown

CATTERY DESIGN

The Essential Guide
to Creating your Perfect Cattery

DAVID KEY

DEDICATION

This book is dedicated to:
the experts who are involved in increasing
our understanding of cat welfare,

the pioneering people already providing
caring and quality accommodation for cats,

and especially to those thinking about setting up a cattery,
we hope this book inspires you!

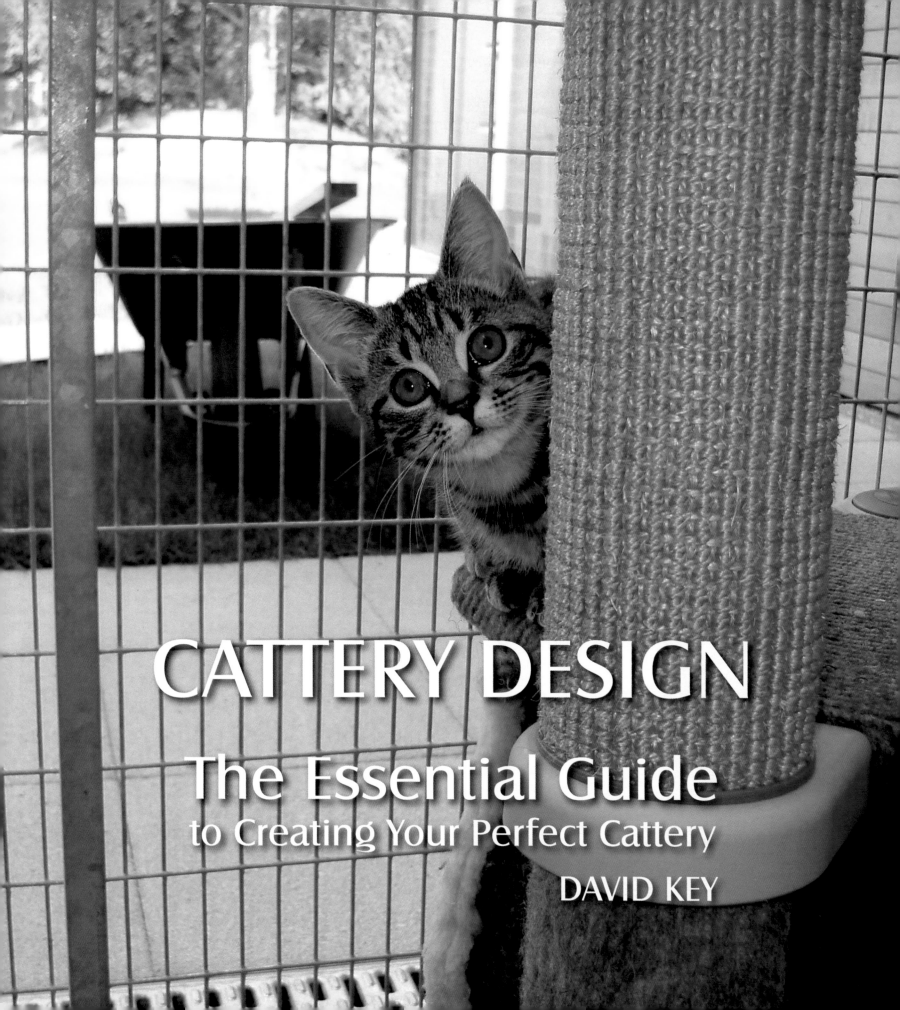

CATTERY DESIGN

The Essential Guide
to Creating Your Perfect Cattery

DAVID KEY

CONTENTS

CONTENTS

CONTENTS

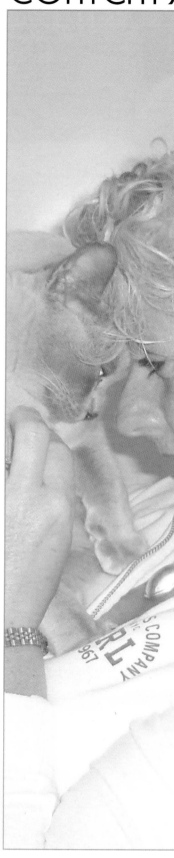

CONTENTS

Foreword by Helen Ralston
Chief Executive of Cats Protection

For thousands of years, the relationship between people and cats has been celebrated throughout the world – from ancient times when cats were seen as mystical creatures to be honoured and sometimes feared… to the present day when, as the nation's number one pet, a cat is part of the family, giving pleasure by its sheer presence as it welcomes you home, or providing company for those on their own.

Part of the pure pleasure of having a cat in your life is ensuring it is cared for in the best possible way. As Cats Protection is the UK's leading cat welfare charity, I am delighted to introduce a book which has, at its heart, the welfare of cats.

Our experience has taught us how complex cat welfare can be – from behaviour to feeding, from environment to socialisation – and when contemplating a facility that will bring many cats into closer contact, how these basics must be considered from all angles.

Designing a cattery, whether for a commercial enterprise or rescue facility, is a serious undertaking, and this book will help you to incorporate into your plans the needs of the cats you wish to accommodate.

The relationship between man and cats is a developing one and we, as cat lovers, have a responsibility to encourage that relationship – and providing the best environment must surely be a firm footing from which to build.

Helen Ralston

Helen Ralston, Chief Executive of Cats Protection

Cats Protection
National Cat Centre, Chelwood Gate,
Haywards Heath, Sussex RH17 7TT
Tel: (National Helpline) 08702 099 099

www.cats.org.uk
Reg Charity 203644

There are no ordinary cats

Colette

Cats Protection
Giving cats an extra life

Formed by a group of cat lovers in 1927, Cats Protection has grown to become the UK's leading feline welfare charity. Today, through our nationwide network of Adoption Centres and voluntary Branches we rescue and rehome 60,000 cats and kittens every year.

Growing need

It's hard to imagine that so many cats need our help, but when you look at how the cat's popularity has grown – (there are a **staggering 9.7 million domestic and feral cats in the UK**, making puss the number one pet) it's no wonder that the demand on our services is greater than ever.

And our services are wide ranging. As well as our core work of rescue and rehoming, the charity promotes the benefits of neutering, **helping to neuter more than 100,000 cats every year**, and offers a wealth of expertise and knowledge through its wide range of literature, informative website and national Helpline.

Cats come into our care for a variety of different reasons – some have been abandoned, some are the result of a divorce or house move, whilst others are simply given up when their owners can no longer look after them.

Seeking happiness

Although our cats come from very different backgrounds they ultimately all want the same thing – a loving home to go to and a second chance of happiness

Helping our cats to 'seek happiness' is the charity's devoted team of 5,500 volunteers, who come from all walks of life, offering different skills and experiences.

From hands-on welfare work such as fostering cats and hand-rearing kittens, to the practicalities of running a Branch such as bookkeeping and fundraising, our volunteers help out in whatever capacity they can.

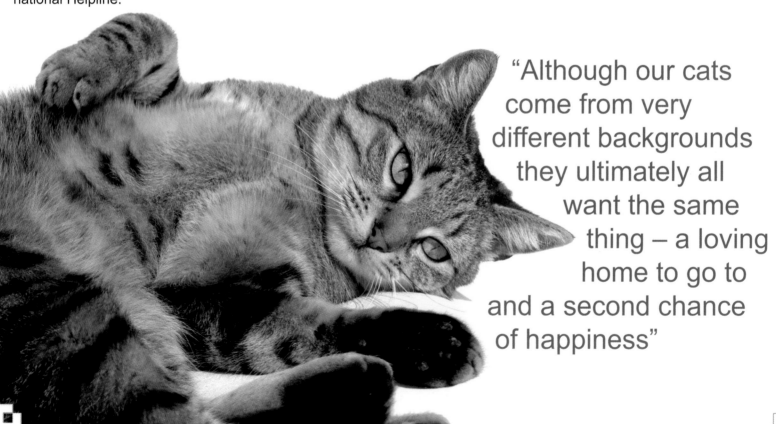

"Although our cats come from very different backgrounds they ultimately all want the same thing – a loving home to go to and a second chance of happiness"

How you can help
There are many ways in which you can support our work

Get involved!
We're always on the look out for people to join us.
Have you considered offering your business skills and expertise to assist in the running of one of our Branches? Are you able to give a little time, have some spare energy and enthusiasm that could benefit cats who desperately need your help?

Make a donation
We receive no government funding and therefore rely on cat lovers like you to help continue our vital welfare work. Whether you choose to give a one-off donation or commit to a monthly gift by direct debit, your contribution will be very gratefully received.

Help us in our fostering programme
Could you consider offering a cat a short-term home whilst a new one is found? Whether you already have a multi-cat household or cattery, are planning one for the future, or just want to help give more cats a better life – please get in contact with us about fostering or volunteering.

Spread the word
Your day-to-day life will bring you into contact with cat lovers who might be able to consider giving a cat or kitten a second chance in life.

Adopt a rescue cat or kitten
Our Adoption Centres and Branches around the country have many cats awaiting new homes.

For further information please:

- Phone our Helpline on 08702 099 099

- Visit our website at **www.cats.org.uk**

- Write to us at Cats Protection, National Cat Centre, Chelwood Gate, Haywards Heath, Sussex RH17 7TT
  Reg Charity 203644

"Getting actively involved with Cats Protection is immensely fulfilling and provides you with the wonderful experience of helping many cats"

INTRODUCTION

ACKNOWLEDGEMENTS

Contributing Authors

Grateful acknowledgement and sincere thanks to Helen Ralston of Cats Protection for writing the foreword to this book, and to cat welfare experts Dr Irene Rochlitz and Nadine Gourkow for their invaluable contributing articles on cat welfare and housing, environment enrichment and how to improve cat welfare in the cattery.

Dr Irene Rochlitz
BVSc, MSc, PhD, MRCVS

Centre for Animal Welfare and Anthrozoology, Department of Veterinary Medicine, University of Cambridge, Madingley Road, Cambridge CB3 0ES, UK

Irene is a research associate with the Centre for Animal Welfare and Anthrozoology at the University of Cambridge. She is a veterinary surgeon, and has a Master's degree in Veterinary Oncology and a PhD in Feline Welfare. She combines work in veterinary practice with research on issues affecting the welfare of companion animals. Her interests include companion animal behaviour, the assessment of quality of life in companion animals, and the welfare of domestic cats. She is on the Feline Advisory Bureau's expert panel list of speakers, for topics related to cat rescue and welfare. Irene edited and co-authored the book *The Welfare of Cats*.

Nadine Gourkow
MSc, B.Ed, BCCAB

Animal Welfare Manager for the BCSPCA, British Columbia Society for the Prevention of Cruelty to Animals, 1245 East 7th Avenue, Vancouver, BC V5T 1R1, Canada

Nadine holds a Masters in Animal Welfare Science from the University of British Columbia and is a Companion Animal Behaviourist (BCCAB) with the American Association of Companion Animal Behavior Counsellors. Since 1998, Nadine has been the Animal Welfare Manager for the British Columbia SPCA and developed the CatSense™ System used in 36 BC SPCA shelters to improve welfare, adoptions and facilitates adaptation of shelter cats to their new home post-adoption. Nadine has won an International Award from The Latham Foundation for the Promotion of Humane Education for her book and Video/DVD *The Emotional Life of Cats*.

Contributing Organisations:

Case Studies and Expert Tips:
Grateful appreciation to our UK, USA and Canadian Case Study contributors who have each generously provided information on their unique organisations:

- **RESCUE AND CHARITY:** British Columbia SPCA, Blue Cross Lewknor, Blue Cross Torbay, Cats Protection Derby, Cats Protection National Cat Centre, Feline Advisory Bureau, Mayhew Animal Home, RSPCA Blackberry Farm, RSPCA Halifax, Wood Green Animal Shelters, Wythall Animal Sanctuary.

- **BOARDING:** Kitty Hill Resort for Cats, Harpenden Cat Hotel, Oakdale Cattery, Preston Hills Cat Hotel, Purradise Boutique Hotel, Pyrton Cat Hotel, Templepan Boarding Cattery.

- **PRODUCTS AND SERVICES:**
  Agora Management, Pedigree Pens, Kennel Sales, PetAdmin, Purr...fect Fence

The Blue Cross Animal Welfare Charity:
Grateful thanks to John Rutter, Chief Executive of The Blue Cross for his enthusiasm and kind permission to illustrate cattery buildings, fittings and materials in our photographs.

Proofreading:
Grateful thanks to Diana Stimson and Martin Brice for their invaluable contribution to proofreading.

Design, Layout, Editing:
The greatest thanks must go to my wife Kay. Without Kay's considerable input and pure dedication, it would not have been possible to produce this book and accompanying website with the depth of information and advice they have, or in the professional and easy-to-read format presented.
It is one thing to write the pure, hard facts, it is entirely another matter to edit and present them in an engaging, appealing way with the 'special touches' that she has added. Kay's love of cats has given her an added incentive to try and provide as much information as possible, in order to improve the welfare of cats in catteries everywhere.

DAVID KEY

David Key is a **Consultant in Kennel and Cattery Design** and has advised hundreds of potential and existing kennel and cattery owners worldwide – ideas, improvements and planning through to designs, building and technical details.

For over 20 years David has also been responsible for **The Blue Cross Animal Welfare Charity** animal and staff buildings and property at their cat and dog adoption, companion animal and equine rescue and rehoming centres. During this time David founded an **Animal Welfare Charity Design Forum**, with the aim of sharing information between leading national animal welfare charities in the UK to prevent costly design, materials or building mistakes.

David has been professionally involved with animals for over 30 years. His experience spans companion animals, wildlife and wild animals and he has provided guidance and advice to animal welfare organizations, rescues, boarding, veterinary clinics and animal hospitals, quarantine, architects, police forces, customs and excise, breeding and multi-pet owners. David's interest started by helping out with a friend's show kennels while still at school, and occasionally working with the local RSPCA Inspector. This progressed to working at local boarding kennels and cattery for over 10 years and later at a zoological gardens. This unusual combination of animal work and practical skills developed into an interest in buildings, particularly relating to animal accommodation.

In 2000, David and his wife Kay created the *Kennel and Cattery Design* business to help promote the kennel and cattery design books, help people find resources and suppliers , and provide an international service for people looking for information on how to build and start up a kennels or cattery. Kay runs the business on a day-to-day basis and David provides consultancy and technical building advice, as well as continuing to look at design issues, construction methods and materials that help to improve animal welfare accommodation. David and Kay live in Oxfordshire, UK with their much loved rescue cats and dogs.

When not writing books, looking after Blue Cross property and advising people on kennel and cattery design, David manages to squeeze in some time for cross-country skiing and mountaineering in Norway, Greenland and Canada.

Kennel Design

David's first book *Essential Kennel Design* was published in 2000 in answer to requests from charities, sanctuaries, authorities and potential/existing kennel owners for more information on materials, designs, building-related issues, cost planning and general information on detail that was lacking in many of the books available on kennel building-related issues. In addition, the Kennel Design website was developed to make the information widely available:

www.kenneldesign.com & www.boardingkennels.org

Cattery Design

The cattery design book and website aim to provide much needed inspiration and guidance to give owners accurate information, and allow them to construct to the best possible standards within budget. The standards of many existing catteries are even more shocking than kennels, and the lack of previously available guidance on building and construction may partly explain this.
We hope this book has a HUGE impact!

www.catterydesign.com & www.boardingcatteries.org

David in Norway pursuing another passion – snow

If David was a cat,
he'd be a Norwegian Forest cat!

AIM OF THIS BOOK AND ACCOMPANYING WEBSITE

We believe it is essential to give as much information as possible to potential or existing cattery owners.

Our mission is to raise the expectations, standard and design of catteries by providing owners with advice and information on options and choices.

With this book and the accompanying website www.catterydesign.com we give you the inspiration, information and support you need to build the best standard of cattery you can, to match your requirements as well as the cats' needs and create a building that is easy to maintain. To do this you will need to understand how a well designed cattery helps reduce stress and provide a healthy and happy environment in which cats can be accommodated.

We often find that people want to provide more than one type of cattery, especially if they already have a customer base. Breeders, groomers, veterinarians and quarantine catteries consider offering a boarding facility to increase income, just as people who want to create a boarding cattery may want to help cats further by providing rescue accommodation, and some rescues think about offering boarding as a way of raising funds to help more cats! There will be additional considerations for multiple catteries, especially when dealing with cats of unknown health history.

Whatever function your cattery will be used for, it is important that you spend your build money wisely, and we want to help ensure that you have the information to do so.

We encourage you to think deeply about the style and quality
of business you want to create, because
quality and caring catteries are greatly in demand

It is not enough to just describe how to construct a cattery, because to make the right choices you need to understand exactly what makes good design, and how this is healthier for cats.

Happy cats will make your cattery successful, and we want you and your clients to be proud and delighted with your cattery!

WHAT IS IN THIS BOOK

Who was this book written for?

This book will give insight to everyone involved with cats, (welfare organisations, boarding, breeding, charities, rescue centres, quarantine, multi-cat owners, designers, authorities, architects and surveyors, colleges and universities) to provide an awareness of the changes in design, and options available.

This book will provide you with an encouraging, easy-to-read guide with hundreds of photographs, an overview of systems and designs, and show you how cat accommodation can be improved with cat welfare knowledge.

International flavour

The international flavour of this book is useful to potential and existing cattery owners. It provides ideas from different countries, highlights different philosophies and guidelines, and will reach a far greater number of people wanting help and advice to create or upgrade a cattery – yet it also shows that cats have the same needs, no matter where they live!

It is interesting to see the similarities between the United Kingdom, America and Canada in terms of statistics and trends. Today, with cats being the most popular pet, cat owners spending more on their pets and having higher demands/expectations – there is now, more than ever, a need to provide enough accommodation to meet this demand.

The most important concept when creating a cattery:

Awareness of cat welfare is an integral part of helping us create cattery buildings and management skills that are as cat-friendly as possible. The combination of understanding what cats need, and knowing what the construction choices are, means you can create the perfect cattery for your situation and budget.

What this book contains:

■ Large, full-colour photographs
To provide you with inspiration and ideas, this book is lavishly packed with colour photographs, many of which are full page or double-page spreads so that you can see lots of detail – just like looking through a window!

■ The surprising extent that the cattery/unit style can affect cat welfare
Understanding just how much accommodation standards affect cats. How to improve the quality of life for a confined cat and what is appropriate therapy for cats housed in less than ideal conditions

■ Case studies
United Kingdom, American and Canadian organisations show how unique each organisation is (which is often what makes it successful), and to illustrate important points by showing how they are put into practice in real life. As you will see, there is always something that could have been improved on, and always plenty to be pleased with!

■ Design, material and equipment options
Descriptions, advantages and disadvantages of different layout/design styles and unit types, materials and equipment all combine to help you make an informed choice for your own situation

■ Best practice and avoiding mistakes
Advice on best practice for planning/zoning and building a cattery. Common mistakes and how to avoid them. What you must do, and what not to do. What cats require, and legislation governing catteries

■ Further resources ...where to find further resources and information. Links to informative websites as well as recommendations for further reading

■ Cat quotations ...and the occasional quotation to make you smile!

OTHER WAYS WE CAN HELP YOU

www.catterydesign.com

How our cattery design website can help you:

- Business Plan
- Property Audit
- Directory of suppliers, products, manufacturers, services - making it easy to buy suggested items in this book online
- Cattery Designs (plans/blueprints)
- Books
- Help and advice
- Latest information
- Support, encouragement and inspiration!

If you enjoy the case studies in this book, you might like to contact us about your story. We can publish this on our websites and provide links to your website to help generate new visitors for you.

Just go to www.catterydesign.com

www.boardingcatteries.org

If you already have, or are considering starting a boarding cattery, we have a website with special search facilities to help generate new business for you.

Just go to www.boardingcatteries.org

Our contact details are:

Kay & David Key
Kennel & Cattery Design, PO Box 146, Chipping Norton, Oxfordshire OX7 6WA, UK
Phone: +44 (0)1608 646454
Email: kaykey@catterydesign.com
Websites: www.catterydesign.com
               www.boardingcatteries.org

We list country phone dialling codes and the current UK time on our contact page to help you get in touch easily.

CARE AND MANAGEMENT

The most important factor for a successful cattery is its care and management.

It would probably be worth putting that statement on every page! However, it is obvious that a well-designed building can only improve matters. Whether for cat welfare, staff morale, easier cleaning and maintenance, or all of these improvements, this book will help you understand the building options available, to get the best result for you.

Everyone has an opinion about what makes a good cattery!

If you could include every cat welfare-friendly suggestion in this book it would be wonderful! However, with building and property prices, site constraints and a finite budget, you must find the right balance to build the best standard you can.

> Always remember that it is an option for you to build half of your ultimate design at the standard you want. It will cost less initially, be faster to build, and will start your income earlier so you have funds to build the second half at a later date

As you will see, you can create a cattery that matches as many of your ideals as possible on a small scale, stand head and shoulders above the 'standard/commonly used' type of cattery and have your clients do your marketing for you!

The Commercial Cattery

A commercial cattery of even six units can provide a good income if a high quality and caring service is provided together with good accommodation. A higher fee (for boarding this is possibly even double that of a standard cattery) will reflect the level of personal care, socialisation and understanding that is offered in a way that a large cattery would be unable to match. Once your income is established, you will then be able to increase the number of cats you can accommodate, or you may prefer not to lose the personal touch, and increase profit in other ways.

The Rescue Cattery/Shelter

A rescue centre has many options to improve cat welfare and increase the adoption success rate. There are ways buildings can assist you, such as creating separate areas for socialisation, getting to know potential owners and understanding how to make the accommodation more cat-friendly. For organisations coping with a very tight budget, there are ways you can improve the cattery without significant cost by using environmental enrichment and cat therapy.

How to Create Your Perfect Cattery - Design Development Chart

On the next page you will find a chart that lists the sort of things you will need to think about in order to create a complete design for your cattery. Whether you fill the chart in as you go along or read through the book first before completing it, this chart will form the basis of your cattery design, and ensure you think about the essential requirements of your building/s to get the ideal result for your situation.

Now we are ready to start creating your perfect cattery!

CREATE YOUR PERFECT CATTERY

ITEM:	MY DECISION:	PAGE:
Cattery function/s:		57
New build/conversion/upgrade:		239
Cattery only:		38
Site located/purchased		85
Feasibility of planning/zoning permission:		
• Spoken to Planning Officer • Spoken to Animal Welfare Officer • Spoken to Traffic & Highways Officer		72
Local legislation/guidelines to comply with:		
• Licence/permit & animal welfare • Environment • Building		136
Cattery aspect:		96
Cattery layout/shape:		
• U, L, I, II, square/rectangular • Indoor, Outdoor, Semi-Outdoor		182
Location of ancillary buildings/items:		
• Reception, Isolation, Admissions • Car Parking • Laundry, Toilet/s • Storage, Refuse		97
Total number of units:		39
Unit capacity breakdown:		
• Single units • Double units • Multi-cat units		40
Size of units:		136
Height of units:		200
Type of units:		
• Full-height, walk-in/Penthouse • Holding Pens/Admissions • Mother and Kitten • Socialisation/rehoming • External exercise area/socialisation room or playroom		200
Corridor/walkway widths:		
Corridor/walkway internal/external:		198
Corridor/walkway covered:		

USE THIS DOUBLE-PAGE CHECKLIST TO HELP YOU CREATE YOUR PERFECT CATTERY DESIGN.
(YOUR FINAL DESIGN INVOLVES MAKING DECISIONS ON ALL THESE ELEMENTS)

ITEM:	MY DECISION:	PAGE:
Project manager:		238
Building method:		240
External construction material:		268
Internal construction materials:		316
Thermal insulation:		292
Floor finishes:		296
Wall finishes:		316
Metalwork: (Size of mesh and Metalwork treatment		324
Unit panel/sneeze barrier construction:		326
Lighting:		340
Heating:		341
Cooling:		346
Ventilation:		347
Condensation:		353
Fixed furniture: • Shelving, Ramps/ladders, Walkways		368
Moveable furniture: • Bedding, Aerobic centres, Scratching posts, Seating		372
Environment enrichment methods:		357
Utilities: • Heating, electricity, water		434
Drainage method:		416
Sewage disposal:		443
Water disposal:		455
Kitchen units and equipment:		418
Laundry machinery:		106
Cleaning/disinfection policy:		424
Cleaning/disinfection methods:		426
Website name/s purchased:		468
Secure fencing for your own cats: (especially if this is a new property or near a busy road)		232
Landscaping:		87

REMEMBER THIS CHART! Place a bookmark between these pages, (or remember
page 23!) to help you complete this chart and develop your design

It is difficult to obtain the friendship of a cat. It is a philosophical animal, one that does not place its affections thoughtlessly

Theophile Gautier

CATS ARE NOW
THE MOST
POPULAR PET AND
TODAY'S CAT
OWNERS WANT
MUCH MORE FOR
THEIR CATS

WHY QUALITY CATTERY DESIGN IS ESSENTIAL

There are still far too many sub-standard catteries in existence.

The aim of this book is to both help people build new, quality accommodation for cats and improve or replace sub-standard ones. Over recent years there has been a significant improvement in the quality of animal accommodation in good boarding or breeder establishments, charities and sanctuaries. Knowing what new products are available, and what all the options are will help you define what fits your requirements. This is all aimed at helping you get everything you want right at the start, and preventing you from being disappointed with the finished result when you start to use it in real life.

The increase in standards can also be partly attributed to:

- ### Professionalism
  A new generation of people wishing to create a better standard of cattery, often with qualifications or experience in animal care, or who already have experience of running a business or working with cats.
  For people who are thinking of using redundancy money to achieve their dream of opening a cattery, a stress-free job with no commuting and above all secure, will be even more appealing – after all, the job of looking after other people's cats cannot be outsourced to Asia!

- ### Lifestyle
  More people wanting to change their lifestyle, wishing to improve both their personal lifestyle and provide quality accommodation, wishing to do something worthwhile with their lives, to love what they do and to 'make a difference'. This is often in conjunction with seeing what local catteries have to offer and thinking "I can do better"

- ### Financial
  A greater capital investment than ever before is now required, which seems to be acting as a filter, mainly leaving the people who really do want to run a cattery for the love of it, and most importantly, to do it well

- ### Awareness and expectation
  An increase in visual awareness of standards and increased customer expectations caused by greater television and internet coverage, and increases in the amount pet owners are prepared to spend on their cats

- ### Knowledge A better understanding and knowledge of the housing requirements for cats. This book will make
  that information readily accessible to all

- ### Construction The choice of building materials and designs available

- ### Legislation:
  Many older catteries are struggling to get their boarding licence renewed to comply with up-to-date regulations. These catteries will either need to invest in new buildings for the future, sell the business or close down

- ### Client demand
  To run a cattery, especially a new business, it is better to keep 10-20 cat units in use constantly, than to have the associated running/construction costs of a larger cattery, which will take time to fill, or have empty cat units initially

- ### Caring catteries reduce stress to increase success
  With smaller, quality businesses you also get the benefit of better cattery management, happier cats and staff, better income or greater rehoming rates, repeat business, a better public image, strong business development, a trusted, personal and caring service that looks better to customers, and feels more personal and inviting to them

Although a well-run establishment with quality, caring, enthusiastic staff can overcome many design faults by providing a high level of care to the cats and their owners, – buildings constructed to a high standard can **only** be beneficial and improve the efficient running of the property

Animal welfare organisations have helped to remove the notion that catteries need to provide only a secure environment with little emphasis on the animals' needs and requirements. The advances in products, materials, equipment and design for animal buildings has been immense in the last decade, and it is often the welfare charities that lead the way (they need to have robust, healthy buildings for animals and people and often build or upgrade new centres in many different locations).

Recent studies clearly describe the needs and requirements of cats, so we should use this information to our advantage, and create much healthier and more stimulating environments – whether it is for two weeks boarding, a temporary stay while a new home is found, or permanently in a home environment.

Hopefully, by the end of this book you will see how quality design and specification is extremely important to all aspects of your business, and be able to assess the features that will make your cattery building work efficiently.

Making it a Success

Success comes from cat welfare and public perception, a sense of pride and satisfaction, and providing a healthy, pleasant working environment for staff that will allow greater time to focus their attention on the cats.

The **only disadvantage** to building a quality cattery is the initial capital cost! However, our clients have shown that this can be recouped quickly, as the fees/rehoming rates are increased.

In the long term of course, robust, quality, correctly designed and specified cattery buildings can **reduce expenditure** and **become an investment** for the owner's future.

THE DEMAND FOR QUALITY AND CARING CATTERIES

Today, there is a high and increasing demand for good, quality catteries with a caring service.

We are delighted to find that the majority of people coming to us for advice now are extremely caring, professional and dedicated people determined to set up the best cattery they can. The amount of passion, research, work, commitment, investment and dedication required will quickly become apparent – and if it is not for you, you will soon find out! Having purchased this book, it is obvious you are already quite committed to the idea of running a cattery. So, if you find out that the more you understand and learn, the more determined and passionate it makes you – then you are probably doing it for the right reasons and we will do our utmost to help you achieve your dream of building or upgrading your cattery.

It is *wonderful* to see someone go from thinking about the whole lifestyle and career change as an idea, to planning exactly what they want and getting it built, whilst avoiding costly mistakes that are usually made with building catteries – and finally opening their cattery. Running your own business and doing something you love changes your life! This will become apparent when you start reading the case studies in this book (starting with the next few pages) and also illustrates how this not only changes your life, but the lives of your clients and their cats.

If creating a cattery is what you dream of, then naturally you will want to provide the best accommodation and care, earn a good living, have fun and really enjoy what you do: providing a safe, healthy environment for cats.

It's a bit of a roller coaster journey,
but having all the right information to hand
will make things much easier!

"A lifestyle rather than a job, running a cattery is a way of life. Your clients will place complete trust in you and rely on you for absolute security and excellent care for their cats. Living on site is strongly recommended to ensure the smooth running of the cattery and it should never be left unattended for more than short periods of time when cats are in residence

Although running a boarding cattery is all about cats, a great deal of time is spent talking to and reassuring owners and maintaining a high quality business image. Ability to communicate clearly and calmly is vital. If you do not like people, this is not the job for you! Taking on a cattery requires a large financial outlay and although it is possible to make a reasonable living, you may not necessarily make a fortune! Do work through a business plan and take advice on finance and all that is involved."

Feline Advisory Bureau, UK

"Cat boarding has traditionally been available as an adjunct of dog boarding. However, with cat ownership increasing rapidly, it is growing and changing, and kennel owners, as well as cat owners, need to be educated in the area of cat boarding."

American Boarding Kennels Association, USA

"The most important management requirement for a successful breeding program will be the design of the cattery. In most instances, the cattery itself is part of your household. The care and comfort of the cats is of primary importance when designing the cattery, and it will pay in the long run to take the time to properly plan your cattery area.
A cattery owner doing all that it takes to produce healthy, happy cats and kittens truly is a professional. You must know cage building techniques, construction and maintenance procedures, security measures, and sometimes even the legal aspects of licenses and permits. Add to the list animal health practices, sanitation, grooming and care. Then, top it all off with show rules and breed standards, and a good knowledge of genetics. Once the package is all put together, remember to keep abreast of current developments in all of these areas, as our technology-driven age continually revises and updates all of our knowledge."

Cat Fanciers' Association, USA

CASE STUDY:
A MODEL BOARDING CATTERY

Organisation: Harpenden Cat Hotel
Location: UK, Hertfordshire
Cattery Type: Semi -outdoor
Cattery Function: Boarding
Number of Units: 16
Unit Size Sleep: 1220 x 1220mm (4ft x 4ft)
Unit Size Exercise: 1220 x 1830mm (4ft x 6ft)
Date Built: 1999

www.cat-hotel.co.uk

A RENOWNED BUSINESS WITH NATIONAL PRESS COVERAGE, SETS AN EXAMPLE TO POTENTIAL CATTERY OWNERS, EXPLAINS WHY RUNNING A QUALITY, PERSONAL, DEDICATED SERVICE IS EXTREMELY SATISFYING AND THE WAY FORWARD

HARPENDEN CAT HOTEL

BRIGHT, MODERN UNITS

All units are south facing, full height PVCu with a double glazed window by the shelf in the sleeping area. The covered area outside the sleeping quarters is PVCu from the floor to 3ft, and then glass to the ceiling. The front outside area is mesh to provide fresh air at all times. There is a safety corridor, and a heat-reflective roof covers the whole cattery.

Since opening Harpenden Cat Hotel, Nicky Tyler has generously advised other new boarding catteries and helped them achieve the same standards across the country. **As a champion of the quality cattery**, 'Your Cat' magazine decided to do a 3 page feature on them entitled 'Choose only the Best'.

Something of a trademark now, Nicky's beautiful 30 year old ornamental maple trees decorate the peaceful garden area immediately outside the cattery, with colourful hanging baskets. A radio is on throughout the day to soothe the cats. The cats have views of open countryside with plenty of wildlife to watch, and even the horse menage (Nicky long ago noticed how much her own cats loved to watch the horses going through their paces and even following them!)

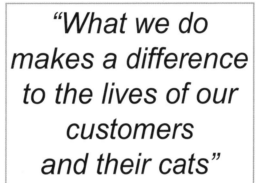

"What we do makes a difference to the lives of our customers and their cats"

PAMPERED PETS

It was a joy to see the strong relationship that Nicky has developed with the cats she boards. As she mentioned a few times, cats do not 'lie' and you can immediately see from their reactions that they are very used to kisses and cuddles with Nicky and we had quite a hard time choosing from all the great photos we took of her with her very happy boarders!

Nicky's cat customers are very much 'pampered pets' and she completely understands how their owners must feel leaving them. It is not unusual for even her male customers to be in floods of tears leaving their 'babies'! So she encourages owners to place their cats into their units rather than just leaving them, or without seeing where they will be staying. Nicky likes owners to settle cats in, leaving when they feel happy. It is important to her that cat owners are relaxed and not rushed. Epitomising the successful, small, quality business providing a dedicated service to customers who want the best, they decided not to expand or have staff, to ensure individual attention and develop their relationships with both human and cat customers.

Photographs by David & Kay Key and Nicky Tyler

What are you most pleased with?

The units! We decided to use Pedigree Pens to supply our cattery because their units were of an exceptional standard and were designed to meet all the requirements from our research. We also found them a very forward-thinking company, and extremely helpful at all stages, even now - several years after we opened!

What would you do differently?

The only thing I would change is to use tiles instead of vinyl, purely from a long-term maintenance/replacement view. We recently changed the flooring to this lovely gold colour, which is light, bright and feels warm and welcoming. It's amazing how cat owners notice even the smallest change, from hanging baskets, scratching posts, even the garden sculptures!

HARPENDEN CAT HOTEL

PROPERTY, LAND AND BUILDING COSTS

A combination of the following factors is leading to better accommodation for cats:

- High property/land prices and increasing building costs (off-putting to those not serious about running a cattery). In business terms, these are called 'barriers to entry'

- Increases in cat welfare understanding and legislation/standards

- Increases in product/materials quality and availability

- Increases in expectations and awareness from the public (TV, internet etc)

- Attraction to professional people prepared to invest in a lifestyle/career change

Property and Land Costs

If you already own suitable land to build your cattery on, you are very lucky!
Property prices have increased dramatically in the last decade and it is now much more expensive to buy land, or property with land. There are rural grants available for up to 50% of the building cost and farmers are being encouraged to diversify into other markets. Farmers should be aware of the many differences between the stock they have been used to, and dealing with companion animals (pets) and their owners. As we shall see later, there are continual increases in the understanding of cat welfare, and the increase in animal accommodation standards.

Global house price boom and bust has been driven by two common factors:

- Low interest rates encouraging people to borrow more

- Lower confidence in equities after stock market dives, made property more attractive – are things now reversing?

The current trend is for equities increasing and property prices remaining stable or falling – so it makes sense to **only invest in a long-term prospect that you really care about**!

The global housing boom In come the waves Jun 16th 2005
From The Economist print edition

The Economist House Price Index 1997-2005*	
South Africa	244%
Ireland	192%
UK	154%
Spain	145%
Australia	114%
France	87%
Sweden	84%
Netherlands	76%
USA	73%
Belgium	71%
New Zealand	66%
Italy	69%
Denmark	58%
Canada	47%
Switzerland	12%
Germany	-0.2%
Japan	-28%

From our experience with many people wanting to build or upgrade their cattery or kennels, the increase in property prices seems to filter the people prepared to invest in their animal accommodation. The higher land and building costs in turn demand higher fees to help pay for them, and as we shall see from the pet market industry statistics – owners are spending more on their pets.

Increasing the Value of your Property

There is no doubt that placing a quality business on a property increases the value of that property.

Despite the increased costs of rural properties, many on main roads will be less attractive to most house buyers, but of inherent value to the potential cattery or small business owner, as it increases the ease of access to customers and also increases the awareness of 'passing trade' about your business. Free advertising!

Keeping Your Own Cats Safe

If you are thinking about starting a cattery, it is highly likely you have more than one cat yourself and you will obviously need to think about the safety of your cats if you are going to be living near a main road, or have traffic on your premises. Chapter 7: Cattery Types and Unit Styles includes suggested alternatives to keeping your cat confined safely, but in a larger space. This should be of great interest to you whether you decide to go ahead with a cattery or not.

Building Costs

The average inflationary construction cost is approximately 8% per year. This doesn't sound like much until you realise that even in a short period such as three years, the building cost has increased by 25% !

Equivalent to building a house

Do not think that because it is a building for cats that it will be less expensive to build than a house (for traditional masonry construction).

For traditionally constructed buildings, you will often find the specification is very similar to that of a domestic house. The foundations, internal and external brick and block work, insulating and roofing materials etc are the same. This means similar purchase and installation costs. If you think about it, you are actually building small rooms all needing heating, lighting and decorating, which will be more time consuming, fiddly and expensive than dealing with large rooms!

These cost implications are mentioned purely to prepare you if you are not familiar with building and property costs!

So, if you are still keen to look at the possibility of opening a cattery, we will move on!

CATTERY ONLY, OR KENNELS TOO?

There are two options: to have a cattery only, or a cattery and boarding kennels. However, it is obvious that cat-only facilities are a better choice for cats, and animal welfare organisations recommend cat-only facilities for boarding.

Cattery only

We are now seeing a definite move towards cat-only facilities, and businesses of a smaller, manageable nature with more emphasis on personal service, care and quality. As you will see in the remainder of this chapter, there are several reasons for this change of emphasis and why the smaller, cat-only facility is proving to be so successful.

Obviously, it is better for cats to be in a cat-only facility (or at the very least a considerable distance away from the dogs)

An owner who has only a cat will always prefer to use a cat-only boarding facility. They will prefer the peace, tranquillity and calm atmosphere. This can also be reflected in the daily charge. For many single people, couples, the elderly, and those particularly keen on ensuring their cats' welfare is of prime importance – a cat-only facility is the only option for them.

> People naturally gravitate towards either cats or dogs, even if they like both species.
> The danger is that cats will always come second when you also have dogs on site, purely because there is more urgency to walk dogs and clean kennels

Cattery and Kennels

It is currently very common in the USA to have both a cat and dog facility on the same site, housing a large number of animals, whereas in the UK there is a much greater number of cat-only facilities. For owners who have both a dog and a cat, it is far more convenient for them to have one multi-purpose facility that caters for both, and there will probably always be a place for this type of operation. When owners are going on holiday it is always a rush, and particularly so if they have children. It is fair to say that convenience is part of the equation and it may not make sense to them to have to use two separate boarding establishments. A dual-purpose facility can work equally as well.

However, if you do take the kennels and cattery option, careful consideration needs to be given to the initial design and layout to provide a private, quiet and secluded area for the cats, which is far enough away from the kennels. Although better noise-wise, this can have a **disadvantage** for the cats, in that the cattery is often some distance away from the main core centre of activity, and consequently it removes the opportunity for the cats to watch the daily activity associated with staff and visitors coming and going.

INCOME AND DECIDING ON THE NUMBER OF UNITS

A high quality, caring, smaller cattery business is much easier to keep fully booked all year round

A smaller, high quality and caring cattery also:

- Costs less to build and set up

- Has less/no staff issues

- Easier to sell in the future

- More profitable as fees can be higher

- Allows you to develop the business at your own pace

- More satisfying as you can spend more time with each cat, and think creatively about their care

- More rewarding as you can develop relationships with your clients to provide a more personal service

However, by far the biggest factor in deciding how many cat units to have is your budget. Please remember that this can be broken into phases, you don't have to do it all at once!
Income is an important part of your business plan and you should work out your potential income as well as building and running costs. By carefully looking at the figures now, you can give yourself the best cash flow and profitability from the start.

Boarding management books suggest working out your '**worst case scenario**' on income, which is **averaged** as being a 'third-full' as a guideline (excluding multiple cats), and working out your '**average income**' to work towards, that being 'half-full'. Historically, it's not usually suggested that you work out your '**maximum**' figure. However, we suggest you work to a higher rate if you are running a quality and caring service with up to 20 units – as you are more likely to be full than someone with 100 units to fill! In fact, we know from our clients that **85% occupancy is easily achievable for quality boarding establishments providing a personal, caring service**.

You obviously cannot just charge a higher fee without knowing what the minimum, average and maximum prices are in your area, or providing that 'something extra'. These must be researched (our online Business Plan helps you assess your potential income). You will need to know what other catteries charge in your area when working out the feasibility – and it is most important to visit these catteries to see **what level of service** they provide for their fees.

In our experience, a quality and caring higher standard cattery can charge <u>double</u> the fee of a low to average standard cattery; (average fees are £5-£6 in the UK and $10-£12 in the USA). **This means that you can build half the number of quality units and your income will be the same (or more) than building twice that at a lower standard.**

A new factor to take into consideration is that, thanks to the internet, cat owners are now assessing catteries from much farther afield than the traditional 20-30 mile catchment area. If holidaying in the same country, cat owners now book a cattery at their holiday destination so they are nearby! Adopters may see a rescue cat on a website or webcam! Obviously this arrangement is not suitable for all cats, but you should certainly take this into consideration for marketing and fees.

You usually get what you pay for!

Create Flexible Accommodation

What impact would 2 or 3 cats from the same household have on your income and ability to accommodate them? As you will see in the 'Understanding The Pet Market' section in the next few pages, 40-50% of cat owners have more than one cat, so you will need to provide ample flexibility for your business.

We suggest that at the very least you provide various sizes of cat unit to suit different activity levels, requirements and numbers of cats from the same household. However, **ideally, every unit should be able to accommodate at least 2 cats**, and some larger options will be useful for 3 or more cats sharing. In some circumstances a multi-cat family will not get on as well as the owner suggests or would like, so it may be necessary to provide accommodation for quiet, nervous or bullied cats separately from their house mates. You should also think about providing accommodation for special needs such as low shelving for elderly cats, blind or deaf cats, larger and more stimulating units for very active cats, kitten-friendly units etc.

By looking through the statistics for your business plan on the catchment area, the average number of cats owned per household, and the number of households with cats for various countries (even researching down to local town and village level), you will soon get a feel for the number of 'cat families' in your area.

It is amazing how quickly people find out that a lovely, friendly new cattery has opened, and recommend it to their friends!

A better income for the quality and caring commercial cattery

Playing around with figures such as your fees/rates will show you how you can have a smaller, quality, caring cattery (which is of course exactly the style of business we are actively encouraging!) and charge accordingly. Of course it is worthwhile working out what your 'maximum capacity' is – you will know what your ceiling income will be – although it is unlikely you will have every cat unit allocated for every day of the year, at least you will know what your 'limits' are.

There will be seasonal swings (such as Christmas, Easter and Summer holidays) when you could fill your cattery several times over – but there may equally be less busy times (February is notorious for being quiet). However, for a more personal, caring cattery with fewer units the bookings may be continual!

Playing the 'what if' scenario with your income can be extremely useful, and you will need to plan ahead to counter the 'no-show' clients who just forget to turn up or cancel.

> By matching your fees with the quality of the buildings and service you provide, you will find that you can make more money, or more adoptions when working with fewer cats

> The more time you spend with the cats you are looking after, the happier and less stressed they will be and so will their owners, your future customers!

Thinking Laterally
You can make as much money by selling a designer collar or other cat items to your existing clients as you could boarding their cat for a weekend – and it requires no more units, just space for stock.

Happy Cats
You know when your cats are happy, playful, not quite themselves, or even miserable, don't you? Your clients will be just the same. If cat owners don't feel that their 'baby' was happy staying with you, or looked after well enough, it is highly unlikely that they will actually tell you – you just won't ever see them or their custom again.

> Taking time to talk to owners about their cat, both before and after their stay, is important

On the next few pages we have an example of a highly successful boarding cattery with just six units, followed by descriptions to clarify what is meant by sub-standard, luxury and state of the art cat accommodation.

CASE STUDY:
THE PURRFECT SMALL BUSINESS

Organisation:	Purradise Boarding Cattery
Location:	USA, California, El Granada
Cattery Type:	Indoor
Cattery Function:	Boarding
Number of Units:	6
Unit Size:	3' x 4' x 7'6"/920 x1220 x2290mm
Date Built:	2003

www.purradisehotel.com

A BUSINESS OF JUST SIX UNITS PROVIDING A PERSONAL, CARING, SUCCESSFUL SERVICE WITH BRIGHT COLOURS AND FUN THEMES. THE HEARTWARMING AND HUMOUROUS GUEST PHOTO ALBUM IS A JOY, AND SPEAKS VOLUMES ABOUT THE CARE GIVEN!

PURRADISE BOUTIQUE HOTEL

HOW IT ALL STARTED

Cecily Hatchitt, founder of Purradise with the title of 'Chief Kitty Keeper', spent over 25 years in marketing project management and called it a day during the technology sector slump of 2002/3. An American by birth, Cecily has spent over 30 years living in Switzerland, France and the UK. Cecily's home overlooks the Pacific Ocean in a semi-rural location and she is fortunate to have a large area of unused space in the house, along with dedicated husband Neil, who could turn his hand to pretty much anything on a practical and business level! As a lifelong animal lover, the pieces fell in place and *Purradise, A Boutique Hotel for Cats* was born.

The findings of extensive research into cat boarding facilities within the surrounding counties revealed disturbing results. Generally, the cat boarding facilities fell into the category of mixed dog and cat boarding facilities in concrete, bare, echoing buildings, bark and howl deafening, reeking of disinfectant, and prison-like. In a notable instance, cats were being caged immediately opposite caged dogs who were barking, nervous and sometimes irascible! A worst-case example called for owners to take a number and stand in line at the check in with their cats. Staff would take the carriers and the cats would disappear into a 'no-go-for-clients-zone'. "Next in line" seemed to be the standard and only greeting!

THERE HAS TO BE A BETTER WAY!

In discussions with local veterinarian and expert animal care specialists, it was determined (without much effort) that cats benefit from comfort, stress-free and loving environments, just like the rest of us do!

Purradise concept:
- Cats-only in private hygienic spaces
- Multi-level suites (no cages), background music
- Diversion (play, grooming, windows, open spaces)
- Comfort (plush, colourful themed furnishings)
- Love (oh so much given on a regular basis) as seen in the photos, cats don't relax like this without affection!
- Personal attention (imagine, on-site personnel!)

With six individually fun-themed suites which are 80ft^3+ each (and the cats fully make use of this) with: multi-levels, windows, private hiding places, climbing places, walkways, verandahs, companionship, vigilance, safety, hygiene, love, love and more love. **With such a low guest capacity, Purradise is able to offer a one-on-one service to soothe guests and clients alike with personalised offerings including:**
- 'Limo' taxi service, relocation services, errands
- Grooming and veterinary appointments
- Email and voicemail updates
- By-appointment check-ins/outs and guest visiting hours

Photographs courtesy of Cecily Hatchitt

What are you most pleased with?

The trust and friendship I have developed with clients and guests alike. From very small beginnings, and with no background to speak of, I have established a solid business with an excellent reputation among veterinarians and other pet professionals. These relationships enrich not only my business, but my life.

What would you do differently?

As Purradise was built into an existing space in our home, we had to make do with facilities that were there. This meant heavy reliance upon weather conditions and the available space in our garage and yard for cleaning purposes. An ideal scenario would be to have a purpose-built area with full plumbing and drying facilities, with easy access.

CLIENTS

Cecily says: my guests' parents see me one-to-one, the owner of Purradise, talk to me, share their purrsonal life, loves, grief and joys and also… give me their house keys and their babies to care for.

Client example 1:
The victim of a broken relationship, Freckles came to stay while her owner relocated from California to Europe. She had already been through considerable emotional upheaval, having been suddenly made into an 'outdoor only' cat due to allergy problems with the new household.

Purradise was contacted at 11:30pm at night and rallied to the 'emergency'. We provided a limo, clerical and personal care to facilitate a smooth and happy result for both client and guest. We made certain that Freckles was emotionally and physically fit to endure a twelve hour international flight.

Example 2:
Hannah & Scully, frequent boarders, stay at Purradise while their avid swimmer-athlete parents train and compete in Hawaii. Hannah & Scully enjoy the serenity and security of Purradise as well as the 'limo' transportation home to greet their parents!

Example 3:
Miss Aimée, Itty Bitty Kitty & Patience – three outstanding guests who each have individual needs. Itty Bitty Kitty in particular has a medical condition and Purradise provides her with medication administration. Additionally, Miss Aimée and Patience are occasional boarders.

WHAT IS UNIQUE ABOUT US

- Cats only
- A private home, not an 'industrial' building
- Individually built and designed suites
- Limited capacity – 6 suites only, not dozens
- Use of colour to portray a 'non-clinical' environment
- One-on-one relationships
- Purradise guests know my voice, smell, touch and spirit. I believe we communicate with love

MY REWARD

The most emotionally satisfying moment for me is the beautiful transition from a frightened, disoriented "I'm-at-the-vet!/my parents have abandoned me!" cat, to calm guest, as they suddenly nuzzle, blink and head-butt into my open palm, tuck into their food and snuggle down purring into their bed in full recognition of Purradise being a loving, safe and comfortable place.

…and of course, there is immense satisfaction in getting to know so many wonderful cats!

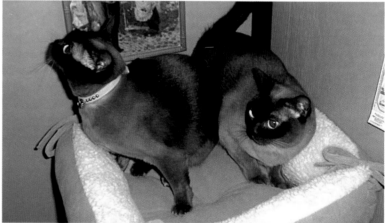

PURRADISE HOTEL

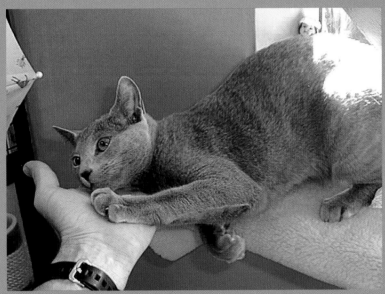

PURRADISE HOTEL

HOW CATTERIES DESCRIBE THEMSELVES

Having looked at hundreds of cattery websites worldwide – there seem to be three phrases used by cattery owners: luxury, five star and even state of the art. These descriptions can commonly be found for sub-standard and very basic buildings! Coupled with no, or few photographs, this is obviously confusing for clients.

Many older properties that haven't had any investment still describe themselves as luxury. We found that approximately 90% of websites checked also referred to their businesses as 'luxury'. Considering the poor quality of many catteries – there is obviously a chasm between reality and promise!

A recent comment from a licensing officer when asked to explain what was a good cattery by a member of the public, said:

"There are only a few 'Hiltons', then there are a few more 'travel lodges'
- and everything else is alCATraz!"

However a cattery is described, the building will always speak for itself

In this section will clarify the difference between basic, sub-standard, luxury/five star and state of the art.

The Basics

The basic, minimum requirements for a cattery are:

- Shelter and safety
- Somewhere to hide, climb and perch up high for safety
- Provision of health and veterinary care when required
- Fresh water and food
- Fresh air, daylight and sunshine
- Somewhere to rest and sleep
- Daily routine with familiar, knowledgeable people
- Warmth
- Companionship
- Scratching posts, Toys
- Something that smells of home and the owner

Luxury and Five Star

'Luxury' is a very subjective word. To satisfy yourself that your cattery actually is 'luxury' you will need to visit several other catteries to establish for yourself what this actually means to you.

Luxury to People

This might be described as having a five star hotel, TV, pretty views, expensive furnishings, good food and drink, landscaping, flowers and hanging baskets, a choice of where to go and things to do, and an escape from it all.

Luxury to Cats

Somewhere safe and warm (underfloor heating, heated beds and sunshine) plenty of attention, things to watch and do, a variety of different beds and places to sit or rest, plenty of space and freedom to move around, being able to jump or climb at will, soft music, calm surroundings, enjoying the company of and a relationship with calm and softly-spoken carers, exciting games involving something to catch or chase, plenty of wildlife or domestic birds/animals to watch and, of course, freshly prepared chicken, ham or tuna/mackerel or sardine treats! To provide this level of service, you have to go beyond cat owner knowledge to a more professional understanding of cat behaviour and needs.

A Holiday?

Thinking in human terms, boarding catteries often describe themselves as a holiday for the cats, a hotel, or a retreat.

Whatever the size of the unit, the cat is still **in a different environment and has been moved out of its familiar home** for a temporary stay elsewhere – **this is extremely stressful**. The cat is 'moving house' and doesn't know how long for. Didn't you say 'that's the last time I do that for a while' the last time you moved house? This is why you need to think carefully about cat welfare and how you can improve it at your cattery. By offering short-stay introductions to your cattery, especially for cats who have never been in a cattery before, you can establish a relationship with the cats, and they will know what to expect from you on longer visits.

Let's remember, cats don't have the luxury of being able to choose to come and stay with you! Use your ingenuity, think up a variety of ways to keep the cats happy and it will also be great fun for you, provide enormous satisfaction and ensure your clients return again and again and recommend you to their friends.

It is a mistake to think that cats are 'low maintenance' because they are not 'walked' and can use a litter tray.

Every cat is an individual character and will need to be cared for correctly and entertained.

Not doing so will result in boredom, inactivity, abnormal behaviour, stress and ultimately illness

---

Sub-standard and Outdated

There are still far too many of these sub-standard catteries in existence.

All buildings have a limited life, and there comes a time when further investment cannot be justified and a complete rebuild is the only course of action. At this point, owners either close or sell up to avoid the investment costs, or upgrade.

These photographs show you examples of buildings that are sub-standard and outdated. Happily, all of these buildings have since been demolished and replaced with new catteries. When you compare these photographs to anything else in the book, you will soon see how times are changing!

Above: this building was demolished due to a failing floor, single-skin roofing, dividing panels not sealed at floor level, narrow corridors and generally difficult and unpleasant environment for staff to work in.

Above: old timber cattery with narrow corridors, low ceilings, all-wood construction.

Above: stacked two units high, timber doors (black), paving slab floor (red)

Above: old cattery with steep ramps, no sneeze barriers (panels to give protection from cross-infection), gaps under the division screens (again, inviting the spread of disease)

Left: dark, cramped indoor unit with no outlook for the cats, an impossibly steep ramp to gain access to the heated sleeping box

Above: close-up photo showing inside the sleeping box

State of the Art

'State of the Art' describes something that is the highest level of development at a particular period. Usually showing architectural flair to attract human visitors, innovation or successful ideas, ahead of their time. Architects are used to providing state of the art for people, but very few will understand what makes a cattery achieve this status.

A state of the art cattery is a **very** high specification design and finish building which is fit for its purpose. It is usually only the major charities or large organisations who can afford to build to this very high standard on a large scale.

Lower left: Cats Protection National Cat Centre built in 2004. All others: The Blue Cross Centre at Lewknor built in 2005

UNDERSTANDING THE PET MARKET

Anyone seriously considering opening a cattery will need to know what the 'market' is for the type of organisation they want to run. The attitude people have towards pets evolves, and you need to be aware of this as it will affect the success and requirements of your cattery. This will affect you whatever type of cattery establishment you are thinking of. The rising number of people living single, busy lives now means we are treating our pets, particularly cats, as child substitutes. Young, affluent single people now treat their cats to all the comforts of home, buying gourmet foods, accessories, and presents.

Longevity: On average cats live for 12-14 years, but they can live for up to 20 years. The oldest cat on record (Puss, a tabby in Devon, UK) is reputed to have been 36 years!
Estimated number of owned cats (millions):
UK 9.2m | USA 78m | Canada 4.5m | Europe 60m | Australia 3m | New Zealand 0.9-1.5m

Almost 50% of UK and USA cat-owning households will have 2 or more cats

Reasons for Cat Ownership

In a recent survey by Cats Protection UK, owners are 3.5 times more likely to be **female**, male owners are most likely to be aged 45-54 and female owners more likely to be aged 35-44.

According to Cats Protection:

- **The main reason people keep cats is for companionship and love.** Cats are perceived as being low maintenance, affectionate, independent, mysterious and perceptive

- **Sharing feelings and bed space:** Many people prefer to share their feelings with their cat rather than a human. Younger people can enjoy a better night's sleep with their cat on their bed rather than a partner!

- **Reducing stress:** A cat can help his/her owner to reduce their stress levels and relax more

- **Better companions:** Cats are often perceived as a better companion than a current or last partner!

- **Enhance 'pulling power':** Women were more attracted to men who like cats, seeing them as nicer people!

What sort of relationship describes how you feel towards your cat?				
	Single men %	Partnered men %	Single women %	Partnered women %
Like a baby/child	14	26	54	45
Like a good friend	65	51	35	42
Like a partner	7	1	3	2
Just a pet	0	18	6	6
Other	9	4	4	1
from a Cats Protection UK Survey				

Cat Ownership on the Increase

Cat ownership has now overtaken dog ownership. Today's lifestyle has more people living alone, or couples going out to work, more people working from home and wanting urban living, and so the self-sufficient, free living, independent cat is coming into its own. Cat ownership is greater in the more affluent and urban areas and in owner-occupied dwellings. Dog ownership is decreasing.

In the USA over 50% of cat owners have more than one animal at home, while dog owners tend to have only one pet.
In the UK 38% of cat owning households have more than one cat, while only 22% of dog owning households keep more than one dog. The UK 2003 feline population was approx. 9.2 million. DOUBLE the number it was just 30 years ago.
The recent growth of cat ownership in the UK far outweighs dog ownership. It is estimated that the annual growth rate since 1995 has been 18.5% for cats, compared with 6.8% for dogs

Keeping Up-to-date

You will need to keep in touch with new advances, products, news and the multitude of health, veterinary, behavioural and care queries that cat owners may throw at you! Signing up to email newsletters or cat magazines is a very quick and easy way to achieve this. We provide a list of useful website addresses at www.catterydesign.com.

Internet/Web

With the easy accessibility of the internet, more pet owners are able to seek out the kind of cattery that 'fits' what they want or expect for their cat, rather than just choosing the nearest. In better quality boarding establishments for example, owners are finding that cat owners are travelling far further than the traditional catchment area of 20-30 miles. It is also becoming more common to go on holiday and take your pets with you to a boarding establishment nearby.

If you are going to invest in building or upgrading a cattery, it is essential you know what the market is. There is no longer a need to charge 'what everyone else is charging' when you are providing a far better facility and service, and able to cast your business net much farther afield by using the internet. We will talk more about your website later.

Pets are Good for You

Just thinking about and caring for another living being helps nurture feelings of empathy and understanding, and makes us feel less alone. Pets provide joy, love, comfort, friendship, understanding of life, are 'part of the family', they even help to keep us healthy and teach us commitment and responsibility.

Several international studies have shown that pets are good for people!

Pets help to lower blood pressure, heart rate, cholesterol and triglyceride, reduce stress and anxiety, offer instant relaxation, help to prevent heart disease, provide greater psychological stability, lower health care costs and help to fight depression, headaches, insomnia, indigestion, help us recover faster from illness and lower the frequency of allergies and even helping with alzheimers and living in a retirement home.
So, as well as loving and caring for your pet, owning one can improve your mental and physical health!

Pets can help educate **children** about life. In this hi-tech age it is even more important to have a foundation for learning about nature, nurture and unconditional love that humans may be unable to provide. Pets can even increase the attention span of children with learning difficulties.
The benefits of pets to the **elderly** are enormous, including providing a link to the outside world.

CATTERY RAISON D'ETRE

CATTERIES ARE ALL
ABOUT 'HOME'.
WHETHER IT
IS TEMPORARILY
BEING AWAY,
OR FINDING
A NEW ONE

People that
hate cats
will
come back as mice
in their
next life!

Anonymous

RESCUE

Rescue centres, shelters and sanctuaries all provide safe and secure accommodation, food, water, veterinary and day-to-day care for abandoned or unwanted cats while they try to find them new owners and homes. Given the increased likelihood of illness or disease from animals whose backgrounds you may not know, it is always a challenge for rescues to reduce or control this risk – but there are ancillary buildings that can help. Isolation is one example, but also having a socialisation room to introduce cats and potential owners and help them bond, and an admissions building where cats are brought first to settle in and be assessed – you can read more about these buildings later.

Rescues want to rehome cats as quickly as possible, and every effort made to settle the cat in and reduce stress will pay dividends when it comes to finding a new owner. However, sometimes shelters decide to keep a cat as a permanent resident, or with a fosterer if it has been through a particularly bad time, or is proving difficult to rehome because of a chronic illness or difficult temperament. The high turnover of cats and possibly staff will mean a harder impact on the buildings, and therefore it is imperative that the long-term maintenance options are considered. It is no use choosing cheap material if it has continually to be replaced! It is in your best interests to build a cattery that can cope with your current needs, and ideally your future ones, and one that can also handle the wear and tear it will take long-term. The more thought you can put into getting it right on paper and planning for the future, the more pleased you will be with the final result.

Working for a national animal welfare rescue myself, I know how difficult it is to balance ideals, building costs and long-term benefits against current budget, resources and site constraints. The best advice I can give you is to build to the best standard and size you can, with as much daylight as possible. Not only will you need to make the buildings cat-friendly, but you will also have to think about the staff who work there, volunteers and visitors, as well as potential owners. As happened to me recently, it is very gratifying to overhear visitors walking away from a cattery commenting on enjoying a visit, rather than being depressed by the number of cats needing homes or the conditions in which they are kept.

Whereas larger organisations may employ pet behaviourists, smaller organisations may not have this luxury and rely on managers and staff to discover the latest findings or research on accommodation. The resources below may help.

Useful organisations:

- **Cats Protection** The UK (and probably the world's) largest cat rescue charity
  www.cats.org.uk

- **Humane Society of the United States**
  USA's largest animal protection organisation
  www.hsus.org
  www.animalsheltering.org
  www.safecats.org

- **Feline Advisory Bureau**
  A charity dedicated to promoting the health and welfare of cats through improved feline knowledge
  www.fabcats.org

- Association of Pet Behaviour Counsellors
  www.apbc.org.uk

Useful books:

- *The Welfare of Cats*, Irene Rochlitz

- *The Domestic Cat*, Dennis C Turner & Patrick Bateson/*The Behaviour of the Domestic Cat*, John Bradshaw

- *Rescue Cattery Manual*, Anne Haughie

- *What is my Cat Thinking?* Gwen Bailey

Dogs have owners, cats have staff

Anonymous

BOARDING

Boarding catteries should provide safe and secure temporary accommodation for cat owners on holiday, in hospital, moving house etc.

These are commercial operations that should be run in a professional and caring way. They accept that the cats cared for are precious to their owners, who soon realise what is a good quality business is when compared with sub-standard catteries.

The cost of modern buildings is high and a considerable investment. Consequently, owners need to ensure they provide a good, quality service to gain repeat business and build a good relationship with their clients to maximise their income.

Having helped hundreds of people create boarding facilities, we can tell you that the trend is definitely towards providing excellent accommodation, larger units and less of them, and a personal, caring service. These catteries have an extremely high occupancy rate and charge higher fees to reflect the quality of their investment. They are also recommended as examples by the authorities to others wishing to start a cattery, and recommended heartily by their clients and vets.

Cattery Management Information

As well as the cattery buildings, the other aspects you need to understand are the best practices for running and managing a cattery. The *Boarding Cattery Manual* from the Feline Advisory Bureau focuses on setting up and managing a cattery. We recommend you purchase the *Boarding Cattery Manual* (buy online from us at www.catterydesign.com) and the following books about running and managing a cattery whether you are thinking about starting up, rebuilding or taking over an existing business. You will learn more about this organisation on the following page.

Useful organisations:

- **Feline Advisory Bureau**
  A charity dedicated to promoting the health and welfare of cats through improved feline knowledge
  www.fabcats.org

- **American Boarding Kennels Association**
  An organisation whose goal is to be an educational centre and forum for cat boarding operators or those interested in learning about the operation of a cat boarding facility
  www.abka.com

Useful books:

- *Boarding Cattery Manual*, Claire Bessant

- *The Domestic Cat*, Dennis C Turner & Patrick Bateson/

- *The Behaviour of the Domestic Cat*, John Bradshaw

- *The Welfare of Cats*, Irene Rochlitz

- *What is my Cat Thinking?* Gwen Bailey

BOARDING CATTERY ADVICE

Feline Advisory Bureau, UK

Boarding catteries are just part of the work of the Feline Advisory Bureau. FAB was set up in 1958 by a handful of people who wanted to be able to provide better care for their cats.

Almost 50 years on and this ethos is still as strong as ever and FAB's excitement at working with this most wonderful animal has not lessened.

The charity has grown considerably to the point where we now influence the care of over 1 million cats every year

Over the years our work has provided information and expertise to people working with cats across a wide range of professions, as well as to cat lovers and owners.

VETERINARY TREATMENT

When we began, the cause of cat flu had not been identified and a vaccine for it was still some way off; many cats died from infectious diseases and in general they were treated as if they were small dogs. Many other diseases were not recognised, let alone treated.

Thanks to our work, we understand cats so much more and realise that they are indeed unique.

Many diseases are now preventable or treatable, and our cats are living longer and healthier lives. However, cats being cats, there are still many mysteries to unravel - from behaviour problems to the recognition of pain, and poisoning to disease control. With the help of its own feline expert panel (a group of veterinary surgeons funded by us to specialise in feline care at UK veterinary universities) we collect information on both rare conditions and common problems.

You will find over 400 pages on our website, put together by these experts in cat care. From behaviour problems to diabetes, vaccination, digestive problems, skin problems and much, much more, our information is constantly updated with new findings or treatments. These experts see cats on referral from vets in practice (just like being referred to a consultant by your doctor) and train the vets and nurses of the future. They speak at conferences and meetings, both in the UK and across the world to audiences ranging from veterinary specialists to cat owners, all with the aim of improving cat care.

ENVIRONMENT AND LIFESTYLE

And we are not just interested in veterinary treatment and catteries, our experts realise that a cat's environment and lifestyle can have a great influence on its health and wellbeing, both mental and physical. We're interested in the whole cat!

The more owners understand cats and their behaviour, the better they will be at spotting problems and giving tender, loving care and support when a cat needs it

FELINE WELFARE

We now occupy a pivotal position in feline welfare, supporting both cat owners and carers and the veterinary profession, and, perhaps even more importantly - helping to bridge that divide. With cats at the centre of all our work, we have tackled areas where high quality, reliable knowledge will improve cat care - from veterinary care to catteries, breeding to rescue.

At the core is the cat owner and our work not only provides the best information for day to day care, but reliable high quality information when a problem arises.

FELINE ADVISORY BUREAU

UK CATTERY GUIDELINES

One of the main objectives when the charity was set up in 1958 was to improve the standards of boarding catteries.

At that time there were no guidelines at all for anyone wishing to board cats and there were many appalling boarding establishments. Through the work of a few dedicated people, we began to develop the ideas for the design, construction and management of catteries to ensure the safety and care of the cats. In 1963 the Animal Boarding Establishments Act was introduced in the UK. Although this stipulated that a licence was required to run a boarding cattery, it gave no information on standards and how they could be achieved.

It wasn't until 1995 that the Chartered Institute of Environmental Health introduced its Model Licence Conditions and Guidance for Cat Boarding Establishments in the UK (into which we had some input) which goes into much greater detail about cattery construction. This is the document which is used to gauge whether catteries should be licensed by the local authority.

> However, the CIEH guidelines are not always used by local authorities, and standards of catteries found acceptable to license vary greatly around the UK

BOARDING CATTERY MANUAL

For this reason we decided to update its information and produce a comprehensive Boarding Cattery Manual and a Standard for Construction and Management of its own.

Although it is written to help cattery proprietors run a good business, it makes no apology to have as its main remit, the health and welfare of the cats boarded in the cattery.

High standards are not necessarily about luxury - keeping design and construction as simple and practical as possible will allow for ease of care and cleaning.

> Owners want to be sure they are leaving their cat, a member of the family, in safe and caring hands

Giving cats warmth, space to exercise and providing a caring environment is much more important than trying to emulate the owner's home. While owners may think they like the idea of carpets and soft furnishing and a home-from-home environment, they may not understand the added risk of passing on infections that this can bring.

The manual and standard set out the principles of good design and management, aimed at minimising the risks to cats in a cattery of infectious disease, injury, escape or depression/boredom and to maximise the care given to them. It explains why these requirements are necessary and how they can be achieved. Different designs of cattery are possible and will keep changing in the future - the important thing is always to consider what the design is for, to aim to keep cats safe and make the care of them as straightforward as possible for the proprietors.

However, the manual also covers management, health and disease of cats in the cattery context, complying with the law in terms of medicines, veterinary consent etc.

It also looks at disinfection regimes and standard operating procedures for many cattery procedures.

UK LISTING SCHEME

The aims of the FAB Boarding Cattery Listing Scheme in the UK are to raise standards of construction and care in boarding catteries, raise awareness of good standards of boarding amongst the public, and provide information for cat owners on how to find a good boarding cattery.

Where to find out more about the Feline Advisory Bureau:
Feline Advisory Bureau, Taeselbury, High Street, Tisbury, Wiltshire, SP3 6LD, Tel: +44 (0)870 742 2278

www.fabcats.org

The
smallest
feline
is
a
masterpiece

Leonardo da Vinci

BREEDING/SHOWING

Many breeders will not have planned for the situation they find themselves in, it 'just grew' from one cat. Planning for the current and the future is always time well spent! To make the best use of your space, location and budget, you will need to ask yourself such questions as: is for the long-term and will you specialise in another breed in the future?

Environment + Socialisation = Breeder Success

It is well documented that kittens from a busy household get used to everyday sights, sounds and smells will have an advantage, and be better able to cope with everyday life when they go to their new home. You will need to focus on the quality of the environment the kittens are brought up in, which will shape their whole lives. There are plenty of ideas on how to achieve this on the internet, just search on 'socialising (or socializing) kittens'.

The better prepared your kittens are for real-life homes, the less stress they will be caused and express as hiding, scratching and spraying which owners may not know how to cope with and simply give their cat up to rescue. **Cats Protection in the UK alone rescues and rehomes around 60,000 cats a year** and the Humane Society of the United States estimate that 3-4 million pets are adopted each year, with a shocking **3-4 million pets being euthanised (put to sleep) each year, pedigree or not**. This is no small problem.

So, how can breeders help ensure their kittens have the best start? As well as specifying to new owners that pet cats should be neutered, perhaps you could provide or at least recommend books on caring for their cat, feline behaviour and how or where to find solutions to problems. As well as a grounding in day-to-day care and maintenance for the owners, this will help ensure that your kittens are not abandoned or given up to rescue because of owner ignorance about these natural behaviours (see books to recommend to cat owners below).

Breeders will need to pay particular attention to the amount of space provided for each cat, as well as space for storage, grooming, kitchen, waste and isolation. A high amount of stress is caused from cats being confined and we will read more about this later in this book, and how to improve life in the cattery. A crate or cage does not allow cats to jump or climb, an innate part of what being a cat is all about, so we will explore some safe alternatives.

Useful organisations:

- **Feline Advisory Bureau** www.fabcats.org

- Association of Pet Behaviour Councellors www.apbc.org.uk

- Governing Council of the Cat Fancy UK www.gccfcats.org

- The Cat Fanciers' Association USA www.cfa.org

- The International Cat Association www.tica.org

- American Cat Fanciers' Association www.acfacats.com

- Cat Fanciers' Federation www.cffinc.org

Useful books:

- *The Welfare of Cats*, Irene Rochlitz

- *The Domestic Cat*, Dennis C Turner & Patrick Bateson

Books to recommend to cat owners:

- *Cat Confidential*, Vicky Halls

- *Cat Detective*, Vicky Halls

- *What is my Cat Thinking?* Gwen Bailey

QUARANTINE

The standard for quarantine **should** be the highest standard available, because the cat is kept in the same accommodation for six months.

The licensing regulations for quarantine are very specific and come under the jurisdiction of DEFRA (The Department for Environment, Food and Rural Affairs UK)

Thankfully, the need for quarantine has lessened in the UK because of the introduction of the Passports for Pets scheme. However, there is still a requirement for quarantine for animals coming from some countries. Further information is available from the organisations listed below.

Useful organisations:

- Passports for Pets
  freespace.virgin.net/
  passports.forpets

- DEFRA
  www.defra.gov.uk/animalh/
  quarantine

Useful books:

- *The Welfare of Cats*, Irene Rochlitz

- *The Domestic Cat*, Dennis C Turner & Patrick Bateson

- *The Behaviour of the Domestic Cat*, John Bradshaw

VETERINARY

Typical layout and design for veterinary use requires cages that are hygienic, easy to clean and have the aim of limiting the amount of movement for a hospitalised cat. These are generally used only in the short term, as in these circumstances it is in the animals' best interest to promote fast recovery after surgery for example.

Useful organisations:

- The American Association of Feline Practitioners
  www.aafponline.org

- American Veterinary Medical Association
  www.avma.org

- British Small Animal Veterinary Association
  www.bsava.com

- Royal College of Veterinary Surgeons UK
  www.rcvs.org.uk

- British Veterinary Association
  www.bva.co.uk

- Feline Advisory Bureau
  www.fabcats.org

Useful books:

- *The Welfare of Cats*, Irene Rochlitz

- *The Domestic Cat*, Dennis C Turner & Patrick Bateson

- *The Behaviour of the Domestic Cat*, John Bradshaw

One small cat
changes
coming home to an
empty house,
to
coming home

Pam Brown

PRIVATE/PET MULTI-CAT OWNERS

In the USA approximately 60% of cats are kept indoors, whereas in the UK this is only 10% (but rising) as most are allowed to roam free.

The organisations below provide cat owners with helpful information on all aspects of cat care, health and cat-related issues, including:

- Cat care leaflets

- Dealing with illness or disease, first aid

- Indoor V outdoor considerations and keeping your cat safe

- Neutering

- Moving house/lost cats

- Asthma

- Senior/elderly cats and kittens

- Living with babies/children

- Grass and catnip

- Multi-cat households

- Feral/free-roaming cats

- Behaviour problems

Useful organisations:

- **Cats Protection**
  www.cats.org.uk

- **Feline Advisory Bureau**
  a charity dedicated to promoting the health and welfare of cats through improved feline knowledge
  www.fabcats.org

- **Pet Care Trust**
  www.petcare.org.uk

- **American Boarding Kennels Association**
  www.abka.com

- **Humane Society of the United States**
  www.hsus.org

  www.safecats.org

- **The Indoor Cat Initiative**
  www.indoorcat.org

- **Cats International**
  www.catsinternational.org

Useful books:

- *Cat Confidential*, Vicky Halls

- *Cat Detective*, Vicky Halls

- *What is my Cat Thinking?* Gwen Bailey

3 PURCHASE AND PLANNING

DON'T WORRY! THERE ARE SIMPLE STEPS TO HELP GET YOUR PLANNING/ZONING PERMISSION

WHAT YOU MUST COMPLY WITH

People usually have exactly the same queries about running/building a cattery wherever they are in the world, so the information contained in this book is relevant to everyone setting up a cattery.

Finding out about legislation is usually the quickest part of the journey, as all you need to do is contact your local authority! In every country, things always differ greatly between regions, nothing is ever applied 'country-wide'.
Even when there are actual country guidelines, some authorities are strict regarding compliance with them, yet others have not even adopted them! Some countries have legislation or guidelines, and others (such as Ireland) have none.

GETTING PERMISSION TO BUILD A CATTERY

Whatever country you live in, the first thing you should do is to contact your local authority regarding Planning Permission/Zoning and Animal Welfare or Boarding legislation or guidelines, as most types of business require permission.

For Building Permission, you will need to find out about:

- Planning/Zoning Permission to build or replace a cattery

- Legislation/Animal Welfare Laws that will affect you

- Getting a licence/permit if you are going to be boarding cats, running a sanctuary or breeding

There are usually two types of permission, one is **outline** permission (where you may not yet own the property and would like to see if permission would be granted with an overall plan of what is proposed) and the other is **full** permission where more detailed information and plans are required. From past experience, I would suggest that it is advisable to obtain the services of an expert, one who is familiar with the local authority and who knows the topography. This is normally in the form of a planning consultant, architect, surveyor or even a quality building contractor.

How to find your local authority:

You can find the contact details for your local authority in the phone book, or on the internet. We also provide an online list of where to find the local authority websites and phone numbers, and legislation by country and region where known on our website. Confusingly, in some countries you may find that catteries are listed just as kennels, or 'cat kennels'.

Where to find contact details for your local authority:
- Look it up on your authority tax bill

- Look it up in your local business pages or phone book

- Look it up on our website: www.catterydesign.com

Who to Speak to

Planning/Zoning Permission

Contact your local authority's planning/zoning department for a planning/zoning application for building on or upgrading your property and discuss the possibility of opening a cattery at your location. This will give you a good indication of how much ease or difficulty you may have with your application. They will take into consideration views from the traffic/highways department and the animal welfare or licensing officer.

In dealing with a planning application, local authorities can either:

- Approve it outright

- Approve it subject to conditions

- Refuse it

Supporting Statements:

Discuss the possibility of obtaining written statements from your existing contacts (such as your vet, cat club, cat rescues and animal warden/animal control officer) regarding the need for good, quality catteries in your area. They may also provide interesting or helpful information (such as all the other catteries in your area are often fully booked, how they perceive the local standard, which catteries will be closing and what the need is for good catteries). If your contacts are willing to put their comments in writing, you can use these as 'supporting statements' to submit with your application and strengthen your case.

Licensing Application

Commercial catteries will require a licence in the UK and North America. Rescue catteries currently do not need a license in the UK, but a permit will be required for North America. Speak to your local authority's licensing officer regarding your licence and application (this will be your environmental health/animal warden/animal control officer depending on your location) – they may also be based at your local authority.

Environmental Issues

Speak to your local authority's environment officer/agency regarding the impact of the cattery on the environment and in particular about waste disposal, (your planning/zoning officer may also be able to help you with recommendations).

Your environmental health officer will probably be based at your local authority, but here are links to the main environment agency websites:

- UK: www.environment-agency.gov.uk
  Scotland: www.sepa.org.uk

- USA: www.epa.gov

- Canada: www.ec.gc.ca

- Europe: www.eea.eu.int

SITE LOCATION

One of the greatest difficulties is in choosing the correct site for your requirements. These requirements are very subjective, but the important point to remember is they should take into account your needs in ten years; not only the next two years.

One of the first decisions you have to make is whether you opt to build on a 'green-field' site or purchase an existing cattery. Both options have factors for and against.

To highlight the pros and cons of both options, some of the more salient points follow.

HOW MUCH LAND IS REQUIRED?

Generally, the *minimum* amount of land you need is 1/4 acre for a boarding cattery.

You will need to incorporate car parking, reception, storage, laundry, kitchen, gardens/ponds/things for the cats to look at, as well as your cat units and an area of private garden for your own use, and of course for your own cats.

How big is ¼ acre?

- **Metric:**   30m by 33m   (990 metres square)
- **Imperial:**   100ft by 108ft (10,890ft square)

What does ¼ acre look like?

- **16 x small gardens/yards:** **Metric:**   7.5m x 8.25m each
  Imperial: 25ft x 27ft each
- **4 x Lawn Tennis Courts:** **Metric:**   23.7m x 10.9m wide (258m square) each
  Imperial: 78ft x 35ft (2,730ft square) each

PURCHASE OF AN EXISTING BUSINESS

If you make the choice of purchasing an existing business, it provides you with the **advantages** of a ready-made client base, an audited income, existing buildings and infrastructure. The **disadvantages** of buying an existing business are the payment for the 'goodwill' and possibly purchasing buildings that are past their useful working life. Goodwill is a negotiable sum and relates to the popularity of an established business, which is treated as a saleable asset. This varies from business to business and can be a substantial amount.

Some of the questions that you need to ask and satisfy yourself that this is the correct establishment to purchase are:

- **Location** – Is the location right for my needs?

- **Existing Licence** – Is the existing licence adequate? Does it have any spare capacity for any future expansion?
  Future Licensing – Will the licence be renewed without extra costs or conditions to bring the buildings up to the local authority and your own required standard?

- **Expansion** – Is the site suitable for expansion and development? Will the local planning authority allow any further expansion?

- **Car parking** – Is there sufficient for customers, staff, delivery vehicles etc?

- **Existing Accommodation** – Are the existing animal accommodation and associated buildings suitable for your requirements?

- **Legislation** – Do the catteries comply with current local standards? To obtain an animal boarding licence the establishment needs to ensure that it complies with local guidelines. (In the UK it is the owner who holds the licence, not the business).

- **Infrastructure** – Is the infrastructure adequate for the current demands being imposed on it?
  (e.g. electricity, gas, water supply and drainage). Is there any spare capacity for future expansion? All of these areas are the lifeblood of the premises, without them daily activities can be made extremely difficult. We will look at this in greater detail later in the book

- **Drainage** – Does the drainage system work correctly?

- **Complaints** – Have there been any complaints to, or any restrictions imposed by the local authority regarding noise, opening times, vehicular/foot traffic, pollution etc?

- **Residential Accommodation** – Does the site have the right amount of residential accommodation? Is there suitable space available to construct accommodation if required?

- **Access** – Can the access be maintained all year? Does the land suffer from flooding, making part of the property unusable during the winter months?

- **Planning and Zoning** – Do all of the buildings have planning consent? For more information on this see the following section on Planning

Some of the most informative details can be obtained about an existing property by spending time watching the staff go about their daily routine. What might be a minor irritation to them in terms of building design and layout could prove to be unworkable for you. Generally, there are very few catteries available for sale that do not require additional works to bring them up to the required standard. This should be remembered when negotiating the purchase price and used in your favour. There are more tips on the next page, where we will hear from a selling agent who specialises in cattery and kennel businesses.

BUYING A CATTERY BUSINESS

Peter Reed MNAEA, MICBA, Kennel Sales

DECIDE WHAT YOU WANT

When buying a property, doing your homework is extremely important. You are buying with your wallet, so buy for financial reasons, do not let your heart take over! **What is it that you want to buy and for what reasons?** How many facilities have you seen? Do friends own one? Visit ten facilities around you, pay attention to the construction, style and condition. Having found a style that you like, try to find the price of the units 'as new' for comparisons to work with.

Consider the location: do you have connections, family, relatives and friends nearby? Are you happy with the location, giving consideration to both plus and negative points? **Good catchment areas are expanding and developing residential areas, with pleasant surroundings**. Avoid dying areas with noticeable decaying in the locality, flight paths, proposed by-passes, pylons, sewage treatment plants, railway lines, landfill sites and areas liable to flooding. **Check the type of land and drainage**, agricultural fields with crops, livestock or with possible treatments which can give concerns for allergies, smells and noise. **Any competitors in the area need to be checked out** including the quality of facilities, service and fees. They are your competition, and no matter how good or bad they are you are, hopefully, aiming to be better! **The accounts are all-important -** it is upon these the business will be assessed by accountants and bank managers. **Having considered all these points (good and bad), what is the property worth to you?** Bear in mind there are possibly far more potential purchasers considering this property than you might imagine, and that one day you will also want to sell the property to someone going through the same thought process as you are! Find an independent financial adviser who will give independent advice, preferably with kennel-financing experience.

WE'RE HERE FOR THE LONG-TERM

A number of purchasers come to our office/kennels and cattery just to talk about the nature of the business. Intending purchasers have had work experience before buying their cattery. We talk with purchasers of kennels about setting up a cattery, and also purchasers (who have been unable to find their ideal cattery) about starting one up from scratch. Customers (not always buying through ourselves) talk to us about the best ways of expanding, modernising or replacing their facilities. We have even visited owners thinking about selling, shown them where they are going wrong (giving themselves more work than necessary), talked them out of selling by showing them how to run their facility more efficiently. They spread the word, and we shall get the property on our books one day!

Upon completion I say to most purchasers: we are still here if they want to talk about anything to do with a cattery or kennels, where to buy things, how to deal with certain circumstances, just phone us, and even if we can't help you, we probably know someone who can! **In February 2006 we celebrated 21 years of selling kennel and cattery businesses.** We would like to sincerely thank our customers for their help, encouragement and many recommendations, **making us the largest specialist agency selling kennels and catteries**. So not only will you have the services of the largest specialist agency, on a 'No Sale, No Fee' basis - we pay all advertising costs (doing more advertising than any other), a non-restrictive contract and with a commission rate starting at 1%. Cynthia, my wife and business partner has acquired 18 years of hands-on experience of running a kennels and cattery, showing and breeding Ragdoll cats, and her experience helps many purchasers during the first few months of ownership, with queries from cleaning equipment to customer service. We are ourselves now looking to expand our own cattery!

BUYING OR SELLING IN THE UK?

Interested? We hope you will be. If you are thinking of buying, selling or indeed already trying to sell your cattery business (privately or through another agency without success), why not give us a call? **We know discretion is important, we ourselves are boarding kennels and cattery owners**, so don't be shy, just give us a call, even in the evenings on:
01277 356641 at Kennel Sales, Ladybird Kennels, Roman Road
Ingatestone, Essex, CM4 9AD, UK.
www.catteriesforsale.co.uk or www.kennelsforsale.co.uk

SELLING A CATTERY BUSINESS

PLAN AHEAD

When thinking about selling your facility, work to a time scale. About 3 years before you do anything dramatic, start work behind the scenes. Bring the accounts up to date, as it is upon these that potential purchasers are going to try to raise their mortgage. The accounts will be looked at by bank managers, accountants and financial advisers who may have no knowledge of the cattery business, despite giving advice based on the accounts.

When selling anything, first impressions count. Imagine yourself as a purchaser, can you see any faults, necessary repairs, rubbish to be cleared or tired paint work? None of these will stop a sale, but may give intending purchasers greater confidence, rather than focusing on what costs they will incur immediately after having bought the property.

Keep an eye on local similar residential properties. Your property, when valued, will start with a comparison to local residences. This will be added to the approximate value of your facilities, taking into consideration their construction, age and condition. This will be further added to by the business, based largely upon the trading accounts. Obtain any information on possible planning permissions to the property, or local developments that might affect it.

CHOOSING AN AGENT

Call in an agent with an understanding of the business and see what comparable properties they have sold recently. Some will continue offering properties on their register when already sold by a rival (giving the appearance of offering more properties and being bigger than they actually are) so check who sold the properties you are interested in! Often properties are offered by different agents and perhaps owners too, and when sold, some agents may still show the property on their register as 'sold' for some time. When we are the selling agent, we confirm the property was sold by us, and when. The date is there for all to see, and for valuers to use as needing comparisons.

We remove all properties sold through other agents from our register after contracts have exchanged.

Before making a decision, request agents send information of their services/charges before they visit.

- Are there fees for: visiting your property, registering it, advertising, or even for removing it if it doesn't sell?
- Check fees are based upon the eventual selling price, and not on an inflated asking price
- Will they explain their terms fully before you sign any contract? Ask for a copy of their contract before they visit. You then have time to consider the implications, or ask your solicitor to cast an eye over it, before you agree to whatever terms are offered

Check the difference between terms:

- **Sole Agency:** The vendors instruct one agent to act on their behalf, normally for a set length of time, and thereafter may continue till a sale is achieved
- **Joint Sole Agency:** The vendors instruct two agents to act together on their behalf, normally for a set time, and may continue until a sale is achieved
- **Multiple Agency:** The vendor instructs as many agents as they wish, all of whom will act independently and in competition with each other. The best (or sometimes the luckiest) agent that finds the successful purchaser, is paid for their effort
- **Sole Selling Rights:** The vendor instructs one agent to act on their behalf. No matter who purchases the property, the agent is entitled to the fees (even if selling privately to a relative, the agent has the rights to claim their fees!)

A few days making the right decision is easier to live with than an expensive wrong decision. For further advice, speak to someone who recently purchased a property, asking where they obtained the best service.

Whilst it may be easy to offer a property privately (through websites/ adverts) an agent will also:

- Try to cut out the 'sight see'ers'
- Have experience and knowledge to know what seems 'right' or 'wrong' in a transaction
- Check the financial background and mortgage capabilities of interested parties, thus cutting out time wasters and unnecessary solicitors' costs
- Liaises with other agents within a chain, reporting periodically on proceedings or problems
- Liaises with solicitors to try and make the sale as smooth and untroubled as possible

PURCHASE OF A BROWN OR GREEN-FIELD SITE

Brown-field Site

A brown-field site is a plot of land that has previously been developed, used or occupied by a permanent structure, and is a land type that is frequently becoming an option for many businesses. The planning requirements are exactly the same as for any other site, but the main consideration is to establish what the site's previous business use has been. Clearly the risks for the site (or part of it) to have some form of contamination is far greater. Before the site is purchased, you need to know the extend of any contamination, the type of contamination, and the costs for either removing it or sealing it in. Specialist advice should be obtained if there are concerns about the possibility of contamination issues.

Green-field Site

A green-field site is land with or without buildings. For the purpose of this book, it is regarded as land that has had no animal-related buildings attached to it. This option has many long-term advantages over the purchase of an existing business, particularly if you want to develop a larger complex, have clear ideas about what standard you want, or start smaller due to initial budget constraints. A green-field site gives you the option to construct modern, well-designed buildings, to your own requirements. It also allows you to develop the site from scratch, to ensure that the buildings are high standard and in the correct position. It removes any restrictions that may occur with existing premises.The proposed development can also be phased over a period of time, to take into account restrictions on time and finances.

What to check:

- Locating a suitable site that is close to an area of habitation; but not too close as to result in complaints to the local authority e.g. traffic generation
- Satisfying the local authority in terms of planning
- To develop a successful business can take a considerable amount of time; the interim period can financially difficult
- A time delay before any revenue starts to come in
- Does the area have enough capacity to sustain another commercial or welfare centre?
- Ensure you have enough income to cover the first six months ideally. This can be done by continuing employment for you or a partner, or allow sufficient amount in your loan to cover this period
- Use the building time productively to get organised with your marketing and image
- If you haven't worked professionally with cats before, and you have the opportunity to work voluntarily for a rescue organisation, seize the opportunity as it will be time well spent
- If you have never run any business before, a slower start might be more beneficial to you as you can build your confidence and knowledge at your own pace

Additional Costs:

For green-field sites, or major upgrading works are proposed, there will be hidden costs. Some examples are:
- **Services Upgrade** – upgrading utility supplies can be extremely expensive
  All utility providers (e.g. water, gas, drainage and electricity) will charge for any works incurred. The level of works required, the supply increase requirement, and the complexity of the works, dictate the cost
- **Road Access** – these can be either private or public
  Generally you can construct any private road on your land and to whatever specification is adequate for the works being carried out. However, once the road becomes public, it is an entirely different prospect. There will be specifications set by the local authority and generally, this type of work will be carried out by the local authority

PLANNING AND ZONING PERMISSION

As already mentioned, the first difficulty is in locating a suitable site; the second major obstacle is in obtaining permission either for a new site, or to develop an existing business. Most types of business development requires permission from the local authority. Clearly, if there has been any business use on the land, a precedent has been set, which can be highly beneficial to your case.

The local planning authority is interested in any new planning application for many reasons. The more usual ones likely to influence the authority's decision are:

- **Appearance and scale** – External appearance of the development, and the size and scale of the development

- **Neighbours** – Any authority will be concerned about how your application could affect your neighbours. Loss of light to their property, loss of privacy, increased traffic and disturbance are all possible reasons for refusal

- **Topography** – How the buildings will sit on the land

- **Environment** – Minimising the impact on the environment

- **Traffic** – Not creating or perpetuating unacceptable traffic or transport conditions, reducing the need to travel (sustainable development)

- **Risk** – Avoiding the development of land that is unstable, at risk of flooding, or that would be likely to increase the risk of flooding elsewhere

- **Highways** – Providing a safe access to the highway. (There are set standards for accesses, these are known as visibility splays. The splay required by the authority will depend on the location, the type of road etc)

- **Car Parking** – Authorities set standards for the number of spaces required on new developments

- **Archaeological Areas** – Areas of archaeological importance can influence any new development

- **Trees** – These can restrict development. Before any new development is undertaken it is worth checking to see if the trees have any preservation orders

- **Services/Utilities** – Any existing utility services within the boundary. It is not uncommon to find either on the site, or close to it, utility services such as gas, water, drainage, electricity or radio masts. *[E.g. one site with a 250mm/10" mains gas pipe running across one corner has a restriction that no building can be constructed within 3m/10ft either side of it!]*

- **Rights of Way** – If a public right of way crosses your site, it could prevent the siting of a new building. It is possible to have this diverted – however, it can be a lengthy process

- **Contaminated Land** – There are risks and costs involved with dealing with contaminated land

- **Wildlife** – Any old building/s that have not been used for a number of years (particularly in rural areas) might have become the home for endangered species such as bats, owls etc. Many of these species are protected under wildlife or environmental legislation. (The authority might insist that a professional survey is carried out before granting planning permission if there is a suspicion that the property might house endangered species). Other animals that will be of interest to local authority will be certain reptiles, newts etc

- **Party Walls** – Shared walls with your neighbours

Summary of Planning Route

1. **Location** of suitable green field site or existing business

2. **Establish what new development is required**

3. **Basic design sketches to show to the Planning Officer**

4. **Pre-Application meeting with Planning Officer** to go over the proposed scheme in greater detail, establish if planning consent is likely to be of concern to the officer (this is important – there is little point in submitting an application if it will never be granted planning permission). Some reasons for refusal have already been identified, further reasons are that the development is in an area designated Green Belt, Conservation Area or is a Listed Building. If any of the above applies to your site, this could have major implications for your application. The Local Structure plan will show if any of these apply. It would also be worth checking prior to purchase of the property

5. **Proposed scheme/design drawn up** to the required standard

6. **Application is submitted with payment**, signed declarations, scaled drawings of the proposed buildings, car parking, roads etc, a scaled location plan (1:1250) for most applications (if the site is extremely rural the authority might ask for a larger plan, say 1:2500 for identification purposes). It is normal for most authorities to ask for five copies of each drawing and plan. It is also useful to include a covering letter or supporting statement about the development. This allows the councillors a better insight at a personal level about your proposal

7. **Application is registered with the authority.** A receipt is sent to you and a reference number is allocated to your proposal. The acknowledgement letter will show when a decision should be made: this is normally between eight – twelve weeks after receipt)

8. **Application is advertised by the authority**

9. **Allow approximately four weeks then contact the authority** to see how your application is progressing.
   Generally you need to know:
   - Any potential issues or problems
   - If there are problems, what needs to be done to overcome them
   - Will the decision be taken by committee or by the planning officer
   - When will the committee be considering your application

10. **Continue to monitor the development.** Speak to any neighbours who might be affected by your proposal, (if the neighbours don't have any objections, ask them to write to the authority to support your proposal)

If there are concerns about your application, you need to address these. Ignoring these concerns is likely to result in a refusal. **If it seems that the application is likely to fail**, you can either let it run, then re-apply, withdraw the application (you will not be reimbursed any of your fees) or appeal against the Authority's decision.
If there are no major issues and the application is successful, if will either be passed outright, or have conditions attached. If successful, the development will normally have a time limit of five years in which it must be completed.

If the application is unsuccessful, or you appeal, I strongly recommend that you take the advice of a professional planning consultant.

Planning Tips

As already mentioned, planning can sometimes be a very complicated and protracted business. An application deemed suitable for the granting of planning permission at one location might not be granted permission at another, which on paper all seem to have similar characteristics!

The following planning tips should be helpful to your situation:

Permitted Development

Certain types of development are exempt from planning permission. This is legal and allows smaller projects to proceed without having to go through the planning procedure.

However, these 'permitted development' rules generally only apply to domestic situations, which do not involve any form of commercial business and are confined to curtilage of your property. This is somewhat of a grey area and should be checked with the Planning Officer for verification.

Time Limits

Planning permissions are normally valid for only a set time period from the date of the permission being granted; although the authority may, in exceptional circumstances, substitute a period either longer or shorter. There is no guarantee that any new application submitted due to time-lapse will be granted permission. Planning policies are constantly changing. In some cases this might be to your advantage, and in others a disadvantage! It is worth checking with the authority from time to time to check this.

Planning Fees

All applications for planning permission have to be accompanied by the relevant fee; the scale of fees being subject to regular increases.

Obviously, the larger the scale of the development, the greater the fee. The planning application will not be valid unless it is accompanied with the correct fee. There are a few, exceptional cases where no planning fee, or a reduced fee is payable, details can be obtained from the planning authority.

Clearly, if the correct approach has been carried out and sensible discussions have taken place with the planning authority and advice taken, any major obstacles will hopefully have been avoided.

Wildlife and Country Legislation

Any old building/s that have not been used for a number of years, particularly in rural areas might have become the home of endangered species such as bats, owls etc. Many of these species are protected by legislation (e.g. the UK's Wildlife and Countryside Act 1981) and it is an offence to destroy, disturb or obstruct their access. Again, your local authority will be able to advise you (in the UK advice on any such issues should be taken from English Nature www.english-nature.org.uk or Defra www.defra.gov.uk).

HOW DESIGN ISSUES CAN HELP YOUR APPLICATION

There are a number of things that you can do to help your application in terms of design, these are:

- **Impact** – Consider the impact of any new buildings from a number of view points and distances

- **Match existing buildings** – Impact can be reduced by relating the size, colour and materials to existing buildings. Use materials and colours that are common to the locality and blend in

- **Colour Tone** – Avoid bright intense colours – these can look very artificial and tend to fade more quickly than lighter toned colours

- **New buildings** – New buildings look best when forming part of a group, rather than standing alone. (Isolation buildings being an occasion when this rule will not apply)

- **Siting** – Try to site buildings in the folds of landform to provide shelter and screening

- **Hills** – Avoid locating buildings on the crest of hills

- **Slopes** – On sloping sites, align buildings parallel with the contours of the land

- **Proportion** – Large buildings can look out of proportion with older buildings, consider providing smaller buildings rather than one large unit

- **Roof pitch** – Try to match roof pitches to existing buildings where possible

- **Roofing materials** – Generally, roofing materials should be darker than the walls

Although extremely simple drawings for planning/zoning are still seen occasionally, the level of detail required by many local authorities for new developments has increased significantly over the past few years. Therefore, it is essential that you do as much fact-finding and homework prior to submitting your application as possible.

Check to see if there have been any previous planning applications on the site, or any development carried out in the vicinity – and speak to the owners and neighbours to see if they had any problems. Generally, once the application has been submitted all fees paid are not refundable, even if the applicant withdraws the application, or the authority rejects the application. It is important to keep in contact with the Planning Officer throughout the process to see if there have been any objections, and what the general feeling is about your application

Before submitting a planning application for any animal-related development, contact the Planning Officer to discuss the project in advance

A pre-application meeting will allow the Planning Officer to pass comment before the application is submitted formally
It must be remembered that the authority is not duty-bound to accept the opinion of the Planning Officer!
At present, it is not unusual to find applications taking between 8 – 14 weeks to be processed. Obviously the larger the development, the more detail and information the authority is likely to request.

Planning Conditions

If the application is successful, it is not unusual to find that the authority has imposed certain site-specific conditions.

The normal conditions for smaller scale developments will be:

- **Landscaping** – The authority might insist that a landscaping scheme is to be considered as part of the application

- **External Lighting** – For rural areas, most authorities do not want to see a large amount of artificial lighting and might restrict the use of floodlights etc

- **Parking** – Providing and allowing sufficient parking on the premises for staff and clients, or ensuring that the vehicles can drive in, turn around on site and then drive out facing forwards (for safety reasons many authorities do not allow business operations to reverse out on to a road)

- **Road Signage** – If you wish to erect a business sign, this normally requires planning permission, and sometimes highways permission as well. This will depend on your location and the size of the sign board

ENFORCEMENT OF PLANNING CONTROL

Local planning authorities have powers to ensure that any unauthorised development that has been carried out is rectified.

Unauthorised development is not in itself an offence, the exception being protected/listed buildings.
Once an unlawful development comes to the notice of the authority, it will decide what action is to be taken. This decision is taken upon the nature of the development, any local restrictions, and materials used etc.

There are two ways an infringement can occur:

- A development that has been carried out without planning permission

- A development that has been granted permission, but has not complied with the specific conditions being imposed by the planning authority

DEMOLITION

It may be necessary to demolish existing buildings on a newly acquired site. The reasons for this are to clear part of the site for future development, to remove or make safe any structures in an unsafe condition.

The law regarding demolition is very specific and should not be taken lightly, with statutory requirements that must be adhered to. For any large-scale demolition, expert advice should normally be sought.

In addition to the authority, the owner or their agent must also notify:

- Any utility companies (e.g. gas, electricity)

- The owner/occupiers of any building adjacent to the building concerned

SITE PURCHASE

Ensure that any site you intend to purchase will be granted planning permission, as this is most relevant to green-field sites that do not have an established business use.

You do not have to own the land to submit a planning application to develop it!

There have been a great many potential building plots advertised for sale, which on initial reading look very attractive and reasonably priced. However, many of these do not have any form of planning consent for development, and many **will never** be granted permission. Clearly without planning consent, the land has little financial value.

Before purchasing any plot it is worth checking the site's planning history. This will tell you what applications have been submitted or refused and quite often you will be able to obtain copies of old plans of any proposed development.

Meet the Planning Officer

It is always a good idea to try and meet the local Planning Officer to pass your ideas to them. However, most planning officers will always take the conservative and cautious approach when discussing projects informally. Any comments made by the Planning Officer do not have to be taken literally; planning is a very subjective issue.

Don't be disheartened if they do not enthuse about your project, their job is to assess every application objectively!

Flexibility

Be prepared to amend or alter your design slightly if this means that you will succeed with your application

Delegated or Committee Decision

There is a difference between a delegated decision and a committee decision. All chief planning officers have the power to grant a planning application under delegated powers. This means that there is no involvement of a full planning committee. This normally expedites the planning decision time.

However, the **disadvantage** is that if the application is recommended for refusal you do not haven any opportunity to try and convince them otherwise. It is vital to keep in contact with the Authority and track your application.

Application Refusal

If your application is going to be refused, it is sensible to withdraw it. An application can be withdrawn at any time, up to the point of the decision notice. This, in theory, keeps the site plot 'clean' in planning terms. However, in reference to future applications, the authority will still mark the site. You will need to understand why your application was marked for refusal.

Clearly, there is little point in submitting another application for exactly the same scheme!

If your application is going to be refused, it is sensible to
withdraw it, find out the reasons for refusal,
and address them on re-application.
(This is another reason for monitoring the
application throughout the planning route!)

Planning Appeal:

If your application has been refused planning by committee; the entire process starts to become extremely protracted and complicated. At this stage, quite often there is little room for manoeuvre.

One option is to appeal against the authority's decision. This process is made by an independent inspector who will judge each case on its own merits, local policies etc. However, this is a very risky business and will take at least six months. It is best avoided!

Planning Conditions:

Most planning applications will be subject to conditions. For smaller developments, these normally relate to material types, colour, fencing and landscaping.

It is often far too easy to forget about these conditions until two or three years after the granting of planning permission, only to be confronted with a letter from the authority stating that work needs to be completed in order to make the application lawful.

Four-year Rule

This is an odd piece of UK legislation, but one that could be in force in other countries. It is not something that should be relied upon as a way of securing a building or development of course, but is worth noting:

If something has been built without permission and no action has been taken against it for four years – then the authority cannot do anything about it.

This could be useful, particularly If you are purchasing an existing business which does not have planning permission on any, or all, of the development. This does happen, particularly with rural properties, and is something that should be discovered on legal searches.

LANDSCAPING AND TREES NEAR BUILDINGS

There is no question that a well landscaped site will improve the general appearance of that site beyond all recognition, will soften the overall look, can help with noise reduction (particularly by screening off private areas and non-animal work) and will enhance the property for your visitors/public.

Most planning applications will require some form of landscaping to the site; the extent required will vary according to the site, its location and the size of the development.

If you propose to (or are required to) carry out landscaping operations, it is worthwhile discussing your requirements with a qualified landscape contractor or architect. Advice will be needed on the types of tree suitable for your location and how far they should be planted away from the buildings; this is particularly important.

Remember a mature oak or elm tree can grow to over 65ft/20m in height – imagine the effect on the buildings and foundations in 20 years' time.

Landscaping on a site should ideally be planned as part of the main construction, to allow for the most suitable species in relation to buildings, underground drainage pipes, service mains, etc. The proximity of neighbours' services, buildings, etc should also be taken into account.

A registered landscape contractor will advise on and design a suitable scheme for a site as part of his contract. It is also common practice for them to advise on any necessary replacements for trees/shrubs that have died, and to provide a **maintenance programme for the first year** following completion of the contract.

Tree Preservation Orders

In UK law, trees with a diameter of over 75mm (3") are regarded as permanent assets attached to the property/land; therefore, they cannot be felled, removed or topped without permission. This relates to 'timber-like' trees only, and not ornamental shrubs or bushes.

Owners of trees are responsible for ensuring that any tree on their property is in a safe and sound condition and does not obstruct public rights of way or highways.

If the land surrounding your property is designated a conservation area by the local authority, six weeks' notification is required before any work can be carried out on a tree. This period allows the authority the opportunity to make a decision whether a preservation order is required for the tree in question.

It is worth remembering that trees in the wrong place can prevent the development of a site!

CASE STUDY:
LOCATION, LOCATION, LOCATION

Organisation:	Pyrton Cat Hotel
Location:	UK, Oxfordshire
Cattery Type:	Semi-outdoor
Cattery Function:	Boarding
Number of Units:	7
Unit Size Penthouse:	1500 x 1030 (5' x 3'5")
Overall size:	1500 x 1800 (5' x 6')
Date Built:	2003

www.pedigreepens.co.uk/boarding

A SMALL FAMILY BUSINESS SET IN A GLORIOUS LOCATION. THE CATTERY IS BUILT IN UPVC, WITH TILED FLOORS AND AN EXTERNAL OPEN TIMBER WALKWAY IN A PERGOLA STYLE TO FULLY COMPLEMENT THE GARDENS

PYRTON CAT HOTEL

THE WOW FACTOR

Owner Michelle Blayachi showed us around with the help of her tour guide Isabella the Maine Coon kitten (shown in the photo below right). The first thing that hits you when you arrive is the stunning location – surrounded by beautiful rolling hills and countryside, nestled at the end of a long private road, it feels very comfortable and safe here. The location is so special that the family just had to secure the property as soon as they could!

It is beautifully quiet, you can only hear the odd cry from red kites flying overhead, the occasional squawk of a free-roaming chicken, and of course a miaow or two from Michelle's cats who seem to delight in showing people around. With this new penthouse cattery of just 7 units, Michelle loves to potter, relaxing with the cats throughout the day. There is already a regular client base.

CUSTOMERS DO THE MARKETING

It is interesting to see how owners of good quality catteries can be so busy with so little advertising, but then as usual, good quality catteries seem to have their marketing done for them by their customers! Every cattery is different and Pyrton's uniqueness is not only due to the location and small number of units, but also to Michelle's relaxed attitude – she doesn't want this to ever be a 'large' business – just a caring, personal one.

SETTING THE SCENE

Michelle's next task is to create a reception and office in the building (shown below right on the opposite page) which is perfectly situated next to the double entrance gates.

The construction of the cattery building is an interesting mix of materials. The units themselves are UPVc, with an outer facing of timber-effect UPVc, with a further open walkway of timber in a pergola style which is used to make the building more decorative and to hold hanging baskets and bird feeders. It certainly works well, giving the building a more relaxed feeling that perfectly matches the beautiful garden setting.

What are you most pleased with?

The continuing relationship and after-care with the manufacturer, Pedigree Pens, which includes a webpage with photos and details on their website. Future plans also include a koi pond at the other end of the cattery to provide even more interest for the cats.

What would you do differently?

The reception – it would have been ideal to have the reception ready at the outset. This is because it is easier to have somewhere to sit with customers, especially during inclement weather! So, a new reception (which will be built next) as a comfortable place to discuss her cat boarders with their owners will be ideal.

PYRTON CAT HOTEL

COMMON, COSTLY ERRORS TO BE AVOIDED!

Above all, have a clear idea of what you want to achieve. Research the project thoroughly, and visit similar properties

---

Common, costly errors to be avoided are:

- **Lack of forward planning**
  Plan well ahead and try to foresee how your business will grow and expand. Allow for this, do not 'sterilise' a site by poor planning

- **Single storey buildings constructed with insufficient foundations for adding a second storey**
  This is particularly relevant if space is limited and the only way for expansion is to build upwards rather than outwards. (This generally only relates to traditional brick/block structures)

- **Piecemeal building instead of a planned, integrated design**
  This is where having a professional site survey carried out is extremely beneficial

- **Inadequate car parking**

- **Inadequate storage facility**

- **Existing structures**
  If converting a site, do not allow existing structures to stop the correct siting of new buildings/facilities

- **Lack of quiet areas**

- **Poor quality finishes**
  e.g. floors/walls which need to be robust

- **Poor location of various facilities** in relation to other units

- **Not providing separate zones** for public and staff

MAKE YOUR MISTAKES ON PAPER - NOT DURING THE BUILDING STAGE!

To err
is
human;
to purr
is
feline

Robert Byrne

ASPECT AND SITE LAYOUT

Aspect

In an ideal world all cattery buildings would face **south/southwest/east** (depending on your location). This means that the cats can do their sunbathing, and exercise runs catch the sun, helping to dry them out more quickly than if they were facing north.

This arrangement also means cats and staff benefit from the warmth of the sun. South/southwest is ideal for the UK, however in hot climates, a directly southern aspect may be too warm.

Clearly, it is not always possible to ensure all the buildings enjoy maximum benefit from the sun, however, it is worth ensuring that some do.
Again, this comes back to the site and design being flexible. For example, if a boarding establishment only uses some of the cat units during the winter months, ideally the warmer aspect units should be the ones that are used. You will need to play around with the site layout to ensure that your cattery has the sunniest aspect, and ancillary buildings are in the most logical and practical place for daily activities.

Consideration of the individual site is important – particularly for coastal or mountainous locations.

Site Layout

The layout and design for your site will depend on many factors such as space, finances and any existing buildings that can be used.

The layout should encompass some very basic design rules that are applicable to all catteries. These are:

- **Security**

- **Access**
  Ease of access for loading/unloading

- **Car parking**
  Adequate car parking

- **Expansion**
  Suitable areas for expansion

- **Storage**
  Suitable storage facilities and ancillary buildings close to the main centre of operation

- **Appearance**
  A pleasing, professional appearance, this can be achieved using suitable colours and materials and professionally landscaped areas

I'm often asked what is the 'best' cattery design. There is no single design of cattery or layout that is suitable for all sites. All requirements are different, and this is particularly noticeable when looking at the requirements of a charity, as compared with commercial establishments.

There are several generic designs and layouts that are well tried and tested and work extremely well, and these shouldn't be discounted because they seem old fashioned!

The UK doesn't generally suffer from major extremes of climate in other parts of Europe, Canada and America. This does simplify matters and remove some the problems associated with these issues.

RECEPTION

This is normally the first building that most clients will go to, and is an extremely important facility. Not only can it also function as an office, shop etc it is the first impression of the property that most people will have. The design and size can be as elaborate and spacious or as simple as you require.

To highlight how flexible/versatile a reception can be, here are some other uses for it:

■ Reception counter/desk
You will need an area where the public can fill out documents, sign cheques, etc. The installation of electrical sockets is a normal requirement for calculators, cash tills, internet access and computers

■ Holding room for cats that are being discharged
This can be part of the veterinary inspection room if required. The purpose is to provide a clean, quiet area away from the main cattery, this gives the opportunity to hold cats if an owner is going to turn up late or has been delayed

■ Manager's office
This is often a dual-purpose room, not only serving as a quiet area in which to retire to concentrate on office paperwork, accounts, etc. It also offers a suitable room away from the main building to discuss private matters with owners and staff

■ Sales area
The installation of a sales area is common practice for boarding catteries and welfare centres; it can provide an easy form of additional income. The sales goods can be basic items such as toys and cat treats through to bulk sales of cat food or litter

■ Staff accommodation
Do you require staff to live on site? If so, how many? The building of accommodation above the reception can serve a dual role: it utilises space, it provides additional security for the site and is a cost-effective method of providing accommodation. One disadvantage to this is that the staff are always above a source of activity, even on their days off. This can limit the type of staff you wish to employ

■ Public & staff toilet
A public toilet is highly practical. It is normally a planning requirement to provide a disabled toilet
It is always preferable to try and provide separate toilets for staff and clients

■ Staff room
With heating, washing facilities, hot/cold water, fridge, microwave and soft furnishings. It can be of great benefit for staff to get together over coffee to chat and discuss the centre's activities

■ Shower A showering facility is becoming a standard fitting for large charities. It shows a positive attitude to health and safety issues

■ Veterinary inspection room This can be part of the main reception, or incorporated within the cattery

■ Storage room
Again, an often-overlooked area, and one that can make a major difference in the smooth running of the business and help to maintain a professional image

ISOLATION

All animal establishments are normally required by the licensing authority to have an isolation facility to contain and prevent the spread of infectious diseases.

In the UK for example, the Chartered Institute of Environmental Health (CIEH) insist on the following requirements:

- One isolation unit for up to 30 cat units, and pro-rata above that

- A minimum separation of 10ft/3m from any other animal units in existing facilities, and 33ft/10m for any newly constructed animal buildings

Due to the limited use most isolation units receive, it has been a normal practice to construct them to a lesser standard than the main cattery. This is a false economy!

Thought should be given to ensure that the isolation units are of an equal standard, if not higher than the main units

---

The reasoning behind this is simple: an isolation unit needs to be thoroughly cleaned and disinfected after each use in order to prevent any cross contamination to future users. The cleaning process may involve the use of mist spraying, steam cleaning or chemical means, and the construction should take these issues into account.

It is always a contentious point as to how many isolation units should you have. The requirement should be judged on the type of facility constructed and the type of animal being cared for.

Commercial Cattery Isolation

Many cattery owners who are caring for fully vaccinated animals argue passionately that there is actually no requirement for an isolation facility. They feel that if an animal is unwell it should be with the vet and receiving full, professional medical care. This being better for the cat, it removes any potential legal implications and is far more responsive in the event of medical complications.

Obviously, this assumes that your veterinary surgeon has 24 hour cover, has the correct facility to hold and isolate cats with possible infectious diseases, and is willing to provide this service.

Some cattery owners will use their isolation unit for cats that have been brought in by their owner without the necessary documentation to show that the cat is fully vaccinated!

Rescue Cattery Isolation

In an ideal world, it would be better to have two separate buildings with at least 2-3 units in each.

Again, the reasons are simple:

There is no point in putting a cat that is simply 'looking off colour' into the isolation building with another cat that is obviously ill and under veterinary treatment.

It is far better to adopt a flexible approach with more buildings. This enables you to segregate the animals and hopefully, prevent any cross infection.

Clearly, if you have a major outbreak of a virus/disease that has infected a large percentage of the cats in your care, a few isolation units will be totally inadequate. Hopefully, these problems can be minimised and better isolated, with improved building design as suggested later in the book.

Obviously the isolation facility should be totally self-contained, with its own access, hot water supply, protective clothing, food supplies, food bowls and cleaning utensils.

Ideally, the person responsible for this unit should not be working with healthy animals.
If this is not possible, then high standards of 'barrier nursing' should be employed, with the use of washable PVC coveralls, wellington boots and disposable gloves.

All of these measures will create additional work and they are not always guaranteed to be 100% effective. However, without them, the problems will be much, much worse.

For any rescue or charitable organisation, having adequate isolation is ESSENTIAL.

Risk can be reduced further by providing an admissions unit

We will look at admissions units in more detail next.

ADMISSIONS

The aim of the admissions unit is to minimize the risk of an outbreak of disease in the main building, thus preventing the temporary closure of the homing cattery. They have a clear and defined use for welfare centres and sanctuaries, which have to **admit cats from unknown backgrounds and keep them for several weeks**.

Rescue Catteries

The installation of an admissions unit is not a new concept; however they have gained popularity particularly with sanctuaries and welfare centres. **The idea is to use the buildings as a form of 'pre-isolation' prior to admitting the cat into the main rehoming sections.**

Like an isolation unit, it should be totally self-contained (ie. separate access, hot water, utensils and if possible, staff).

Obviously the number of units required is dependent on the total number of animals coming into your care. If the average monthly figure for cats being rehomed is 60, then the number of admission units will be approximately 30, this taking into account that the cats will be in this unit for fourteen days.

Obviously, several factors should be taken into account before such a unit is constructed, these being:

- **Cost implications**

- **Planning and space restrictions**

- **Time considerations**
  How long will the cats be kept in this building, type of animals coming into your care, do they have a documented background and are they vaccinated?

- **Waiting List**
  If you have to close, what happens to the cats on your waiting list? Is there an alternative sanctuary/centre for them to go to?

- **Financial**
  Can you afford to keep the cats for an extended period of time

- **Staff**
  Can you afford the additional staff to run this unit?

Commercial Catteries

Admissions unit use for boarding cattery owners is somewhat limited, as the average stay is 1-3 weeks and the **background, health and vaccination record of the cat is known**. Boarding catteries will tend to use holding units to provide flexibility if owners are delayed, these will be discussed in the chapter on Cattery Styles and Unit Types.

PUBLIC ACCESS AREAS

Clearly you do not want the public to have free access to the site, unless under supervision.

In order to be aware who is on the premises, the design must channel all clients through a barrier system. Not only does this prevent unwanted visitors, it also secures the site and minimises the chance of a cat being let out either intentionally or unintentionally.

Security

Security is paramount for any animal establishment!
For commercial cattery owners, it is taken for granted by the cat's owner that it is in a safe and secure environment.

> The loss of a cat through poor security is tantamount to negligence and has the potential to damage your business. The loss of a cat through escape is potentially the most serious and damaging of all circumstances you may encounter

However, after a short period, it should become second nature to check all gates and doors to ensure that they are closed properly.

The loss of a cat might not be directly your problem. Occasionally owners will bring their cat into reception by either carrying the cat in their arms, or in a cardboard box – these are all potential areas for the loss of a cat at your premises.

In one incident, an owner was bringing the family cat in to board for approximately eight weeks while their house was undergoing renovation. The owner knocked on the door to say that the cat had just escaped from the box in the car, and had run off. As the cat was unknown to the staff, there was only a description of the cat to go on – black and white wearing a red collar.

A full six weeks had passed by and the cat was not seen. However, early one morning a very thin black and white cat wearing a red collar was seen under a hedge. A trap was placed and baited with pilchards – and within half an hour the cat was caught! The owners were contacted and arrived shortly afterwards to greet one very thin, but happy cat.

The moral of this story is not only to educate your clients to use proprietary cat carriers, but also not to give up hope. If a cat escapes, s/he doesn't generally go too far away from the place of escape.

Car Parking

Larger catteries and welfare centres should have designated parking for staff and for the public.

Thought must be given to the number of staff that is likely to be employed and the availability of public transport. If the site is isolated and staff have no other way of getting to it except by their own car, adequate parking must be made available.

The number of spaces required for the public is often difficult to estimate, but a general guide would be parking for a minimum of six vehicles.

Some authorities adopt the planning guidance for various activities, (e.g. residential, hotels, retail, etc). The closest category for catteries is veterinary establishments.

The recommendations for these are:

- 1 space per vet plus 2 spaces per vet for patients
- 1 space per professional staff
- 1 space per 3 non-professional staff

The space required for various types of vehicles is as shown below:

VEHICLE TYPE	LENGTH		WIDTH		TURNING CIRCLE	
	Imperial	Metric	Imperial	Metric	Imperial	Metric
Small car	10 ft	3.05 m	4.5 ft	1.41 m	28.25 ft	8.6 m
Medium family car	14.5 ft	4.47 m	5.5 ft	1.71 m	34.25 ft	10.46 m
Large saloon car	17.5 ft	5.35 m	6.25 ft	1.90 m	41.5 ft	12.7 m
Van (1 tonne)	14.5 ft	4.4 m	6 ft	1.78 m	40 ft	12.2 m
Van (2 tonne)	19.5 ft	6 m	7.25 ft	2.24 m	43 ft	13.1 m
Dustcart (10.8 tonnes)	24.25 ft	7.4 m	7.5 ft	2.29 m	46 ft	14 m
Fire appliance (8.3 tonnes)	26.25 ft	8 m	7.5 ft	2.29 m	50 ft	15.2 m
3 axle skip lorry	23 ft	7 m	8.25 ft	2.5 m	57 ft	17.4 m
Rigid lorry (16.2 tonnes)	28 ft	8.5 m	8.25 ft	2.5 m	68 ft	21 m
Articulated lorry (38 tonnes)	49.25 ft	15 m	8.25 ft	2.5 m	39-50 ft	12 –15 m

LAUNDRY

The issue of laundry equipment, type of bedding to be used, and infrastructure services should be addressed at the **outset** of the development; it should be considered as an **integral** part of the project.

The problems associated with cleaning animal bedding can be a major source of irritation, expenditure, time and energy to the cattery owner who has not addressed this issue. The end result being unsatisfactory arrangements that in the long term, are often more costly.

Correctly addressed, this problem becomes just another part of normal day-to-day activities leaving you to concentrate on the more important issues. The installation of suitably sized laundry equipment is essential for any modern animal establishment using fabric bedding. The provision of a laundry will depend on the type of bedding that is used.

The three most common options available are:

- Special cat beds

- Vetbed® (PetLife International Ltd www.vetbed.co.uk)

- Blankets, sheets or towels

Which option to be used is a matter of personal choice, availability and cost. From a practical and personal point of view, the proprietary **vet bedding or cat bedding** is recommended. The **advantages** are they are light, hygienic, easy to wash, dry very quickly, provide high levels of comfort for the cat and are aesthetically pleasing. The **disadvantage** is the high initial cost. However, given that cats do not generally chew bedding, this shouldn't be an issue!

The use of blankets/sheets/towels is a close substitute. For rescue centres, it is surprising how easy it is to obtain old bedding free of charge! The **disadvantage** over vet bedding is that larger pieces are required to provide the same level of padding and comfort, and it takes considerably longer to dry. **This can be a major problem when faced with a large quantity of washing!** Whatever the bedding chosen, you will need a suitable washing machine/s to cope with the loads being generated on a daily basis.

A domestic machine is not normally adequate for larger establishments, and will not be able to cope for a prolonged period of time. The only answer is to install a commercial machine. The minimum size should be able to cope with loads of approximately 18 lb (8 kg). Ideally, the larger machine that you have space for and can afford, the better. A machine with a capacity of approximately 25-30 lb (11-15 kg) will provide a cost-effective, reliable, long-term solution.

Special Note for Rescue Catteries

Generally, the preferred option for larger charities is to install one central laundry room for the entire site. This option allows for the installation of single, larger machine which is cheaper pro rata than smaller, individual units. The **disadvantage** of this option is that it does not offer any flexibility if a machine breaks down. However, with a reliable company that provides a good breakdown service, this should not be a major problem.

The other option is to install smaller machines into each cattery building. Clearly, this system ensures that you will always have at least one machine working at any one time. The decision is one of personal choice, site layout, building design and size.

Drying

To be able to clean the bedding is one thing; the next problem is trying to dry it. Remember that you cannot always rely on drying the bedding naturally; especially in countries where the weather is too unreliable! Therefore, you are going to need some method which will allow fast, effective drying.

Clearly, the simplest solution is to install a suitably sized tumble dryer to match the washing machine. It is pointless having a large commercial washing machine and only a domestic tumble dryer!

In order to make full use of the washing machine, an equivalent sized tumble dryer needs to be installed. Generally, it is accepted that the dryer needs to have a slightly larger capacity than the washing machine.
For the larger commercial machines to operate effectively, they normally require a three-phase electricity supply for the washing machine, and a gas supply for the tumble dryer. A pre-heated supply of hot water will reduce the running costs and help speed up the wash cycle. All of the larger tumble dryers are normally heated by gas, as the use of electrically heated dryers is prohibitively expensive.

Purchasing Equipment

Although this equipment is not cheap to purchase, there are several options available to the cattery owner. The commercial machines are sometimes sold off from launderettes and hospitals, or can be purchased from specialist auctions. The **disadvantage** with this form of purchasing is the uncertain service history and lack of installation information.

A far better option is to contact one of the specialist manufacturers and suppliers providing industrial size and quality machines. For further information that might affect your laundry facility, please see the chapter on Environmental Legislation.

Helpful Hint:

Ensure that the entrance door is at least 926mm/3ft wide, as this will allow the installation of the larger machines without having to remove doorframes etc

Note:

- If the laundry is in a large commercial centre or charity, the door will need to have at least half-hour fire resistance

- Try to ensure that the laundry area has at least one external wall, this will allow the tumble dryer flue to be directly vented to the outside. This gives the most cost-effective installation and improves the efficiency of the machine. It also allows easy installation of adequate ventilation or 'make-up' air

- Install a floor drain outlet within the laundry area, this will allow any water to drain away from wet bedding or floods etc

- A solid, concrete floor is needed for all commercial machines

- Do not try to mix the laundry area with the boiler room, blanket fluff and boilers are not compatible!

- Ensure that the equipment you purchase complies with local water by-laws (see the chapter on Environmental Legislation)

Toilet Facility for the Disabled

As already mentioned, for any larger scale of development it is likely that the local planning authority will insist on the provision of a toilet for the disabled when granting planning permission.

If only one public toilet is available on your site, it should be suitable sized for wheel chair users.

Storage Facility

This is another area that is much underestimated. The problem of not providing suitable and adequate storage can be extremely tiresome!

Ideally, there should be two types of storage. One for the bulk deliveries (litter, food etc), and another small facility close to the core working areas. The facilities should be large enough to provide dry, vermin-free storage and have suitable access for vehicular and pedestrian traffic.

The building will need to have a range of suitable shelving to help make full use of it. This is normally in the form of purpose-designed warehouse shelving systems, floor pallets, or secure bins with lockable lids. Another important aspect to consider is the off-loading of deliveries and moving of supplies once on the site. Apart from the time factor, the health and safety of staff has to be considered. The weight of some cat litter can be considerable!

It is worth going to farm auctions, government surplus sales etc to try and purchase suitable equipment to move supplies around the site; it is far cheaper than buying new.

REFUSE AREA

This is another area that tends to get overlooked, often resulting in inadequate provision with dustbins being left around the site, creating a poor impression and all due to lack of forward planning. However, before an area is dedicated, thought should be given to establish what method of collection is available for the disposal of the waste generated.

The most common systems used are:

- Plastic bags

- Standard Authority plastic wheeled bins – capacity from 90-330 litres

- Small skip type wheeled bins – capacity from 500-1,100 litres

- Open/covered skips, delivered/collected by purpose-built vehicles with capacities of 2,000-16,000 litres

Before a contract is placed with any supplier, questions that need to be asked are:

- What is the most suitable arrangement for you?

- How much waste will be generated?
  This will determine the size of the area to be provided, (as a general guide an establishment with around 40 kennels and 30 cat units will generate approximately 2,000-3,000 litres per week)

- Is the area accessible for the proposed collection vehicle?

- Can the area be isolated and screened off from the main buildings and public?

- Is the area accessible for the operators during unsocial hours, without disturbing the cats or staff?

- What type of surface is available? Are there any steps or ramps?
  (It can be extremely difficult manoeuvring a full 1,100 litres down steps, or over gravel and soil)

- How frequent is the collection service?

- If plastic bags are going to be used, some form of caging may be required to prevent dogs/foxes from damaging the bags

The latest Building Regulations in the UK – Section H6 of the Approved Documents states that:

"adequate provision shall be made for storage of solid waste. Waste storing areas should have an impervious floor and also provision for washing down and draining the floor into a suitable system"

Clearly this is highly dependent on the size of the development. However, it does need careful consideration.

On one recent project, the local authority insisted on the installation of a foul water drainage system in the open storage area –even though the waste bins are fully sealed with close fitting lids!

INCINERATOR

While the installation of an incinerator might seem a cost-effective solution to removing a large percentage of the waste generated on the site... beware! It has hidden costs and legal requirements, and may prove to be more problematical than first envisaged.

Incinerators come in many sizes and levels of efficiency; they all aim to achieve the same end result, which is to transform the waste into a less hazardous, less bulky or more controllable form. The problem with most of the waste generated from catteries is that is tends to be metal from cans of food (which could be recycled!), waste products that have been soiled with faeces/urine, faecal matter and cat litter. All of these present their own difficulties, the former is not suitable for incineration in small domestic units, while the latter is classed as clinical waste and comes under strict legislation and control.

Most, but not all local authorities deem animal faeces and materials contaminated with faecal matter as clinical waste, and are therefore not suitable for collection under normal refuse systems. However, this varies enormously and it is worth checking with local registered waste carriers to seek their views.

If you intend to install any form of incinerator, please ensure that you contact the local authority to establish what the current legislation is, and what permissions are required.

The basic designs for incinerators are:

- **Open burning/smouldering**
  This is only suitable for burning clean, dry materials such as timber, paper, etc

- **Non-fuelled prefabricated systems**
  These are generally simple metal boxes with regulators and flues. These are most useful for burning general waste in a more controlled form than the above

- **Fuelled prefabricated units**
  These tend to be specialist systems for the incineration of specific waste and are designed for that purpose. This type of system is used in hospitals, research establishments, quarantine and other secure operations

Clearly, with the cost of the incinerator and the legal costs, it starts to become expensive. You will also need to include any costs to provide a room, cover for the incinerator, or fenced storage etc.

CAT WELFARE

WE WILL NOW
FIND OUT JUST
HOW MUCH
ACCOMMODATION
CAN AFFECT CAT
WELFARE & HOW
TO IMPROVE IT

CAT WELFARE REQUIREMENTS

Whatever your reasons for wanting to build a permanent structure, the construction issues, the cats' needs, and basic requirements are the same.

No matter where you are in the world, all catteries and cattery management techniques should have similar aims, these are:

- To ensure that adequate and nutritious supplies of food and water are available

- To provide a safe, warm, dry and stimulating environment for the animals in their care

- To protect from extremes of climate

- To provide health and veterinary care when required

- To allow the cat to display normal behaviour and make choices

- Freedom from emotional and physical distress

Up until recently, there was less emphasis placed on cat requirements than compared with dogs. However, in the last decade cats have become a more popular pet than dogs, owners are expecting more for their cats and spending more on them, and scientific studies have emerged which are challenging us to look carefully at future standards and requirements – all of this adds up to the drive towards better accommodation.

FOCUSING ON WHAT CATS NEED

It is important for you to understand what cats need and the ideals you should aim for, rather than merely complying with what was acceptable in the past, is currently in use, or the minimum legislation you will be required to comply with.

The problem with many existing catteries is that they have taken the 'minimum' requirements and read this quite literally is 'the standard' to achieve!

In the rest of this chapter, feline veterinary and behaviour welfare experts (with a special interest in housing requirements for cats) will help you start to understand just how much the quality of accommodation affects cats.

However, just before we hear from our experts, we will look at a quick summary of what recent scientific studies have shown in terms of what distances cats prefer to stay apart, and the possible quantity of space required.

QUANTITY OF SPACE

Studies have shown that cats prefer to keep a distance of 1-3m(3-10ft) apart

In 1999 a study was done to assess the differences in behaviour of indoor-only cats.

It found that **half of the time was spent away from other cats**, but when they were together they kept a distance of 1-3 metres (approximately 3-10 feet) apart. We can therefore use this information to help us understand what cats require in terms of space when confined, especially in multi-cat environments:

The minimum width/depth of a two-cat unit should be 1200mm/4ft

Other studies have given recommendations of a **minimum** 1.5m² (16ft²) per cat with another 0.75m² (8ft²) for each additional cat

When you compare these sizes with the minimum sizes shown for various countries in the chapter on Legislation and Standards, you can see there is a large variation in what is suggested as suitable accommodation for cats.

The reasons for the discrepancy in suggested sizes may be due to:

- Cats being small animals (so they don't need much space)
- Historical reasons (that's the way it's always been done)
- Cost
- Lack of awareness
- Lack of easily accessible information

Studies have also given **full-height** recommendations. This means they should be suitable for **human** height

This full-height recommendation is important...

Although **cats exercise isometrically** (think cat pilates!), being **descended from tree-living cats** means they also have a **need to be up high** (for safety and watching what is going on) and to be able to climb and jump to get there.

HOUSING AND WELFARE

Dr Irene Rochlitz

HOW CATS RESPOND TO HOUSING

Cats are more likely to respond to poor housing by becoming inactive and by not showing normal behaviours (such as feeding, grooming, urination, defaecation, exploration and play), than by showing obviously abnormal behaviours (such as over-grooming or pacing).

The way a cat is housed and looked after will have a profound influence on its welfare.

It is important to remember that whether the cat will be housed in a particular environment for two days, for two weeks or two months is of little relevance to the cat, as its welfare is largely determined by the conditions it lives in day-by-day. That is why high standards of housing and care should apply to all environments in which cats are kept, including catteries and shelters.

MAXIMISING VERTICAL SPACE – WHY HEIGHT IS IMPORTANT

Domestic cats, having evolved from the semi-arboreal **(tree-living)** African wild cat, spend less time on the floor of their pens than on raised surfaces, and high structures (which provide vantage points) are used more frequently than low ones.

As the vertical dimension is so important for cats, enclosures should be of adequate height, at least 1.5m/5ft so that the cat can stretch fully and jump freely.

Walk-in enclosures are ideal, as they also allow caretakers to enter and interact closely and comfortably with the cats. If an enclosure is too small, there may be an increase in aggression between cats or cats will attempt to avoid each other by becoming inactive.

QUANTITY OF SPACE

A study of pairs of indoor-living cats found that while the cats spent half of their time out of each other's sight, for most of the time that they were together they kept a distance between themselves of 1 to 3 metres/3 to 10 feet. A reasonable conclusion from this study is that when cats are together, there should be enough space so that they can maintain distances between themselves of at least 1 metre/3 feet (this can include vertical distance).

Other studies have attempted to determine the minimum size of enclosure that cats need, particularly in situations where space is at a premium. It is generally accepted that there should be at least $1.7m^2/5'7"^2$ per cat for group-housed cats in shelters.

THE IMPORTANCE OF RELATIONSHIPS AND ROUTINE

Cats do not like unpredictability, such as irregular contact with unfamiliar cats or humans, or an unfamiliar and unpredictable routine.

BALANCING HYGIENE WITH ENRICHING THE ENVIRONMENT

The control of infectious disease is very important, especially when there is a lot of movement of cats in and out of the cattery or shelter. Care should be taken that management and environmental enrichment procedures do not increase the risk of disease transmission.

However, it is also worth remembering that an over-emphasis on the need for sanitary conditions can lead to barren housing conditions.

SINGLE CAGES FOR VETERINARY USE

In some instances, it may be necessary to house cats singly in small cages, for example when they are hospitalised in a veterinary practice.

The cage should have at least $1.5m^2/16ft^2$ of floor space, and ideally should be **no less than 1m/3ft high and contain at least one shelf**, which will allow the cat to rest on an elevated surface and still be able to stretch in the vertical direction.

Placing the cage on a shelf at waist height or higher will make access easier for the caretaker.

SHELTERS AND CATTERIES

The Chartered Institute of Environmental Health has published model licence conditions and guidance for cat boarding establishments in the United Kingdom (CIEH Animal Boarding Establishments Working Party 1995), which serve as a basis upon which local environmental health officers issue licences to boarding catteries.

The Feline Advisory Bureau (a cat charity) in the United Kingdom has published two manuals, one on how to set up and manage a boarding cattery and another on how to set up and manage a shelter.

MORE STUDIES REQUIRED

While much of the advice is sound and based on experience and current practice, there is a need for more scientific input into the best way to house cats in catteries and shelters.

RESEARCH APPLIES TO ALL

Although more studies have been carried out in shelters than in boarding catteries, research findings can, in most instances, be extrapolated from one environment to the other.

ROLE OF SHELTERS

The function of shelters is to provide housing, food and care for cats that are abandoned and unwanted and, providing the cats are healthy, to find them homes as quickly as possible. A cat's stay in the shelter should be kept short, and the cat subjected to as little stress as possible.

DIFFERENT BACKGROUNDS

The population of cats entering shelters is often extremely mixed, differing for example in origin (feral, stray, owned), socialisation status, age, vaccination status and health. In most shelters, the control of infectious disease is a major challenge. Although the shelter environment may not be the primary source of these viruses, it serves to spread viruses between infected and non-infected cats, to reactivate infections and to enhance the severity of disease through stress and increased exposure.

PREVIOUS CATTERY EXPERIENCE

Cats with previous experience of boarding in catteries or shelter-like accommodation, as well as those that have short travelling times to the premises and short waiting times before being admitted, will settle in more quickly and be less stressed.

SIZE RECOMMENDATIONS

In a study of cats in a shelter, a minimum floor space of 1.7 m^2/5'7"^{2} per cat was recommended to ensure acceptable stress levels.

However, these cats were used to other cats, the composition of the groups was relatively stable, and the enclosures well adapted for cats.

In other situations, **more space** per cat may be required.

LONG-STAY CATS

Some cats may be housed in shelters for long periods of time (months or even years), especially if the shelter has a 'no-kill' policy, that is they will not euthanise a healthy animal.

Due to the social disruption, lack of control, and both acute and chronic fear-inducing situations that may exist in the shelter environment, there are serious welfare concerns for these long-stay animals.

THE DIFFERENCE POSITIVE DAILY CONTACT AND HANDLING MAKES

Ensuring that the cat has daily, rewarding contact with humans is important, and may have other beneficial effects.

In a study of the effect of human contact on the reactions of cats in a rescue shelter, cats that received additional handling sessions (where they interacted closely with a familiar person) could subsequently be held for longer by an unfamiliar person – than cats that did not receive additional handling sessions.

This is likely to improve their rehoming potential.

❖

The way
a cat is housed
& looked after
will have a profound
influence
on its
welfare

Dr Irene Rochlitz

CAT WELFARE

Nadine Gourkow

Welfare is better described as a continuum from poor to good. Stress, disease and abnormal behaviour (such as inhibition of feeding) or engaging in repetitive behaviour (stereotypies) are all indicators of poor welfare. The absence of such indicators is however, not sufficient to place the animal on the 'good' end of the welfare continuum.

In the case of cats, indicators of good welfare may include behaviours such as object and social play, affiliative behaviour towards humans and cats (when housed communally), face rubbing, 'normal' use of space, interest in the environment and so on.

Equating welfare to the absence of stress, disease and emotional distress would be equivalent to saying that when a human is not physically or mentally sick, that automatically means that s/he leads a happy and fulfilling life. That is not the case! The environmental and social conditions needed for good welfare vary from individual to individual, depending on their personality, previous learning experience, life stage and so on.

WELFARE STANDARD

In an effort to improve welfare, several humane groups and organizations responsible for animal care have embraced the scientific concept of the 'Five Freedoms' (Farm Animal Welfare Council www.fawc.org.uk/freedoms.htm).

The World Veterinary Association (WVA, 2000), advises that **provision of care in the form of the Five Freedoms is essential to animal welfare** and that every practical effort should be made to achieve them.

The five freedoms for companion animals are:

1. Freedom from thirst, hunger and malnutrition

2. Freedom from discomfort

3. Freedom from pain, injury and disease

4. Freedom from emotional distress

5. Freedom to express behaviours that promote well-being

The Canadian Council on Animal Care states that animal well-being encompasses both physical and psychological health, and recommends that environmental enrichment promotes a full and extensive repertoire of normal behaviour, while at the same time preventing the development of abnormal behaviour.

THE FIVE FREEDOMS

1: Freedom from hunger, thirst & malnutrition:

To meet this freedom, we must understand the feeding behaviour of cats.

- Close proximity between feeding and elimination areas may inhibit eating or drinking

- In communal housing, confident cats may restrict access to resources such as food and water to less confident cats. Positioning of bowls must ensure access for all cats

- Cats in communal housing must be monitored for dehydration and body condition to ensure they are getting proper nutrition

- When cats are under stress, they do not eat. Reducing stress is essential to encourage feeding behaviour

- Pet cats that are anxious may not engage in feeding behaviour unless petted by a familiar human

2: Freedom from pain, injury, and disease:

To meet this freedom, we must recognize behavioural and clinical signs of disease and pain. Internal communication between staff must be efficient, and decisions must be prompt to ensure veterinary care is provided at the first indication that the animal is not well. Geriatric cats housed in communal pens may injure themselves, or experience pain when jumping up or down, to or from a shelf. Steps or ramps must be provided to reduce the risk of injury.

3: Freedom from discomfort:

Comfort needs are species-specific but vary based on individual preference, age and previous experience. **To meet this freedom, cat enclosures must provide a waste-free living area with appropriate ambient temperature, natural light, good ventilation and comfortable bedding.** Communal enclosures in particular must provide for geriatric cats.

4: Freedom from distress:

To meet this freedom, we must provide an environment that enables cats to self-manage stress and negative emotions, (such as by hiding, scent marking) and provide opportunity for social interaction with people and other cats, based on the level of socialisation.

5: Freedom to express behaviours promoting psychological well being:

To meet this freedom, we must provide environmental and social enrichment that enables the cat to engage in a wide range of behaviours normally expected of cats known to enjoy good welfare.

Exercise and social activities such as object play, affiliative behaviour, rubbing, exploring, chasing, pouncing and so on (these activities will vary based on personality and age) will ensure that cats are enjoying physical and psychological contentment.

THE FIVE FREEDOM TEST

To conduct the Five Freedom Test:

- Observe the environment in every room where cats are placed, even if it is for a short time

- Observe cats' body posture and behaviour during every aspect of care

When observing environmental conditions, ask:

- Is there anything that may be preventing this cat from accessing food and water? (i.e. other cat in communal, food and elimination area too close)

- Is the quality and quantity of food appropriate?

- Does the cat's cage look like it is being used normally, not used at all, or destroyed?

- Are feeding, eliminating and sleeping areas separated?

- Is the environment free of items that may cause injury?

- Is there comfortable bedding?

- Is the temperature adequate?

- Does the cat have items to hide in, perch on, pounce on, play with, and scent mark?

When observing the cat, ask:

- Does this animal's physical condition indicate that s/he is healthy (coat condition, weight etc)?

- Does this cat engage in normal behaviour?

- Does this cat engage in abnormal behaviour? (Remember absence of abnormal behaviour does not mean presence of normal behaviour. Both must be present.)

- Does this cat present postures that indicate psychological health (free of fear, presence of play and friendly behaviour etc)?

ASSESSING INDIVIDUAL CAT WELFARE

VETERINARY ASSESSMENT

When a veterinarian is faced with a sick animal, s/he must first make a diagnosis.
The veterinarian will conduct a medical exam that may include such things as blood or urine tests. Once the problem is diagnosed, the appropriate treatment can be prescribed and recovery can be monitored.

CARER ASSESSMENT

When a cat caretaker, welfare practitioner, behaviourist or ethologist is faced with an animal suffering from poor welfare, s/he must conduct a welfare or behavioural assessment (diagnosis). This welfare assessment may include physiological measures, but most often draws on behavioural observations of the animal and evaluation of the environment. Once the specific welfare problem is identified, the appropriate environmental, social, behavioural or pharmacological treatment can be provided.

A trained assessor should observe each cat daily, typically at the same time every day (before feeding and cleaning) and record (+) or (-) indicators of welfare.

If a cat is not drinking or if s/he shows behavioural signs of disease, it is recommended that
s/he be checked by a veterinarian

IMPORTANT CONCEPTS ABOUT THE ASSESSMENT OF STRESS

It is important to observe the change in welfare indicators over time.

Sudden changes in behaviour are indicative that something is wrong

- **(-) Indicators**
  Typically cats will show (-) indicators during the first 3 to 6 days after arriving at the boarding cattery, and will show a decrease in (-) and increase in (+) indicators over the next few days

- **(+) Indicators**
  Cats that show (+) indicators of welfare for all categories observed and subsequently begin to show (-) indicators may be getting sick, frustrated, bored (lack of appropriate stimuli) or be otherwise unwell

- **Stress**
  Stress cannot be assessed based on evaluation of one body part or posture in isolation. It is important to observe clusters of behaviour. Posture and facial expressions may vary based on personality, time of day, ambient temperature and so on

- **Pupil dilation**
  Pupil dilation may be difficult to establish if the shelter is dark (a flashlight may be directed at the cat's face from the side, not directly into the eyes)

Behavioural signs of disease are also assessed, and (-) indicators for health or pain at any time during the cat's stay must be addressed immediately.

CAT EMOTIONS

NADINE GOURKOW

EMOTIONAL RESPONSES

The emotional response is an evolutionary system that ensures an animal is psychologically motivated to avoid unpleasant situations (danger) and to engage in pleasant situations. The emotional system contributes to adaptation/evolution. Specific hormones are associated with various emotions.

Emotional distress is the experience of negative emotions, when the cat is unable to adapt to environmental or social conditions. The cat may inhibit normal behaviour (eating, grooming, eliminating) and show abnormal behaviour (pacing, circling, self mutilation, excessive vocalisation, defensive aggression).

When cats are faced with situations, people or activities they perceive as potential danger, they become anxious. Anxiety is an emotional state that helps the cat focus all his attention on his environment to determine if s/he is in danger.

Once the cat determines that he is in danger, he experiences fear. The stress response is initiated and prepares the body for fleeing. Among other things, his heart rate increases, his immune system prepares for a possible injury and non-essential organs are shut down (digestive and reproductive). If the cat cannot flee, he may try becoming very small and immobile (freeze response) hoping to be unnoticed. If all fails, he will fight to defend himself against the perceived danger.

WELFARE THERAPY

If a welfare problem is identified, cats should be provided with welfare therapy.

Descriptions and therapy for these cat emotions follow:

- Anxiety
- Fear
- Frustration
- Depression

ANXIETY

Anxiety is defined as the *anticipation* of a future danger or threat – whether real or imaginary.

Anxiety is an emotional state which the cat experiences when s/he is uncertain about the environment, usually because it is novel. The cat needs to assess what is happening to him/her and the potential for danger. Posture varies with the intensity and duration of the stimulus and the individuality of the cat

Stimuli known to cause anxiety in shelter cats:

- Arrival of a stranger
- Intrusion into their personal space
- Sudden movements
- Loud noises
- Novel objects
- Novel smells
- Loss of control over the environment

Behavioural indications of anxiety

- Cat at the back of cage usually immobile/frozen
- Eyelids may be wide open, with pupils partially or fully dilated
- Eyes may be pressed shut, indicating feigned sleep
- Reduction or complete inhibition of self-maintenance behaviour
- Cat may lie flat – immobile in the litter box, with eyes peering over the edge
- Body and ears are flattened
- Whiskers are retracted
- Tail is tightly held near the body

Above photographs courtesy of Nadine Gourkow

FEAR

Fear is an emotional state, triggered by the mental assessment of a stimulus as a **definite** danger.

A frightened cat takes on a defensive posture, aimed at protecting his body, particularly vulnerable parts such as ears, neck, tummy and tail.

Stimuli known to cause fear in shelter cats:

- Approach by an unfamiliar human, that cannot be assessed as safe
- Pain, such as that caused by some handling techniques or medical procedures
- Noises
- Anything novel can cause fear

Behavioural indications for anxiety and fear (anxiety and fear are on the same continuum):

- Flattened ears move to back of head. Whiskers pan out and forward to assess distance between him/herself and danger
- Tail is held tightly around body
- Breathing is rapid and shallow
- Pupils are dilated
- Eyes are wide open
- Cat may be shaking
- Cat may urinate or defecate
- Cat may drool excessively
- There may be repeated lip licking

If you approach, s/he will attempt to keep you away at first:

- S/he will spit and hiss
- S/he will deliver quick strikes with paws – claws out

If you continue to approach:

- S/he may turn on his back and expose all his weapons – teeth and claws
- S/he may attempt to grab your hand and bring it to his mouth to bite it

Above photograph courtesy of Nadine Gourkow

THERAPY FOR ANXIETY AND FEAR

During the **first few days** at the shelter, cats are **more prone** to anxiety and fear.
Reducing these negative feelings and stress during the first few days can go a long way towards preventing the onset of disease.

1. Conduct a daily assessment to determine presence and severity of negative emotions

2. House the cats singly in enriched cages until they show a significant reduction in fear and anxiety

3. Pre-spray each cage with feline facial pheromone or place a feline facial pheromone plug-in diffuser in the room

4. Play a CD of gentle classical music

5. Reduce staff rotation or exposure to many volunteers, and provide a regular and consistent routine

6. Spend a few minutes talking (high pitched voice) to the cat and if s/he responds positively, attempt to pet the cat for tactile reassurance

7. If vocal interaction or approach causes the cat to become defensively aggressive, back off!
   Use minimal handling for the first few days and let the cat cool off

8. Encourage incoming cats to eat during the first few days by providing yummy treats when you visit.
   This will also help the cats see you as a friend

9. If you know the cat's name, **always** use his/her name when interacting

FRUSTRATION

There are two main causes for frustration:

1. Non-Reward:

In a natural setting such as the home, cats experience anticipation for scheduled events (i.e. feeding, play time, return of human companion). Anticipation arousal decreases when the expected event occurs. This is called a reward. However, when the expected events are anticipated but do not occur, this is called 'non-reward' and this causes the cat to feel frustrated

2. Impoverished environment:

When animals in captivity are not able to engage in the behaviour normal to their species, they become frustrated. This is true of the cat housed in traditional settings that offer few opportunities for meaningful interaction with the environment. Chronic (on-going) frustration can lead to depression

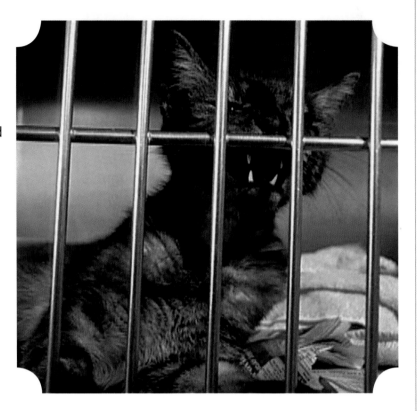

Behavioural indications of frustration:

Cats express frustration differently depending on their personality (extrovert/introvert).

■ Extroverted cats that suffer from frustration:

- Moody (friendly one minute, aggressive the next)
- Seem to be friendly, trying to catch people passing by with their paw
- Be very vocal
- Engage in escape behaviour, such as pawing a cage closure
- Spray or eliminate outside the litter box (also associated with anxiety)
- Sit at the front of the cage, meowing continuously, intensity increasing when you approach/depart
- Seek eye contact
- Engage in escape behaviour
- Continuously try to open the cage
- Pace
- Shred or destroy cage items
- Turn all items upside down (can be a sign of frustration if s/he is not also trying to hide)

■ Introverted cats that suffer from frustration:

The introvert cat may not be noticed if only observed for a few minutes. They choose to relieve their frustration with quiet, repetitive behaviour.

- Over-grooming or focus licking on one area of the body, causing damage to the skin (note that this may also be a sign of a medical condition, or a response to pain)
- Self-mutilation (as above)
- Sucking, chewing or eating non-edible items
- Focusing interest on one part of the cage

Above photograph courtesy of Nadine Gourkow

THERAPY FOR FRUSTRATION

Frustration is more likely to occur once anxiety has *subsided*.

Cats experiencing frustration need an opportunity to have more control over their environment and an opportunity for the expression of a wider range of behaviour.

1. **Communal Therapy** – Frustrated cats **must** have priority for communal living

2. **Individual Change of Scene** – For those that are aggressive to other cats, provide time out of the cage

3. **Play Therapy** – Provide extra items to redirect energy (e.g. batting toy, items that can be shredded). These do not need be to be expensive store bought toys. Some shelters have made use of syringe covers, tampons or pieces of rope

   Provide novelty!

   To ensure that cats use toys, you must also give **new** ones every few days or they will lose interest

4. **Scratching** – Provide items to scratch

5. **Mental Stimulation** – Provide food enrichment and smart toys (e.g. clean yogurt cup taped shut, with a treat inside. Make a hole in the container big enough for the cat to stick his/her paws in and retrieve the treat)

   Be creative!

6. **Visual Stimulation** – You can place an aquarium in the adoption room and light it up at night. Some toys can be attached to a fan and move around when turned on. Bird feeder can be placed outside a window

   Once again, be creative!

7. **Auditory Stimulation** – For auditory stimulation; there are a variety of nature sounds music CD's available. Those with bird and insect songs are interesting to cats

   Do not leave it on all day or the cats will habituate and lose interest

8. **Tactile Stimulation** – Tactile stimulation should not be done with your hands when provided to a frustrated cat. They may injure you, as they are in a heightened state of arousal.
   Provide cats with different textures to lie on

   Choice is the key!

DEPRESSION:

Depression is an affliction experienced by many animals living in captivity.

When an animal is sick or experiences on-going frustration, they eventually seem to give up on life, and show a reduction in many of their normal activities such as eating, remaining alert, and interest in play or exploration. **It is important to be aware that these signs are often also associated with illness.**

Stimuli known to cause depression in shelter cats:

*   Chronic frustration
*   Boredom
*   Sickness
*   Lack of opportunity to engage in normal behaviour

Behavioural indications of depression:

*   Listlessness
*   Anorexia
*   May sit with head hanging for hours
*   Oversleeping
    (cat is difficult to wake up and
    remains sleepy once awake)
*   Complete inhibition of grooming behaviour
*   Withdrawal from previously anticipated interaction
    with a familiar caretaker

There is no individual specific sign for fear, or anxiety or frustration. However, there is some overlapping of signs.

THERAPY FOR DEPRESSION
(NOT RELATED TO SICKNESS)

When frustration is not addressed, the cat can become depressed. Depression is very difficult to treat in the shelter environment. Cats suffering from depression should get priority for foster homes, or be promoted as *Pet of the Week* on your website. They **need** to get out of the shelter.

■ **Touch Therapy -** Provide depressed cats with grooming, touching, petting, massage

■ **Play Therapy -** Depressed cats do not engage in inanimate play, so placing toys in their cage is ineffective

■ **Olfactory Therapy** - Stimulate hunger with strongly scented food such as mackerel or sardines. While the use of catnip is not recommended in the shelter (it makes some cats aggressive), it is useful for stimulating the depressed cat. Use sparingly! You can also place a couple of drops of peppermint oil on a towel in the cage

■ **Visual Therapy -** Move the cat to a high traffic area with lots of activity to stimulate his/her interest

■ **Busy Areas -** Always place depressed cats in busy areas. Next to entrance or kitchen area. Do not place in the communal unless closely monitored.

In critical cases, it may be necessary to see a veterinarian and obtain a prescription for an antidepressant (some anti-depressants may increase appetite). **Cats suffering from depression, that are not treated, have a high risk of dying while in care – because it is difficult to get them to feed, drink or groom.**

Photograph courtesy of Nadine Gourkow

THE DANGER OF STRESS

When cats experience emotional distress, they also experience physiological stress.
Emotions are the psychological responses to a stimulus perceived as unpleasant or dangerous.
This emotional system evolved to ensure that an animal is psychologically motivated to retreat from potential danger, or other unpleasant situations.

Stress is a physiological state that coexists with many emotions, and is the consequence of various triggers.
It ensures that the body is physically prepared to react appropriately when faced with an unpleasant or dangerous situation (e.g. being chased by a predator).
Cats living in confinement are not able to engage in natural responses such as running away, hiding or climbing to safety, causing them to experience on-going stress, unless provided with alternatives.

The stress response prepares the body for fight or flight.

It provides the body with:
- An increase in the level of blood sugar to provide energy to the muscles for a quick escape
- An increase in respiratory & cardiovascular function to increase oxygen and blood to the heart and muscles
- Increased vigilance with pupil dilation (increase in peripheral vision)
- Redirected energy for escape by temporarily curtailing digestive function

This shift in energy enables the cat to:
- Quickly run away and find a hiding place
- Jump or climb to a high place
- Fight off the danger

When the danger is gone, the stress subsides. The body returns to a normal state.

When emotional distress is **ongoing**, stress *remains high* for a longer period than the body is capable of handling.

On-going stress makes disease more likely to occur, and more damaging when it does.
Although we recognize the role of stress in disease, its **impact** is often underestimated

In addition, behaviour that accompanies stress (such as **suppression of feeding behaviour**) depletes the body of the energy required to fight the disease.

The **suppression of grooming** behaviour makes cats more susceptible to parasites and other skin conditions, and over-grooming can also cause damage to the skin. **Over-grooming** is a displacement activity that often follows conflict with another cat, or expresses frustration. Generally, if there is damage to the skin, the cat should be examined for an underlying medical condition.

STRESS FACTORS TO REDUCE

Being stared at

Don't know what is happening

Never been to a cattery before

Owners are upset

Long waiting time

Car travel or long journey
(does not like the car)

Going into a cat basket
(going to the vet?)

Being in a confined space
with a cat that isn't liked, or is a bully

Unknown dogs/not used to dogs

Dislike of being near other cats

Not used to other cats

Surrounded by unknown cats

Intrusion into personal space

Unknown people

Loss of owner

Lack of familiar contact

No outside access if used

Strange sounds

Strange cat litter or tray

Loud noises

Strange food

Loss of comforting smells (own, owner, home)

No grass

No toys

Strange smells

Nothing to explore, pounce on, chase, stalk

Being touched in places not liked

Nothing to watch

Being handled if not used to it

Lack of exercise

Strong smells (disinfectant, air fresherner)

Lack of comfort

No control over environment

New, unfamiliar routine

Being confined

Loss of normal routine

Unable to escape

Nowhere to get up high to safety

Nowhere to hide for safety

LEGISLATION

NOW YOU KNOW
WHAT SIZE YOUR
CATTERY SHOULD
IDEALLY BE, WE
WILL LOOK AT THE
MINIMUM LEGAL
REQUIREMENTS

CATTERY LICENCE REGULATIONS

Always remember that legislation notes suggest the **MINIMUM** standards and are open to a great deal of latitude!

United States, Canada and the Rest of the World

Legislation varies enormously between states/regions, and it would be another book to list them all!

However, it is easy to find out what requirements you will have to comply with – just ask your local authority. You will be able to find this out from the animal warden, animal control officer, or the licensing/permits office.

United Kingdom

Boarding Catteries

The Animal Boarding Establishment Act 1963 requires all establishments to be licensed by the local authority (except where it is an ancillary business or animals are kept at the Animal Health Act 1981 requirements. You must not be disqualified from keeping animals. Boarding establishments are defined as the carrying on at any premises (including a private dwelling) of a business of providing accommodation for other people's cats and dogs.

CIEH 'Model Licence Conditions and Guidance for Cat Boarding Establishments' 1993.

This publication's aim was to provide a framework for all local authority inspectors, to ensure that a consistent approach was implemented nationwide for cattery sizes, systems for hygiene control and standards.

The local authority has a duty to inspect annually and issue a licence for all boarding catteries. The inspectors normally come from the Environmental Health Department, this being the obvious choice as they are used to inspecting food outlets, restaurants, etc. **However, not all authorities have adopted the guidelines as policy!**

It has been accepted that it is impossible to bring all of the boarding establishments up to the required standard overnight, and will need to be phased in over a period of time for **existing** businesses. However, for **new establishments**, there is an expectation that all of the conditions will be met before a licence is granted.

Cautionary Note:

- **Where an existing establishment has a licence and the property is sold**, it should be borne in mind that the new owner might be required to upgrade the cattery at the outset. Clearly, this will have serious financial implications and will require careful research

- **Disallowing timber catteries**: we estimate that more than 90% of the UK's boarding catteries are of timber construction. Having spoken to several authorities regarding their views on the continued use of timber, some authorities are now disallowing the use of timber catteries. We have also found some forward-thinking authorities adding further conditions to the Boarding Establishments Act to improve the clarification and standards for their area.

Rescues and Charity Catteries

Generally, the CIEH does not have any jurisdiction over animal welfare centres and charities, as they are not commercial boarding establishments. In fact, it is the major animal welfare centres and charities that are setting the trends and standards for catteries, with new designs and environment enriching measures! This is partly driven by the requirements, partly to show the cats off in the best possible light to potential owners, and partly attributed to the organisation's statement or standard it feels it should set.

Animal Welfare Bill

"In October 2005 Defra published the Animal Welfare Bill, following its introduction to, and first reading in, the House of Commons.

Amongst other things it introduces a duty on owners and keepers of all vertebrate animals – not just farmed animals – to ensure the welfare of animals in their care.

It will mean that, where necessary, those responsible for the enforcement of welfare laws can take action if an owner is not taking all reasonable steps to ensure the welfare of their animal, even if it is not currently suffering."

- Reduce animal suffering by enabling preventive action to be taken before suffering occurs

- Place on people who are responsible for domestic and companion animals a duty requiring them to do all that is reasonable to ensure the welfare of their animals

Boarding:

- Animal boarding establishments should continue to be licensed. Regulations will clarify the position on home boarders of dogs, but commercial home boarding of cats is considered to be unacceptable

- Licences will run for no more than 3 years on a risk-managed basis

- Local Authorities will issue licences and will have powers to inspect, and to withhold or revoke licences

Sanctuaries:

- Animal sanctuaries should be required to register with local authorities

- Registration will run for a maximum period of 5 years – there will be power for the local authority to inspect sanctuaries on a risk-managed basis

- A code of practice covering issues such as rehabilitation and rehoming will be introduced

DEFRA Animal Welfare Bill, UK

For more information see www.defra.gov.uk/animalh/welfare/domestic

MY SUGGESTED CAT UNIT SIZES

As already stated, with their tree-living origins, it is extremely important to provide shelving and high places for cats to rest, jump and climb on. Most catteries install shelving at various heights to provide a three-dimensional unit that makes the most of the internal height within the cat unit. This is essential, as cats need to climb, stretch, get up high to feel safe, or to hide. This is easily done with a full height, walk-in unit.

My Suggested Sizes:

Having been involved with many organisations that all have their own requirements, ideals, building costs and budgets – for a temperate climate, my suggested solution is for the following style and sizes:

Ideal Cattery Style: Semi-outdoor

Ideal Unit size: Full-height, walk-in units of 2m (6'6")

Sizes:	Imperial	Metric
Indoor sleeping area of:- **PLUS**	4ft x 5ft (20 sq ft)	1220 x 1500mm (1.83 m²)
Semi-outdoor exercise area of:-	4ft x 6ft (24 sq ft)	1220 x 1800mm (2.19 m²)
COMBINED TOTAL:	44 sq ft	4 m²

The above sizes provide a good compromise in terms of the cats' needs, building costs, staff time, and is suitable for two cats. The larger units are also an excellent sales or PR (public relations) point! However, the extra width of a 5ft/1.5m wide unit makes a **tremendous** difference, making it well worth constructing units for this larger size. Of course, if you have the space and budget to increase these sizes, it will be in the cats, staff and business's best interests to do so!

> My suggested sizes will make a good compromise for cats in the care of rescue and boarding catteries, because these cats receive LOTS of human interaction (e.g. grooming, playtime and attention), which helps combat the effects of stress and make for a much happier and more relaxed cat

Due to environmental pressures, local authorities and welfare centres have started to focus on cattery design. In the past, the focus has been more on developing and providing good quality dog accommodation, probably due to the noise factor. Having been left to individuals to make up their minds about the accommodation they build, and with the focus shifting to cats, it is now the ideal time to bring to light the necessity of improving the existing information.

However, with the increase in cat numbers and the fact that (at least in the UK), more cats are homed through charities and sanctuaries than dogs, a far greater emphasis has been directed to improving cat standards. The style and design of the cattery is very subjective, and all of the designs have their advantages and disadvantages. The preferred style is a matter of personal choice and is influenced by several factors.

International Minimum Unit Sizes for Combined Sleep/Exercise

Clearly, there is a major difference in what is deemed a satisfactory level and standard of space:

Organisation	HEIGHT	X 1 Cat Sleep + Exercise	X 2 Cats Sleep + Exercise	Groups
My Recommendation (sleep + exercise combined)	2 m 6'6"	4 m² 44 ft²	4 m² 44 ft²	10 m² 100 ft² (up to 4 cats)
United Kingdom				
Boarding (CIEH) (sleep + exercise combined)	910 mm 3 ft	2.55 m² 27 ft²	3.73 m² 40 ft²	
Boarding (FAB) (sleep + exercise combined)	1.8 m 6 ft	2.55 m² 27 ft²	3.73 m² 27 ft²	14.55 m² 155 ft² (up to 6 cats)
Quarantine (DEFRA) *any cat entering a quarantine facility stays in that unit for 6 months and is **never** let out*	1.8 m 6 ft	1.4 m² 15 ft²	1.4 m² 15 ft²	

UK Quarantine – It is clear to see in the sizes shown for quarantine (and remember, this is from the **Voluntary** Code of Practice! – many catteries do not even reach this standard!) that the **sizes are totally inadequate** to provide the cat freedom and space to allow natural behaviour.

Organisation	HEIGHT	X 1 Cat Sleep + Exercise	X 2 Cats Sleep + Exercise	Groups
United States of America				
Breeding (CFA)	915 mm 3ft	0.92 m² 10 ft²	-	
Boarding (HSUS)	-	-	-	13.5 m² 150 ft² (to 10 cats)
Boarding (Colorado State) Cats up to 2lbs to 5lbs	530 mm 1'9"	0.38 m² 4.9 ft²	-	0.9 m² 10 ft² per cat
Boarding (Missouri State) Cats up to 8.8 lbs	600 mm 2ft	0.28 m² 3 ft²	-	

USA and Canada – It is common for many cattery owners to use small cages and to have separate exercise 'playrooms' for the cats in their care. Obviously this allows some extra freedom for short periods each day. However, this style of cattery does present its own problems in terms of disease control and staff time.

Organisation	HEIGHT	X 1 Cat Sleep + Exercise	X 2 Cats Sleep + Exercise	Groups
New Zealand (Boarding)	-	1.08 m² (11.5 ft²)	0.36 m² 3.8 ft² (per cat)	
Australia (Boarding)	-	1.0 m² to 1 week 1.5 m² over 1 week	-	

United Kingdom

In the UK the concept is for floor area (area^2) and no account is taken of height, use of shelving etc! (We cover quality of space i.e. shelving, furniture etc, in the Environmental Enrichment chapter)

Boarding Catteries

Although the UK minimum sizes are adequate for animals in boarding catteries (which by their nature tend to hold animals for a short duration, the average being 1-3 weeks), **they do not suit the more specialist operations such as welfare centres and sanctuaries.**

The CIEH insist that all new boarding catteries must have the following MINIMUM sizes:

Number of Cats	Size of Sleeping Area		Size of Exercise Area	
	Imperial	Metric	Imperial	Metric
1	9ft^2 (e.g. 3ft x 3ft)	0.85 m^2	18ft^2 (e.g. 3ft x 6ft)	1.7 m^2
2	16ft^2 (e.g. 4ft x 4ft)	1.5 m^2	24 ft^2 (e.g. 4ft x 6ft)	2.23 m^2
4	20 ft^2 (e.g. 5ft x 4ft)	1.85 m^2	30 ft^2 (e.g. 5ft x 6ft)	2.7 m^2

Rescue Catteries

At present there is no legislation for welfare organisations. Like commercial catteries, the quality varies enormously from excellent to dreadful. Again, any charity should have as its absolute minimum standard the FAB/CIEH sizes.

Breeding Catteries

For cats that are permanently in a cattery environment (as opposed to a home environment) then additional consideration needs to be given to ensure the cats have the additional space, safety and stimuli they need. How a kitten is socialised in the first few weeks will affect it for the rest of its life.

"You will need suitable accommodation. A stud house may be built to your individual requirements or bought ready for assembly. It should be well insulated, well ventilated, have plenty of window space and be easy to clean. There should be a run of adequate size for exercise, and a safety run to provide security against escape"

Governing Council of the Cat Fancy, UK

Quarantine Catteries

When the UK introduced animal quarantine in 1901 and amended it in 1974, the aim was simply to provide secure holding facilities for 6 months to ensure that no animal coming into the UK was incubating the rabies virus.

The cats' welfare requirements and standards did not feature in the legislation guidelines!

Even today, the standards are still wholly inadequate for cats that cannot be removed from their holding quarters for six months, as the points below clearly demonstrate.

Accommodation should be built so that cats:

- Can see out of their unit to a reasonable extent, preferably with visual stimuli

- Have an adquate and constant supply of fresh air

Quarantine Temperature:

Provide a minimum temperature of 45° F/7° C.

When you consider that this is 37° F/3° C **below** even the minimum CIEH standard temperature, it clearly shows that little consideration is given to welfare.

Although the demand for quarantine has decreased with the introduction of the Pet Passport in 2000, it is still enforced for animals coming from certain countries.

> *"Initially this applied only to Western Europe and certain rabies-free islands, but it was subsequently extended to some 30 other countries including the US and Canada, and more recently to Russia and much of Eastern Europe. Further changes are possible and we continue to keep a close watch on the situation."*

> *Passports for Pets, UK*

Careful consideration and research needs to be carried out by any cat owner who is importing a cat that needs to be quarantined to ensure that the quarantine cattery has:

- Good facilities

- Taken the cats' welfare into consideration when designing premises

- A progressive approach to the entire process (e.g. staff awareness and training, well designed accommodation that goes beyond the minimum requirements)

- Open policy when it comes to allowing clients information and access

It would be in the cats and cat owners best interest to contact Passports for Pets as the first step:

Passports for Pets: www.freespace.virgin.net/passports.forpets

United States of America

In the United States the concept is for cubic space (area^3)

It is common for many cattery owners in the USA and Canada to use cages for accommodation, with separate exercise 'playroom' for the cats in their care. Obviously this allows some extra freedom for short periods each day.
However, this style of cattery does present its own problems in terms of disease control and staff time.

Boarding & Rescue Catteries

These size requirements will vary from state to state.

Breeding Catteries

The Cat Fanciers' Association (CFA) show the following guidelines as minimum size requirements:

- 1 cat = 30 cubic feet of cage space.
  This is made up of a unit of the following size:

  30" deep x 48" wide x 36" high   (760 mm x 1220 mm x 915 mm)
  This equates to floor area of 10 sq. ft   (0.92 m²)

  If the height of 36" (915 mm) is taken into consideration, it gives a cubic area of 30 cubic feet. (0.84m3)

"First, you'll need 30 cu ft of cage space for each cat, plus free play space, and grooming and maintenance areas. Stud males should have more than the minimum 30 cu ft. Remember, the Board's guideline establishes **minimums***, not optimums. Thus in planning,* **more space is definitely better***."*

"The standard show cage is 4ft long x 2ft wide x 2ft high, 16 cu ft (4'x2'x2'=16ft). Thus, **a show cage is not adequate housing for even one cat** *in the cattery environment.*

Cat Fanciers' Association, USA

USE OF MEDICAL CAGES/CARRIERS/CONDOS

Generally medical/veterinary/hospital cages are stacked two high for cats who are undergoing veterinary care and need confinement and rest. For such purposes these are ideal.

Medical cages or condos (cages with shelves) are commonly used in North America for boarding cats. Thirty years ago this style was also common in the UK, and even now can still occasionally be seen in use in older establishments.

In 1973, a UK boarding kennels and cattery business had a very good reputation and a licence for 80 cats. The cattery was indoor-only, using medical units with the majority being a tiny 30" wide x 24" deep 24" high (760mm x 600mm x 600mm).

At the time, this was accepted as being adequate to house the cat, litter tray, food and water bowls!

Although the cats were housed in these units for only 1-3 weeks, were safe, secure and looked after – the design offered no stimulation or outlook, and had little to do with cat welfare, yet this was just seen as acceptable at the time. The cats of course, were extremely quiet and withdrawn.

For normal fit and healthy cats, this style of housing is far too restrictive and does not provide and allow the cat any freedom or ability to express natural behaviour.

In a commercial situation such as cat boarding, where clients are paying for the service, there is happily an income being generated which can be used to upgrade the accommodation.

It is only when you compare the various types and styles (as we will do in the next chapter) that you can start to see how improved designs can affect the cats' wellbeing, and response to the accommodation and care given.

Clearly this style provides a very cheap way in which to house cats, but it is an option that is outdated and as the latest studies show – not acceptable today.

For rescues and emergency situations where budget does not allow for upgrading the cat accommodation, there are **many** things that can be done in daily management that will improve cat welfare.

Following on the next pages are examples of **just how much can be done to improve the conditions and welfare of cats in small single cages immediately**, and at little or no cost.

This will also be of interest to all types of cattery, as these ideas can be applied everywhere.

ENRICHING SINGLE LIVING

Nadine Gourkow

Single housing is appropriate for short stays. However, to meet the psychological needs of cats, housing **must** be enriched. The following information is designed to help organisations who currently use caging:

- Quality of space is more important than the size of the pen. Fully use any vertical space

- Cats may refuse to eat if litter tray and food dishes are in close proximity

- Cats feel at ease when their space is familiar – containing their own scent

- Cats housed singly need more stimulation than those in communal pens – they will need more social contact (e.g. play sessions)

- Because of lack of space and environmental complexity, cats in single housing have less control over the environment and less choice for behavioural expression – they may be more susceptible to frustration and depression. However, some cats may prefer single housing

- Long-term cats may benefit from being moved around or having their cage rearranged occasionally (be sure to monitor stress)

The single cage should provide separation between functional areas:

- Food and water bowls secured on cage door via a clip

- Elevated bed

- Control over amount of exposure to cattery activities

Provide opportunity to engage in a wider range of behaviours such as:

- Hiding and perching

- Playing with toys to simulate hunting behaviour (batting, pouncing, throwing up in the air)

- Scratching and scent marking

- Opportunity for play with humans

Equipment: The Hide, Perch and Go Box™ (see opposite) provides for the following:

- Facilitates separation of functional areas and feeding bowls can be affixed to the cage door at perch height

- Choice in temperature (cats are sensitive to even minute differences in temperature)

- Opportunity to engage in a wider range of behaviour (hiding, perching, jumping up/down)

- Choice of viewing points and choice of textures

- Enables cats to be surrounded by his own scent inside the box

- Promotes marking (face rubbing on box), scratching

- Provides cats with more control over the amount of exposure to people or cats with visual access to the cage

THE HIDE, PERCH AND GO BOX™:

A cost-effective way to reduce stress and improve welfare for shelter cats, the Hide, Perch and Go Box™ has been designed by an animal researcher and a mechanical engineer, to provide durability and ease of assembly. Boxes are made of coated, water-resistant cardboard.

Benefits:
- Separates feeding, elimination and sleeping areas
- Provides opportunity for hiding, perching and face rubbing
- Provides a choice of material to lie on and difference in temperature and light
- Provides more control over the amount of exposure to the shelter activity to facilitate self manage of stress
- Enables the cat to saturate the cage with his/her own scent by face rubbing on the box, making it more familiar
- Transforms into a cat carrier and buffers sound

HELPING CATS ADJUST TO THE SHELTER

To help cats cope with the novelty of the shelter, the BC SPCA developed the Hide, Perch and Go Box™. Each cat gets his/her own box in their enclosure. It provides them with more control over exposure to shelter activities, and as the box gets saturated with their own scent, they begin to feel more at home and safer. An alternative is to use the bedding that has their scent and provide an upside down box with holes cut that are large enough for the cat to enter.

HELPING CATS ADJUST TO THEIR NEW HOME

To reduce the stress of transport to the new home, the Hide, Perch and Go Box™ is transformed into a safe and sturdy cat carrier. To reduce stress once in the new home, the box is once again transformed into a hiding area. The cat can be kept in a quiet room for the first few days with his box. The box is saturated with his own scent and is a familiar place for the cat. This will prevent the cat from finding a hiding place that may be difficult to reach, and reduces the chance that he will attempt to run away/escape.

Above photograph courtesy Nadine Gourkow

THE FIRST TRIAL

MEET ALEX

Alex came into to the shelter in a trap. He was fearful and showing a strong defensive aggression response when approached. Like most cats entering BC SPCA shelters before the implementation of the Hide & Perch, he was placed in a stainless steel cage with a litter box, a towel, and food and water bowls.

DAILY WELFARE ASSESSMENT

His welfare was being assessed daily. Staff noticed that he was not eating, and drinking very little. He was also showing a strong defensive-aggressive response when approached. By day four, Alex was still not eating. A volunteer was bringing Alex little treats to encourage him to eat, but in vain.

TRIALLING THE SYSTEM

At that time, we were still in the process of developing the Hide & Perch box; it was not yet available to all our cats. However, we decided to take one of the samples to give to Alex.

WITHIN 10 MINUTES...

We took out the items from Alex's cage and placed the Hide & Perch in the cage. Within 10 minutes, he had entered the hiding area.

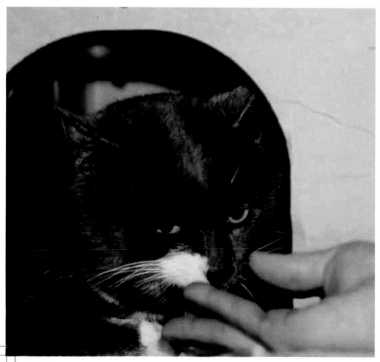

WHAT A DIFFERENCE!

Later that day, Alex was eating from my hand and showing signs of low stress. He was adopted shortly after that!

BCSPCA CATSENSE™ SYSTEM

BCSPCA CATSENSE™ SYSTEM

In the last few years, research into the needs of animals has produced knowledge that can be applied to the care of cats in shelters. Poor emotional well-being experienced by many cats in the shelter environment was found to affect physical health, behavioural expression, and relationships with caretakers. In addition, stress and emotional distress were also found to be common during the first few weeks after adoption. Research conducted at the British Columbia Society for the Prevention of Cruelty to Animals indicated that cats experience better physical and emotional health when given control over their environment, and the opportunity to express natural behaviour.

WHY THE SYSTEM WORKS

When cats can hide, perch, scent mark, control the amount of exposure to human activities or other cats, and experience positive interactions with humans, they adapt to shelter life faster, are healthier and friendlier.

THE RESULTS

The benefits are increased adoptions, with shorter pre-adoption time, reduced rates of sickness and euthanasia, and improvement of general welfare.

MORE INFORMATION

The BC SPCA recommends reviewing the *Emotional Life of Cats* DVD & Manual before using the boxes.

For more information on the *CatSense System™*, or the *Hide, Perch and Go Boxes™* please go to:

www.spca.bc.ca
(special programs)

or contact:
Nadine Gourkow, BCSPCA Animal Welfare Manager
at ngourkow@spca.bc.ca

Above, opposite page and next page photographs courtesy of Nadine Gourkow

GO AREA

Hide, Perch & Go™

SPONSOR LOGO AREA

BCSPCA: HIDE, PERCH & GO BOX™

CASE STUDY:
CONDO? NO CAN DO!

Organisation:	Kitty Hill Resort for Cats
Location:	USA, California, Santa Cruz
Cattery Type:	Indoor
Cattery Function:	Boarding
Number of Units:	30
Unit Size:	6' x 5' x 8' (1.8 x 1.5 x 2.4m)
Date Built:	1999

www.kittyhillresort.com

AN ARCHITECT DESIGNED HER OWN CATTERY WITH CAT WELFARE AT THE FOREFRONT OF HER MIND, SETTING AN EXAMPLE TO OTHERS WISHING TO START UP A SUCCESSFUL, PERSONAL AND CARING BOARDING CATTERY BUSINESS

KITTY HILL RESORT FOR CATS

THE FELINE ARCHITECT

Kitty Hill's owner, Harriet Butts, is an architect who wants to encourage other cat lovers to create cat resorts like hers, that provide private, walk-in rooms with furniture, windows, and lofts for the cats, rather than the commonly used (in Northern America) condo cage system.

Harriet says: We love cats and we take so much pleasure in being able to offer them cat boarding facilities that carefully provide for their absolute comfort, safety and entertainment. Not only do we have the pleasure of caring for cats, we also have the satisfaction of watching our unique and innovative resort set a new standard of care for cat boarding. Copy us - it works *so well* to board cats this way!

BIGGER AND BETTER

We do not ever mix cats from different households together, each room we provide is only for one family's kitty or kitties. No two rooms are alike; they all have their own names and special features. The *Western Dude Ranch* is 4'6" x 10' x 8' high, the *Sun Room* is about 8' x 7' and has windows on 3 sides with a twin bed in it. Our average size is about 6' x 5' x 8' high (1.8 x 1.5 x 2.4m high). All rooms are the same price: $22 per night for one cat (around £12), $36 for two (around £20). We know all too well that ROOM sized accommodation takes up much more space, costs more, and takes more cleaning and care, *but it is well worth the trouble*! As our cat guests relax and unfold themselves day by day, we are able to establish intimate relationships with them and these relationships sustain both them during their stay, and us as we scoop litter and work on their behalf.

We offer skylight lofts, climbing poles, cat-walks, shelf lookouts, ladders, nooks, hiding spots, lounge chairs, beds, bins and baskets. The rooms have operable screened, grilled windows and heated floors covered with padded vinyl.

Extra large rooms, like the *Presidential Suite* and *Samurai Room*, are perfect for multi-cat families. Our rooms are all so different: we have special rooms for reclusive cats, for social cats, kittens, ancient cats, for climbers, sleepers, athletic rowdies and fussy perfect princesses. We even have a black and white room, the *Music Room*, for black and white cats!

SWEET SMELL OF HOME

Owners are encouraged to bring something that smells of them and also some of their cat's familiar possessions - toys, scratching post, blanket, brush etc so their cat will have the familiar smells and comforts of home around them.

Sometimes we get their owners to mail a 'scent letter' which is a fresh sweat-wiped paper as a greeting!

> *"The walk-in room design proves itself to us every single day"*

What are you most pleased with?

When I watch people enter Kitty Hill for the first time, the surprised, delighted and relieved look on their faces just makes me light up inside. This is something I didn't foresee. It is kind of addictive working here - soaking up all the good feelings from cats and owners! I am especially thankful to my sweetheart, Dale Gatlin, for doing such a super job building all our beautiful custom cat rooms.

What would you do differently?

I think Kitty Hill was built a little too open. This works well for humans - light and airy, but it's a little more than the cats need. We accomplish the 'feel-safe factor' by closing-in with drapes for more privacy when needed. In 2006 we will add another 20 large rooms which we will make a little more closed in. I look forward to the fun of building, among others, the French Laundry Room, an Egyptian Room and the Art Studio!

Photographs courtesy of Rob Watson, Stacy Tatman & Harriet Butts

OUR PHILOSOPHY

We have two Cat cuddlers who pet, flatter and cuddle our guests. Anita comes every morning to murmur sweet encouragements, and Annette, who lives at the Resort, cuddles late into the wee hours of the night. We consider this cuddling to be essential, not optional. This one-on-one time helps our guests relax, eat normally, and feel that boarding is entirely acceptable. We want the kitties, and their owners, to be happy when they return for their next visit with us

ROOMS V CAGES: OUR PHILOSOPHY

The traditional rationale for boarding cats in small cages is that :

- Cats feel secure in small spaces
- Cats exercise isometrically and so do not need much room
- Unlike dogs, cats are independent creatures and do fine alone

Well, we disagree!

While it is true that cats love small spaces to hide in, and it is also true that frightened cats feel more secure in small spaces, this does not make it right for a boarding facility to offer ONLY small spaces for boarded guests. Something is *very* wrong if a boarded cat is frightened the whole time.

All cats should have a place to hide, but they should also have a place to come out from hiding and play. Actually, small cages are not very good for hiding either; they offer little to hide behind, or in. Sadly, many cages do not even have enough room for both a regular litter box *and* a cat, so they use little cardboard trays for elimination.

Cage-boarded cats get depressed, they stop grooming themselves, and they don't exercise. They don't have scratching posts, they can't jump or climb, or do much more than turn around and stretch their backs. A short stay in a cage 'exercising isometrically' won't harm their musculature, but longer stays will. We've seen the loss of muscle tone a number of times from cats that have been boarded for weeks in cage-style boarding kennels.

> *"Most people don't approve of boarding cats in cages. They don't want to do it, but often have to because they have few options"*

The cats that visit Kitty Hill Resort are companion animals; they are loved pets who are used to being an integral (if not pivotal) part of their family's life. **The old-fashioned labelling of cats as 'independent' creatures ignores the emotionally connected side of family cats.** In their own ways, they are very involved with their human families, very loving towards them and they miss their families when they are separated. They don't understand why they should be put in a cage, and they don't like it. *Who would?!*

CHANGE IS COMING

A change in attitude towards cat boarding is taking place all across the USA. Newer upscale boarding facilities offer 'condos' which are multi-level cages. **While this is obviously a BIG step in the right direction, we do not feel it goes far enough.** Most people don't approve of boarding cats in cages. They don't want to do it, but often have to because they have few options.

Super-friendly cats are the exception, not the rule, in a boarding situation. There are scaredy cats and shy cats and cranky cats – lots of wonderful cats who are simply not 'ready to purr and be friends' with just anyone in a new, strange environment. How do you establish a relationship with these cats? They certainly do not want a stranger to hold them. Do you reach into their condo to pet them while struggling to keep them from jumping out?

In a room like those at Kitty Hill you can have a seat, get comfortable, and let the cat's curiosity bring him or her out to make friends with you.

CATS NEED SPECIAL CARE

The ROOMS at Kitty Hill help cats in two vital ways; the space we provide allows our guests to move about comfortably, surrounded by their own scratching posts and bedding smelling of home, and allows our staff to establish relationships with them easily and naturally.

This combination creates purring kitties and grateful owners, which makes us happy Kitty Hill cat-lovers!

KITTY HILL RESORT

CATISFACTION

BUILDINGS SPEAK FOR THEMSELVES

As an architect, I am very aware of the way in which the three dimensional reality of a building embodies a human value or idea. A good building is a value made visible, tangible. Once we finished building, I no longer had to explain in words what I was trying to do, the building was more fluent and persuasive than I could ever be! **Rooms at our Resort are perfect for making friends; you can sit on the furniture or lie on the floor and let the cat come out to you from the safety of their own hiding place!**

CAT BOARDING IS HARDER TO GET RIGHT

In terms of psychological health, cats are harder to board than dogs. At Kitty Hill, cats are given comfortable rooms. They have their own toys and bedding smelling of home, and the loving relationships they have with Harriet and the staff sustain them. Except for the phone book and the internet, we don't advertise. **Our clients advertise for us**; they can't wait to bring back a friend or colleague! Kitty Hill's philosophy, embodied in our facility, sells itself – with the help of our kitty guests lounging in skylight lofts (as shown above and right).

"We hope lots of people will follow our example and set up similar cat boarding facilities of their own"

CATS DESERVE THE BEST

Kitty Hill tells the story that its cat guests are treasures of infinite worth, deserving of the best love and shelter we can offer. **We love to watch the amazed delight and appreciation on the faces of our new clients as they enter, look around at something they have never imagined, and immediately love**. Their idea of 'appropriate boarding for cats' is changed forever! Our clients love their cats so much, as I do mine, I think many of them are almost embarrassed about it; they don't always admit the depth of their feelings to others or sometimes even to themselves. **We see lots of tears at drop off and pick up times. Owners have brought us their hearts for our safe-keeping**. As we carefully listen to their special concerns and help them set up their cats' rooms to their liking, we validate their feelings, and reassure them in their vulnerability. Many have never boarded their cats before and tell us fiercely they 'would never kennel their cats'! We who 'work' at Kitty Hill are rewarded with all the gratitude and the thanks we get. And better yet, our nice clients leave, and we get to play with their cats!

RESPONSIBILITY & SATISFACTION

Yes, our responsibility is enormous, but what could be more satisfying? This satisfaction happens on a number of different levels: First of all, we have happy and contented boarded kitties. That's wonderful right there. Second, we have a facility that can be copied by others, so that a greater number of cats can be boarded this way around the world. **We have proved the viability of our business by becoming financially successful**. This is more than enough satisfaction, but there is a third source that is even more important to me. This has to do with the idea of cats as treasures. What does it imply to board a cat in a small cage? It implies that the cat is of small worth, reinforcing the whole concept of the limited worth, rights and value of any cat.

We are changing as a country, moving closer to becoming guardians of our pets, of all animals, of our beautiful planet. I hope Kitty Hill helps to strengthen the sense of worth and value of cats (and all animals) by validating the love and concerns of the owners, by setting a standard for boarding, and by teaching by example. I would love to feel that we helped push the world in the direction of compassion, caring and connectedness, even just a little bit, through our efforts. **On so many levels I feel very fortunate to have started a business which brings me so much comfort and pleasure. It is truly a labor of love, and I would recommend it most highly.**

KITTY HILL RESORT

KITTY HILL RESORT

THE TREND TOWARDS LARGER ACCOMMODATION

There has been a trend to provide larger accommodation, particularly for new commercial, rescue and sanctuary work.

The reasons for this are:

- Allows better facilities for cats (e.g. shelving at various heights to provide a more stimulating environment, and enough room for a seat to make volunteers, owners or potential owners more comfortable)

- Ease of working for the staff. (We recently visited a (licensed!) timber boarding cattery of low standard and hygiene with 2ft mould growths on the concrete slabs – the cattery manager was a rather portly gentleman who could just about squeeze in and turn around in the 3ft/1m wide unit, so it is no wonder that cleaning was difficult!)

- Greater increase in multi-cat households

- Shows the cat in a more natural environment, and hopefully more relaxed

- Is excellent PR and makes good business sense, particularly for commercial establishments when advertising

- The move to have 'something different' and 'better' is leading towards greater prevalence of large 'suite' type units

Single or Double Cat Units

Having spoken to a major manufacturer of prefabricated cattery systems, it stated that the majority of commercial boarding catteries installed have generally been sized to **accommodate two cats** (a double unit). This makes perfect sense once you understand that approximately 50% of cats will be in pairs, and as well as providing flexibility in the cattery, it looks more generous to clients for single cat use.

The reasons for making all units 'double' (suitable for two cats) are:

- Approximately 50% of households have two cats, or more

- Minimal cost difference between single or double unit sizes

- Greater public appeal and perception of the property

- More space for the single cat

- Greater flexibility to the owner

- Ease of working for the staff

Family Units

You can incorporate more flexibility into the cattery by providing a 'removable' panel between units, or a lockable cat flap so that two units can be joined, or used together to make larger runs for families of cats (who are happy to share). You then have the option of closing the cat flap if the cats are not happy to be together in this new environment. The flexibility is also there if a client wants a particularly large unit for their cat/s. On the next few pages we will see an example of a boarding cattery using large suite accommodation, which is becoming more and more popular with newer facilities.

Plus – it is far easier to take good photographs of cat units that are large!

CASE STUDY:
LARGE SUITE ACCOMMODATION

Organisation: Oakdale Boarding Cattery
Location: UK, Cheshire
Cattery Type: Indoor
Cattery Function: Boarding, 29 Units
Unit Size Sleep: 1000 x 1870mm (3'3" x 6'1")
    1300 x 1870mm (4'3" x 6'1")
Unit Size Exercise: 2750mm/9ft long
Date Built: 2004

www.oakdalecattery.co.uk

A NEW, RURAL BOARDING CATTERY WITH LARGE 12FT/4.5M SUITES, ENJOYING THE SUCCESS OF BEING A SMALL BUSINESS WITH A VERY HOME-LIKE FEEL, THE CATTERY IS IN A BEAUTIFUL LOCATION WITH LOTS OF ANIMAL LIFE FOR THE CATS TO WATCH

OAKDALE BOARDING CATTERY

LOVING THE LIFESTYLE

Zoe Gallagher, owner of Oakdale Cattery couldn't be happier with her boarding cattery business. She talks joyfully of the pampered cats who become 'hers' once in the cattery, and her lovely clients. The cattery is a converted stables and it is amazing the difference adding a clock tower, porch and external features has made to the building, set in a lovely rural environment on a farm full of other animals for the cats to watch.

FAMILY-RUN & HOME-LIKE

Zoe and husband Noel purchased the derelict farm 11 years ago and lived in a mobile home while the farm was being rebuilt. Their 7 year old daughter Kitty (!) has now developed a certificate scheme for the cats, and pointed out Shadow, one of her favourites who has been given a 'cute & chubby' certificate! You immediately 'get' the feeling on the farm, which is very much a family-owned and much-loved place. In particular, Zoe enjoys her night-time rounds, with the soft string lights glowing and the red floor, it feels quiet, cosy and relaxing.

HOW THE CATTERY STARTED

Zoe originally wanted to work from home to be with her favourite animals, and after a year of planning and research, the planning application was submitted and granted. Her primary reason for creating a cattery (apart from her love of cats) was to provide a better cattery than she had seen. Having visited several catteries, Zoe was appalled at the standard – especially where owners were not even allowed to see the cat accommodation for themselves. The reasons often quoted were 'it will upset the cats' or 'for health and safety reasons' and one cattery even used small, dark, stacked rabbit hutches! Naturally, seeing this motivated Zoe to build larger than normal 'suites' of over 4.5m/12ft long to provide much more space – she just knew she could do better!

SETTLING CATS IN

Having been introduced to the feline facial pheromone by one of her clients, Zoe now uses the spray (if required) and plug-ins permanently, as the effect on the cats is so noticeable, especially on arrival when cats need to settle in and feel calm and comfortable. Zoe also feels that the more home-like feel of 'solid' walls and large suites with lots of daylight also helps to settle the cats in well.

There is plenty for the cats to watch as inside the cattery in the spacious 3m/10ft corridor, there are large cages with a chipmunk (constantly on the go!) budgies and finches. From the deep shelf in front of their own window, the cats can watch rabbits, chickens, ducks, pheasants, wallabies, donkeys, pygmy goats, llamas, their horse Toby and the farm cattle.

Photographs by David Key and Zoe Gallagher

OAKDALE CATTERY

PLENTY TO WATCH

CAT COMFORT

Particularly noticeable is the amount of hiding places and variety of beds for the cats to choose from. Zoe feels strongly about allowing the cats the freedom to use all of the suite at night too, having seen many semi-outdoor catteries 'lock in' the cats at night. She likes to give the cats as much freedom as possible in her indoor cattery.

ADDING EXTERNAL RUNS

Although currently an indoor-only cattery, there will be an additional outdoor covered space added for the cats directly from the round 'port-hole' instead of the usual cat flap, which are currently being built. This will allow two indoor rooms, plus an outdoor area overlooking one of the ponds.

MAKING IT EASY TO LIVE WITH

Zoe wondered if having larger units would make cleaning more of a chore, but in fact the opposite is true. With so much space to move around in, (being large suites that are full-height), cleaning is easy and not an onerous task like some of the timber or smaller catteries she has seen where there is barely enough room to turn around inside. The roof is ventilated and there are sky lights and windows, so the cattery feels bright and fresh. A building like this would be too large to completely heat, so all the sleep areas are heated by radiators.

BEING SUCCESSFUL

After initial concerns about how successful the venture would be, Zoe now realises she need not have worried. A good proportion of customers find her on the internet, or from veterinary and customer recommendations, but this has increased lately by adding signage on the busy main road, so passing traffic has become more important as more people are now aware of the cattery. Zoe remembers every cat and when the owner phones, she says 'ah, Jamie's Mum!' Another asset to the business is the booking software she uses to keep the paperwork down and prepare notes for the day ahead.

With 400 customers already within her first year of opening, with such success she needs to be organised!

What are you most pleased with?

Thoroughly enjoying the challenge of the business, and of course our cat boarders and their owners who are lovely. Zoe was delighted to recently have been told by the licensing officer that Oakdale Cattery is the best in the area, and that her website is used as a referral for people thinking about setting up a cattery!

What would you do differently?

The floor paint scratches and flakes, so it needs to be repainted, so we will be tiling it in the near future. We originally intended to fit UPVC doors, but ultimately did not because of the extra cost, and not knowing whether we would be successful. However, UPVC would have been a better option in the longer-term maintenance aspect, than timber doors.

OAKDALE CATTERY

OAKDALE CATTERY

A
meow
massages
the
heart

Stuart McMillan

STATUTORY LEGISLATION

The scale of your project has an impact on the level of infrastructure required, and it can also affect the level of legal requirements you will need to comply with.

In reality, the legislation shown on the following pages could apply to any new or existing development. However, the requirements for a smaller scale project will be less onerous than for a larger scale project.
It is obvious that we cannot list regulations for every county in every region in every country. However, like cattery buildings, regulations will be similar (certainly between the UK, USA and Canada), although the wording may be slightly different.

In this chapter we list regulations that cattery owners may need to observe in the UK, but there will be equivalents in many countries, and many of them are a matter of common sense, even if there are no similar regulations for that country. These are examples of the more common regulations that you may need to comply with.

You will see what kinds of responsibilities you may have from glancing through this chapter, such as:

- Building regulations, gas, electric, fire risk, emergency lighting, asbestos

- Health and safety regulations, accidents at work, protective equipment, working at height

- Construction, demolition, design and management

- Environment protection

- Disability discrimination

Statutory Obligations

All businesses are compelled to comply with certain legal obligations and regulations, irrespective of the size of the business; these regulations apply to both the employee and the employer. Like all legislation the rules are complex and constantly changing; therefore only an overview is given of the relevant legislation to ensure that the employer is aware of the effect of the main legislation. Full guides to the UK legislation can be obtained from HMSO Publications www.tso.co.uk and specialised publications such as Croner's www.croner.co.uk.

Building Regulations

Building Regulations are totally separate from planning permission. Although Building Control may be housed in the same building as the planning authority; they are two self-governing bodies; totally independent of each other. Generally, under normal circumstances all schemes require Building Regulation approval. However, it is worth checking with the Building Control officer to establish if all of your proposed development will require permission.

NOTE: Building Regulations can be somewhat of a 'grey area' in the UK. It is worth checking with the Building Control Officer to seek his/her views on this.

Under Class III of the Building Regulations (Greenhouses and Agricultural Buildings) there are exceptions that allow for some relaxation in the requirements, these are:

■ Buildings used for agricultural purposes, or principally for the keeping of animals, which are:

- sited not less than 1.5 times their height from any building containing sleeping accommodation,
- provided with a fire exit which is not more than 30m (98ft) from any point of the building

It is these two points that make this an extremely useful tool for the owners of any new development. However, consideration should be given to ensuring that the structure is safe, has adequate fire alarm and protection and has adequate fire escape provision.

What is Building Control?

Building Regulations require that buildings, which are erected, extended, altered or which have a material change in their use, are capable of performing to minimum standards. **These standards are set to protect the health, safety and welfare of people; to conserve energy and to prevent contamination of land and water**. To ensure that these standards are met requires that you inform the Building Control office of your intentions. Your architect, surveyor or builder will normally address the specific technical requirements of the regulations; however, there is no reason to stop you from dealing with the department yourself.

In most circumstances involving a commercial business or operation the Building Control officer will primarily be interested in:

■ Insulation values of the building

■ Fire protection

■ Heating source type i.e. gas/oil boiler, electricity etc

■ Drainage – Foul and surface water disposal

■ Structure stability, foundations and ground conditions

■ Access and fire escapes

Construction (Design and Management) Regulations 1994

CDM normally applies to existing businesses and in particular larger scale projects which will be longer than 30 days duration. The aim of the regulations is to promote better safety standards and health and safety provisions for construction workers. The responsibility for enforcing these regulations lies with the Health and Safety Executive. The regulations place specific duties on all parties involved with the development, i.e. client, design professionals, contractors and subcontractors. Projects which involve CDM notification to the Health and Safety Executive would normally have professional advisors e.g. architects, who will advise the client and manage the legislative requirements of the act.

Demolition

It may be necessary to demolish existing buildings on a newly acquired site. The reasons for this are to clear part of the site for development, or to remove or make safe any structures in an unsafe condition. The law regarding demolition is very specific and should not be taken lightly, with statutory requirements that must be adhered to. For any large-scale demolition, expert advice should normally be sought. Generally, consent to demolish a building is not required under the Town and Country Planning Acts, the exception to this being for a listed building. However, a person intending to demolish a building or part of it must give notice under section 80 of the Building Act 1984 to the local authority.

The Building Control section of the local authority usually undertakes the control of such work. The notice usually takes the form of a letter describing the impending work and a site plan showing the location and the building.

In addition to the Authority, the owner or his/her agent must also notify:

- Any utility boards i.e. gas, electricity

- The owner/occupiers of any building adjacent to the building concerned

Personal Protective Equipment at Work Regulations 1992

Personal Protective Equipment (PPE) means all equipment (including clothing affording protection against the weather) that is intended to be worn or held by a person at work and which protects him/her against one or more risks to his/her health, safety and welfare.

The main items of PPE for the cattery owner would include such items as aprons and gloves (isolation), eye protection (mixing disinfectants) etc. It is designed to be personal protective equipment for an individual, not for communal use. The person given the equipment should have suitable provision to secure his/her equipment away after use. It is normally the 'last resort' and only to be provided where engineering controls and safe systems at work do not effectively control the risks identified.

The problems associated with PPE are:

- Protects only the person wearing it

- Maximum levels of protection with PPE are seldom achieved; in practice the actual level of protection is difficult to assess

- May restrict the wearer's movements, visibility, hearing and provide additional weight to be carried

Health and Safety at Work Act 1974

The broad aims of the Health and Safety at Work Act 1974 are essentially:

- **To secure the health, safety and welfare of persons** at work.

- **To protect persons other than employees** from risks at work (e.g. those living or working near the business or those entering the premises in the course of business)

- **To control dangerous substances** in terms of acquisition or use

- **To control emissions** into the atmosphere from the workplace

- **Failure to comply with the act**, or any regulations made under it, is a criminal offence and the employer, or even the employee may be prosecuted

- **Health and Safety Policy Statement**
  At present any employer who has five or more employees must prepare a written statement of their general policy on health and safety. This policy will evolve to take into account changes in management, legal requirements and technological changes

Duties of Employees – Sections 7 and 8 of the Health and Safety at Work Act 1974 require every employee to have the following responsibilities:

- Take reasonable care for the health and safety of himself and other persons who may be affected by his acts or omissions at work, and as regards any duty or requirement imposed on his employer or any other persons to co-operate with him so far as is necessary to enable that duty or requirement to be performed or complied with

- No person shall intentionally or recklessly interfere with or misuse anything provided in the interests of health, safety or welfare in pursuance of any of the relevant statutory provisions

Accidents at Work

The legislation regarding accidents at work in commercial premises is contained in the Reporting of Injuries, Diseases and Dangerous Occurrences Regulations 1995 (RIDDOR). The aim of these regulations is to ensure accidents that occur in the workplace are investigated and, where possible, remedial measures are taken to avoid recurrence.

An accident is normally defined as one of the following and is reported to the Health and Safety Executive (HSE):

- Fatal accidents and major accidents/conditions

- Incidents where as a result of an accident connected with the workplace, people not at work are injured and have to be taken to hospital for treatment

- An incident where a person not at work suffers a major injury as a result of work being carried out and has to be treated at a hospital

- Dangerous occurrences and accidents which cause more than three days incapacity absence from work

- Certain work-related diseases

- An accident includes any non-consensual act of physical violence suffered at work

Disability Discrimination Act 1995

It is unlawful for service providers to treat disabled people less favourably than other people for a reason related to their disability. Service providers have been obliged to:

- alter practices, policies or procedures that make it unreasonably difficult for disabled people to use their services

- provide alternative methods of making their services available where the physical features of their premises make it unreasonably difficult for disabled people to access services

- provide auxiliary aids and services to assist disabled people to access goods and services

The extent of adjustments that a service provider is obliged to make will depend on a number of factors, these include the level of activity, financial resources and the disruption the adjustment will cause.

Being Aware

The DDA classes someone as disabled if they have a physical or mental impairment, that has a substantial and long-term adverse effect on their ability to carry out normal day-to-day activities. In addition to clients who use wheelchairs (a very low percentage), or who have mobility problems, there are millions of potential clients affected by some degree of hearing loss, learning disabilities, visual impairment, mental illness or more common conditions such as arthritis. The most important barriers to access for disabled people arise from the physical features of premises, from staff communication and training, and from the business policies and practices that service providers adopt. To achieve full access it is as important that staff are aware of the various disabilities as it is to remove physical barriers to access such as steps, poor signage and dangerous and damaged pathways. A common sense approach towards individual needs, combined with minor adjustments, can make a dramatic improvement. Remember that around 3% of people are born with their disability, and around 83% of disabled people become disabled during their adult life.

Making Adjustments to Your Premises

Service providers have to make 'reasonable adjustments' to their premises so that there are no physical barriers stopping, or making it unreasonably difficult, for disabled people to get and use their services. The DDA requires that you make changes when it is unreasonably difficult for disabled people to use your services, not only when it is completely impossible to use services. The definition of 'unreasonable' means whether the time, inconvenience, effort, discomfort or loss of dignity experienced by disabled people in using the service would be considered unreasonable by other people if they had to endure similar difficulties. Possible adjustments will depend on the scale of service you provide, practicality, disruption, cost compared with turnover. These factors will vary from cattery to cattery. A feature that is deemed reasonable for you to adjust might not be deemed reasonable for another business provider to adjust!

In circumstances where a person with a disability cannot gain access to a business because of the presence of a physical barrier, the business is obliged by the Legislation to consider one or a combination of the following options:

- The removal of the feature that prevents the disabled person gaining access
- Alter the feature so that it no longer has the effect
- Provide a reasonable means of avoiding the feature
- Provide a reasonable alternative method of making the service in question available to the disabled person

Some of the main areas of concern and potential difficulties for disabled visitors are:

• **Car parking** – lack of dedicated parking
• **Main access door** – too narrow or too heavy to operate
• **Cluttered reception areas**
• **Signage** – outdated and poor signage with lettering too small to read
• **WCs** – without adequate door widths and emergency communication facilities

There are actions that can be taken by all businesses to minimise issues, and awareness is one of the critical factors.

There are simple actions that can be taken that do not cost money, such as:

• Not allowing able-bodied staff and visitors to use the disabled parking bays
• Keeping corridors, doors free from clutter and obstacles
• Not using disabled toilets as storage areas
• When speaking to a disabled visitor who is wheelchair bound it is far better to pull up a chair and sit next to them. This is not only polite but also more comfortable for both parties
• If the centre is busy and noisy, it is far better to talk to a visitor with a hearing impairment by moving to a quiet part of the reception or, preferably to an interview room

---

The aim is to allow the disabled person to remain as independent as possible and to enjoy the visit as much as an able-bodied person

---

Environmental Protection Act 1990

The Environmental Protection Act 1990 (Part III) draws together most of the statutory nuisances from earlier legislation, and amends some of the definitions and rationalises them. Under the 1990 Act, there is a duty for every local authority to "cause its area to be inspected from time to time to detect any statutory nuisances which ought to be dealt with". Areas of concern which may affect the cattery owner might be noise, smell, conditions of premises, burning cat litter, waste materials (e.g. cans, litter, animal waste) not suitably contained which might attract vermin and flies and any other nuisance.

Duty of Care

Under Section 34 of the Environmental Protection Act 1990 all producers of waste are compelled to dispose of it in such a manner as not to endanger public health or the environment; this is known as 'duty of care.'

All waste produced on the site has to be transported by a registered carrier and disposed of at an authorised facility.

Under The Environmental Protection (Duty of Care) Regulations 1991 a mandatory system of transfer notes was introduced. Under normal circumstances all waste will be collected by arrangement either by the authority or a local, registered carrier. The definition of waste produced by catteries is under review, therefore it is worth checking with the local authority to clarify local policy (see the chapter on Environmental Legislation).

Gas Safety Regulations

The Gas Safety (Installation and Use) Regulations 1994 were introduced to try to prevent and reduce the amount of dangerous gas appliances in use; these include fires, cookers, boilers, laundry equipment, etc. The regulations are complex but the basic guidelines are simple: to ensure that any gas appliance or installation pipe work at a place of work is maintained in a safe condition. It is the duty of any person who owns a gas appliance or any installation in a premise or part of a premise let by him to ensure that the appliance and installation is in a safe condition. A registered and qualified person should check the appliance and installation at intervals of not more than 12 months. A record should be kept of the inspection and any recommendations or works carried out.

Electricity at Work Regulations

The Electricity at Work Regulations 1989 were introduced in April 1990 and designed to take into account changes in technological developments and more importantly brought a legal compliance to all.

Inspections
It is a legal requirement that the premises provide a safe environment for staff, public and any other visitors and that an inspection of the entire wiring system is carried out every three to five years. Obviously, a new installation that has not been modified or tampered with is far safer than an installation that is 30 years old and has had several modifications over this period.

Portable Appliance Testing
The testing and recording of electrical portable appliances is a procedure that is normally carried out every 12 months for most light commercial operations; it is a legal requirement. Each appliance and if applicable its power lead is tested by a suitably trained person or electrician; on completion of the test it will either pass, or fail and need corrective works. Once these have been carried out it will be tested again and either pass or fail. Once a 'pass' standard has been reached, this will vary for each appliance. A label will be stuck/attached to the appliance with its own unique number or code for identification purposes and should be logged either in a book or on a computer disk, and this should be kept in a safe place.

Control of Substances Hazardous to Health Regulations 1994

The Control of Substances Hazardous to Health Regulations 1994 (COSHH) applies to potentially harmful substances. The COSSH provisions cover practically all substances harmful to health at work e.g. disinfectants, waste etc.

The act is divided into six main provisions:

1. **Assessment -** No employee should be exposed to substances hazardous to health unless an assessment has been carried out. Data sheets provided by the chemical manufacturers will provide the general information required

2. **Prevention or control -** Once substances hazardous to health have been identified, the employer must prevent or control it by various means such as substitution, elimination or ventilation etc

3. **Maintenance and testing of equipment -** Employers must ensure employees use any control measures in force. The employer is responsible for ensuring all equipment is inspected, tested and a record is kept of this

4. **Monitoring -** Employers must monitor employees who have been exposed to hazardous substances

5. **Health surveillance -** If employees are exposed to substances that may have been a contributory factor to ill health e.g. dermatitis and disinfectants it may be appropriate to arrange a health surveillance programme. This can range from a full medical check to self **inspection**

6. **Information, training and instruction -** Employees exposed to hazardous substances must be given adequate training, information and instruction to know the risks involved to their health and how to use control measures

Control of Asbestos at Work Regulations 2002

This latest piece of legislation is something of which all businesses in the UK need to be aware.

Asbestos first became noticeable in the 1960's when it was recognised that exposure to asbestos fibres had potential and deadly consequences. Asbestos is still found in many households and businesses today. In reality it is still an extremely useful product. It was used extensively in housing for insulation, fire-proofing materials, thermoplastic floor tiles, rainwater guttering and roofing materials as well as a wide range of commercial applications. It was used extensively in construction during the 1950's until the early 1980's.

The current legislation requires the following in non-domestic premises:

- To survey and to determine whether asbestos-containing material is present (the presumption is that the material will contain asbestos unless it is proven otherwise)

- Assess the amount and condition of the material

- Make, record and keep up-to-date records of the location

- Assess the risk of the material and how the risk will be managed

- Review and monitor the situation

- Provide information to anyone who is likely to come into contact with the material

- Due to the complexities of this regulation, any business should take professional guidance

See www.HSE.gov.uk for more information.

Work at Height Regulations 2005

The Work at Height Regulations 2005 needs to be considered by all businesses. Falls from relatively low heights, up to 2m/6'6" still remain the single biggest cause of workplace deaths and one of the main causes of major injury.

The nature of many roofing materials used in catteries often means it has to be cleaned to remove algae and vegetation etc. The fragile nature of many roofing materials will, in many cases not support the weight of a person; obviously this is potentially lethal.

The aims of the regulations are to:

- Avoid work at height where possible

- Use work equipment or other measures to prevent falls where they cannot avoid working at height

- Where this cannot eliminate the risk of a fall, the use of work equipment or other measures to minimise the distance and the consequences of a fall should one occur

- The use of mechanical lift platforms has become the mainstay for many operations that in the past were carried out by the use of ladders

For further information see www.hse.gov.uk/falls

Fire Precautions (Workplace) Regulations 1997

On 1 December 1997 the Fire Precautions (Workplace) Regulations took effect with explicit requirements for every organisation with five or more employees to carry out a written fire risk assessment. The assessment is to ensure that all areas of potential risk have been identified. **In the main this will cover:**

- Identification of the areas where fires are likely to occur

- Provision of measures to minimise the possibility of a fire starting

- Ensuring that fire protection systems, escape routes, etc. allow escape to a safe place

Every area should be assessed separately and a judgment should be made with regard to the type of combustible materials and possible sources of ignition, types of doors, i.e. should standard doors be replaced with fire rated doors, availability of fire extinguishers, etc.

Portable Fire-fighting Equipment

The installation of portable fire extinguishers is a legal and usually an insurance requirement. Most catteries will have only this type of equipment installed; the installation of fixed, centralised, monitored systems will not be required for most single-storey buildings with good external access points. The type and number of extinguishers required is dependent on the size of the premises and the risks of fire involved; advice should be sought from insurance companies, extinguisher suppliers, and the fire officer. When talking about fire extinguishers we are dealing only with small isolated fires that can be extinguished quickly and safely; we are not concerned with large fires that have engulfed an entire room or a more extensive area. Once a fire has reached this latter stage the only safe action is to vacate the building and call the Fire Brigade.

- **Wall-mounted extinguishers** – These fire extinguishers come in a variety of sizes and substances for use on different types of fire and materials. Advice on the most suitable for your needs should be discussed with your insurance company or provider.

- **Hose reels** – Recommended particularly for floor areas in excess of 800m². Extremely effective on certain classes of fire, they deliver an unlimited supply of water and with sufficient mains pressure can deliver a jet of water in excess of 6m. A standard hose is normally 30m in length and has an internal diameter of 19mm.

- **Fire blanket** – This is used to smother small fires involving liquids and organic materials and would normally be installed near cooking appliances.

All of the above appliances need to be sited in the most suitable place, generally:

- As close as possible to any fire risk
- Close/adjacent to doorways and on escape routes
- At the same location in identical buildings
- Near 'fire points'
- Away from extremes of temperature

The extinguishers need to be securely fixed to walls, approximately 900mm above the floor. This will prevent the base from rusting, particularly in wet environments, and also prevent them being used as 'door stops'! They should be visible at all times and staff should be aware of their location and, more importantly, how to use them. It is pointless having extinguishers on the premises if none of the staff can operate them. Most supplying companies will offer an annual inspection to ensure that the units are fully charged and capable of working; this can also be an ideal time to train staff to operate an extinguisher.
It is surprising how difficult some people may find the procedure of discharging an extinguisher; ANY form of practice might make the difference between a minor fire and a major disaster

Fire Protection

Generally the main areas of concern are: fire alarm system, emergency lighting, fire-fighting and protection.
Most cattery buildings, by their very nature do not represent a significant fire risk; the solid nature of construction and the lack of inflammable materials all reduce the risk. This, combined with a non-smoking policy and regular electrical wiring checks will minimise the risk. In addition, where a relatively small number of staff is employed, (ie. fewer than 20), a Fire Certificate will not be required. The normal procedure when applying for Building Regulations Approval is for the officer concerned to pass a set of the plans to the Fire Brigade. The plans will be assessed and recommendations made for any specific requirements; for most small catteries the minimum recommendation would possibly be for portable fire extinguishers or fire doors with overhead closing devices. Insurance companies may also stipulate the level of equipment required for a particular location and operation. Even if your building does not come under the requirements for Building Regulations or Control, it is good business policy to install basic fire protection as it may save lives.

The basic elements for domestic and small commercial operations can be divided into three elements: Fire detection and alarms systems, emergency lighting and portable fire fighting equipment

Fire Detection and Alarms

There is a vast range of systems available on the market from simple battery operated; stand-alone units to fully integrated systems linked to intruder alarms. The level with which your insurance company and the fire authority are satisfied will depend on the layout of the centre, the size of the building, the number of staff employed and any high-risk operations that might be carried out. However, most animal welfare establishments and catteries are classed as low risk properties and therefore do not normally require a sophisticated system. The purpose of fire detection and alarm systems is to act as an early warning system. The more time there is to take the appropriate action, the less likelihood of serious damage or loss of life. Fire detection should not be viewed as an unnecessary expense, a waste of time or something that may never be used; the sooner a fire is detected, the more chance of limiting the damage. The cost of installing a basic system is an extremely small percentage of the overall project cost. The minimum requirement is a battery-operated stand-alone unit, which will give an audible alarm in the region of 90dB. Clearly this type of unit has its limitations and this must be taken into account when looking at the site layout, distance of the cattery from any residential property etc. A more permanent solution is to install a basic system of heat/smoke detectors linked to a control panel with manual call points and an external audible alarm. The advantage with these systems is that the buildings can be 'zoned' if required. This would enable a staff member to go directly to the fire zone without having to spend time looking for the fire.

Emergency Lighting

The aim of emergency lighting is to indicate the emergency escape routes, to show changes of direction, to show where the fire alarm call points and fire extinguishers are located and also to enable emergency work to be carried out or completed.

The types of lighting available are:

- Some luminaries with emergency battery back up
- Wall mounted plug in, battery-operated units
- A central battery system, which powers all of the luminaries
- A back-up generator capable of providing power to all the lights
  This has the added benefit of being able to provide power to enable the rest of the site to continue to function

Because of the relatively simple construction and layout of most single storey catteries, the normal requirement is for a very basic mains supplied system, which covers the legal requirements and also enables basic duties to continue during a power cut.

CATTERY TYPES & UNIT STYLES

CATTERY TYPES AND CAT UNIT STYLES

The designs shown in this section are primarily aimed at commercial catteries, rescue organisations and charities. Long-stay cat housing and multi-cat families will tend to have their own requirements and much more flexibility.

The design and layout of the main cattery building can be as simple or as grand as you want it to be. The size and design will be influenced by financial restrictions, the size of the site, proximity of neighbours, the number of units you need to build and any existing buildings that may be used, and also any business statement you wish to make to your customers.

Cattery designs are often in straight lines (single or double), L-shaped or U-shaped.

However, it is generally the financial restriction that has the greatest influence on the number of units constructed.

Cattery layouts:

- **Indoor**
- **Outdoor**
- **Semi-outdoor** (this is the ideal)

Unit styles for the above layouts:

- Walk-in, full-height (this is the ideal)
- Penthouse, raised sleeping box

Options for more flexibility:

- Holding units
- Mother and kitten units
- Multi-cat or communal
- Play, socialisation and rehoming rooms
- Communal or outdoor exercise

Options for the home, indoor-only cats and multi-cat housing:

- Large external safety runs (or enclosing a garden boundary) using escape-proof fencing

We will look at each of these options in detail in this chapter.

INDOOR CATTERIES

Indoor catteries have individual, combined or separate sleeping and exercise accommodation areas accessed via a service corridor.

More common in America and Canada (and other countries with extremes of climate), this type is also favoured by some organisations and individuals. The majority of these catteries tend to be conversions of existing buildings, or where external factors (such as noise) are an issue.

There are some additional considerations that have to be taken into account. The main areas of concern are ventilation and lack of natural lighting. However, providing these have been considered at the design stage and adequate allowance made, then there is no reason why this design should not be as successful as any other.

Clearly, this design does have its disadvantages.

My view is that this style (if constructed properly with good ventilation and natural lighting) is equal to other designs for short periods. However, there are reservations about its use for long-term care.

Advantages:

- Temperature control in areas with extremes of climate
- Where a quiet environment is required

Possible Disadvantages:

- Lack of ventilation/fresh air
- Lack of daylight, or poorer quality of lighting
- Lack of an outlook for the cats
- Higher risk of disease

In the UK this style is permissible for boarding, providing that the combined area (m^2) is equal to the combined areas of the sleeping and exercise run. In the USA/Canada and extreme climates this style is more popular.

CASE STUDY:
INDOOR RESCUE CATTERY

Organisation:	RSPCA Halifax, UK
Cattery Type:	Indoor, penthouse style
Cattery Function:	Rescue
Number of Units:	19
Unit Size Sleep:	1m-1.5m x 900mm x 900mm (3'3"-5ft x 3ft x 3ft)
Unit Size Exercise:	1m-1.5m x 2.4m (3'3"-5ft x 8ft)
Date Built:	2004

www.rspca.org.uk

REPLACING AN OUTDATED CATTERY, THIS NEW INDOOR REHOMING CATTERY MAKES FULL USE OF THE LIMITED SPACE ON SITE AND HAS SUBSTANTIALLY REDUCED THE LEVEL OF DISEASE — PROVIDING A CAT & PEOPLE-FRIENDLY ENVIRONMENT

RSPCA HALIFAX

The RSPCA centre in Halifax constructed a new indoor cattery in 2004, replacing a very tired and outdated timber cattery building. The centre is housed on a compact site with steep sloping ground. Consequently, this imposes its own practical and operational issues.

OLD PROBLEMS TO OVERCOME

The centre manager, Julie Cockroft, explained some of the difficulties she has experienced since joining the centre three years ago:

On arrival it was obvious that the centre was experiencing far higher levels of disease than at other centres. This was attributed partly to the design, an indoor cattery with little natural light and outlook for the cats, and due to the materials used, it meant that it could not be adequately cleaned and disinfected. The old cattery was located adjacent to the dog kennels. Consequently, the cats suffered greater levels of stress by being in such close proximity to the kennels.

THE NEW CATTERY

Due to the physical constraints of the site, the decision was taken to construct an all-indoor cattery. This allowed the centre to overcome the issues with noise and stress for the cats, by moving the cattery further away from the kennels and using double-glazed doors/windows.

COLOUR CODING

The new cattery has two wards, the green ward and the cream ward. Each ward is colour coded for the trays and equipment etc. This ensures that the equipment stays in the right place to reduce the risk of cross-contamination.

Each ward has it own kitchen, sluice and store area. By constructing the wards this way, it allows a greater degree of control and flexibility in the event of a disease outbreak. Both wards have a full multi-port extraction system that removes air from inside the sleeping pods and discharges it at high level to the environment. To date, the centre hasn't had an outbreak of cat flu.

CAT-FRIENDLY

It was clear that a great deal of thought and effort is taken to keep the cats healthy and stimulated.

Each run area has a **seat for volunteers** for use when grooming and socialising the cat, **disposable cardboard dishes** are used as a matter of policy to reduce the risk of disease spread, a **wide range of cat toys** are freely available and classical music is played at a low level.

Julie firmly believes that **classical music** is of great benefit to the cats along with the use of plug-in **feline facial pheromone** therapy.

MATERIALS AND ENVIRONMENT

The materials used, stainless steel, glass and ceramic floor tiles provide an easy to clean, hygienic, bright, cheerful and pleasant environment for the cats, staff, volunteers and visitors alike. The ventilation system ensures that the air inside the wards is fresh, and changed at a regular rate.

Correctly built, an indoor cattery can work as well as any other design for short stays. In this particular case, the benefits of a hygienic and quiet building have been clearly demonstrated.

What are you most pleased with?

The peaceful, relaxed environment that allows visitors to concentrate on the cats and a building which substantially reduces disease-related issues.

What would you do differently?

The centre would have liked deeper drainage channels to prevent wash-down water from spilling over. However, the ceramic channel used only comes in one set depth. Also, some opaque glazing in the division panels would have provided more privacy for cats that really will not tolerate another cat.

OUTDOOR CATTERIES

Outdoor catteries have individual sleeping accommodation and individual exercise runs. These are generally accessed from an external safety corridor.

This is one of the more common arrangements seen in the UK, and has been the main design and style used by many boarding establishments over a number of years. The majority of these outdoor catteries are a prefabricated timber construction.

Advantages:

■ **Ventilation**
This design allows excellent levels of ventilation and generally a good views for cats

Disadvantages:

■ **Cold for Cats, Staff and Visitors**
The major disadvantage with this system, particularly for sanctuaries and charities, is that they tend to be cold for the staff and visitors; this can have a marked effect on rehoming figures and number of visitors etc.
This is often exacerbated by the fact that the indoor sleeping section is warm, and the cats are quite happy to stay indoors and out of sight!

■ **Takes up more space**
This design tends to take up more space than indoor or semi-outdoor catteries, as this style often has a sneeze barrier gap (to reduce the risk of cross-infection) normally 500mm/1'6" gap between the units – which does take up a considerable amount of space

■ **Prefabricated construction**
The design is really only suitable for prefabricated construction due to the fact that each building is totally separate from its neighbour. The costs to construct this type of design using brick/block make it uneconomical

Outdoor Cattery
Typical Layout

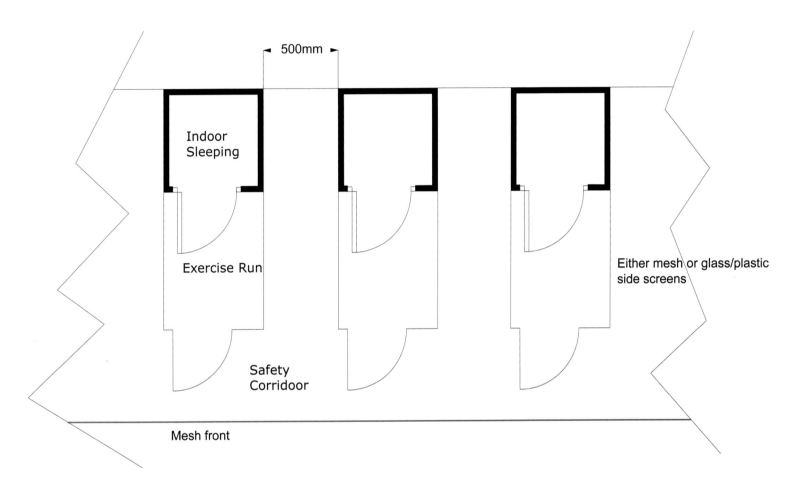

NOTE:
The separation gap left between each unit is normally a minimum distance of 500mm

SEMI-OUTDOOR CATTERIES

Semi-outdoor catteries have heated indoor accommodation and individual, covered exercise runs with the front face open to the atmosphere. Each unit is entered individually from a service corridor.

There are design options which allow access to the external exercise run from the internal corridor, these differences can be seen in greater detail in the following layouts/plans.

This style of cattery is favoured by many commercial catteries, charities and sanctuaries as it offers better viewing from the public's point of view, and usually plenty for the cats to watch.

It also allows staff to work and discuss potential adoptions/bookings with clients under cover, and in the warm in the colder months (or cool in the warmer months, especially if air conditioned!)

The semi-outdoor cattery is generally the most cost-effective and flexible design, and provides many of the required features for the cats' welfare, staff ease of working and public access

Semi-Outdoor
with Reception and Offices

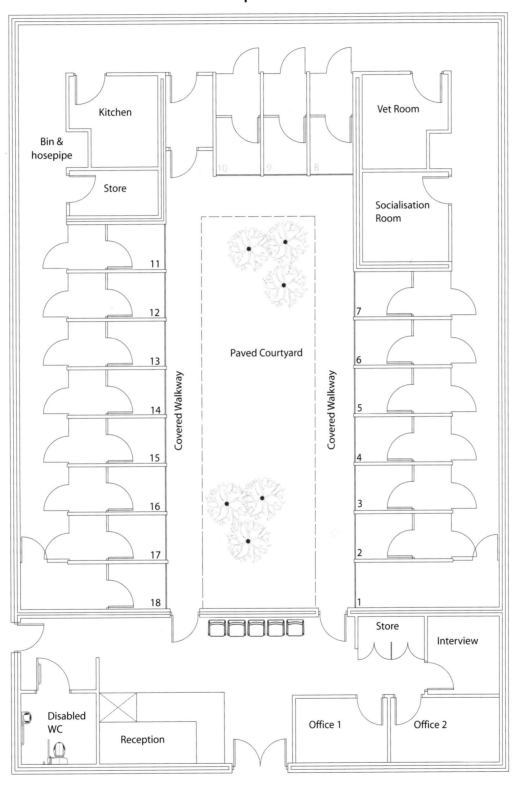

Semi-outdoor
The Blue Cross, Burford UK Rescue and Rehoming Cattery

Semi-outdoor
(Layout of photo shown left)

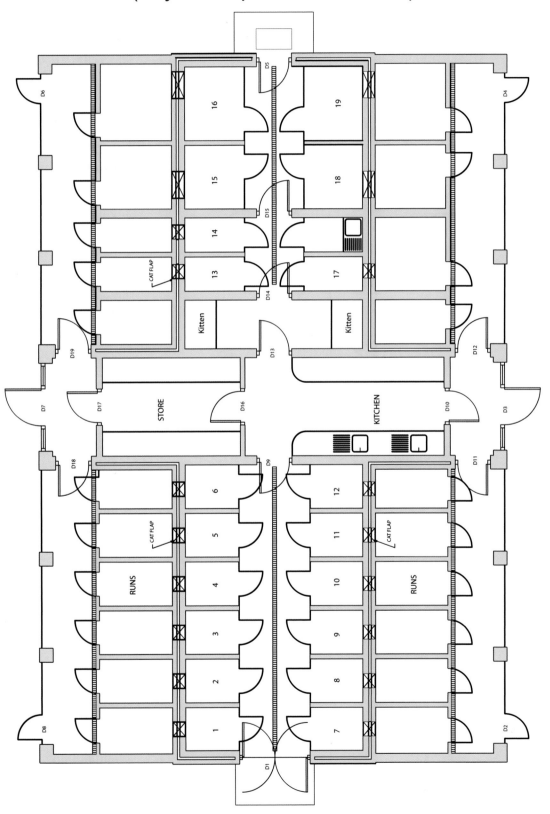

Semi-outdoor
Single Row Layout and Elevations

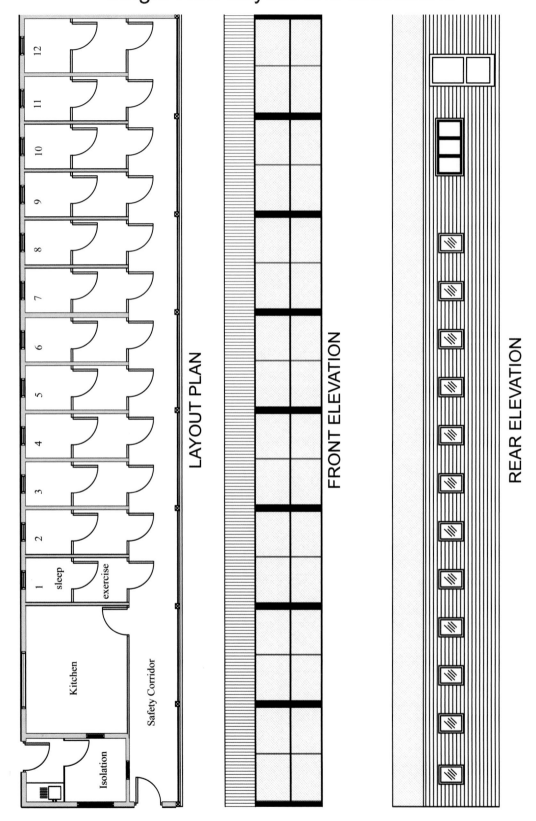

LAYOUT PLAN

FRONT ELEVATION

REAR ELEVATION

Kitchen

Safety Corridor

Isolation

sleep

exercise

1 2 3 4 5 6 7 8 9 10 11 12

Semi-outdoor
Single Row Section

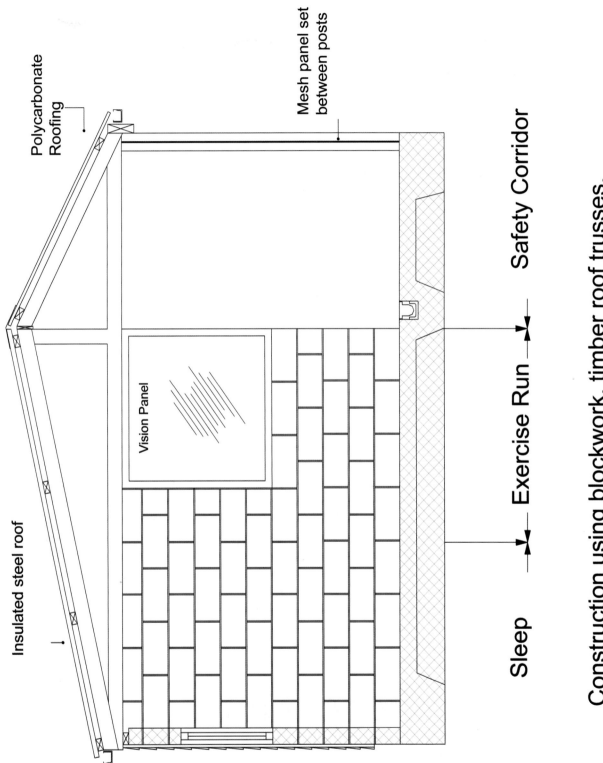

Polycarbonate Roofing

Mesh panel set between posts

Insulated steel roof

Vision Panel

Sleep

Exercise Run

Safety Corridor

Construction using blockwork, timber roof trusses, insulated steel and polycarbonate roof coverings

Semi-outdoor
The Blue Cross, Lewknor UK Rescue and Rehoming Cattery

Semi-outdoor
U Layout wrapping around a Courtyard

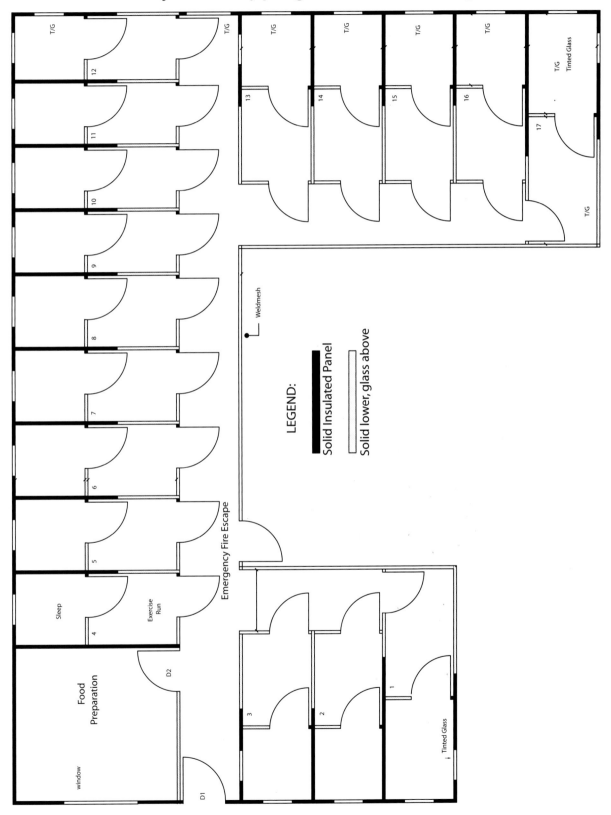

LEGEND:

■ Solid Insulated Panel

□ Solid lower, glass above

Weldmesh

Emergency Fire Escape

Food Preparation

window

Sleep

Exercise Run

Tinted Glass

Tinted Glass

Semi-outdoor
Double Row Section

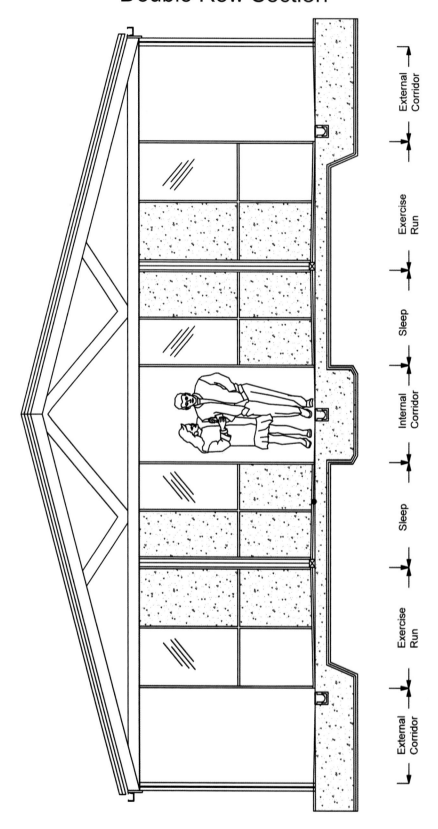

External
Corridor

Exercise
Run

Sleep

Internal
Corridor

Sleep

Exercise
Run

External
Corridor

Semi-outdoor
Double Row Layout

Disabled Public wc

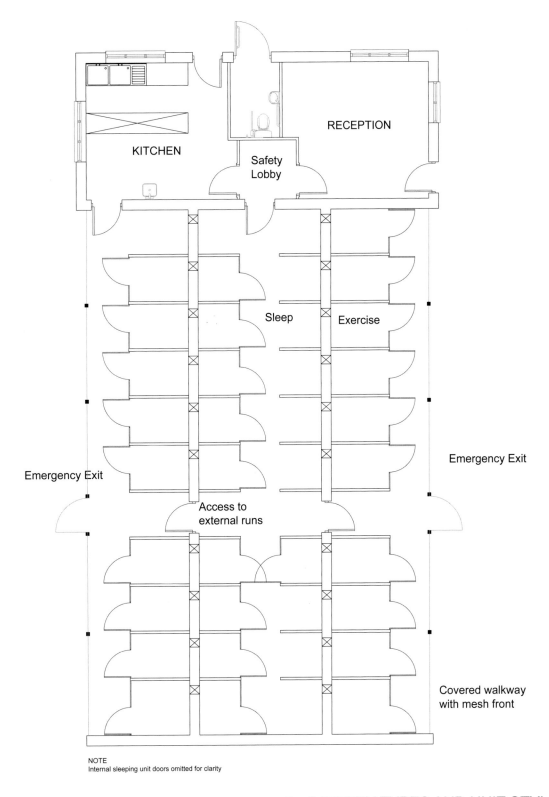

KITCHEN

RECEPTION

Safety Lobby

Sleep

Exercise

Emergency Exit

Emergency Exit

Access to external runs

Covered walkway with mesh front

NOTE
Internal sleeping unit doors omitted for clarity

CORRIDORS

Consideration should be given to ensure that adequate width is provided for safety corridors, and where to position them.

Corridor Width

The minimum width you should consider is 1200mm (4ft), with a preferred width of 1500mm/5ft. If you are running a busy rescue or sanctuary it is worth considering increasing this to a minimum of 1800mm/6ft, as this will allow two wheelchairs to pass each other. Whatever width is agreed upon as being the most suitable and cost-effective, it should be a clear width, without obstructions such as radiators, fire hoses etc. The width of the corridor could be a building regulations requirement for a large charity or sanctuary.

1500mm (5ft) wide corridor which still has working space even with obstructions such as food trolleys

A family utilising a 1500mm (5ft) corridor to get to know a rescue kitten

Internal Heated Corridor

Access to the exercise run is via a full-height door in the sleep area (you could also add an external covered walkway to provide protection from bad weather). An internal heated corridor leading to the sleep area is obviously a **benefit** to staff during the colder months. The internal corridor photograph on the opposite page (top) shows how solid panels (UPVC and glass) can be used to provide sneeze barriers where cat units face each other. Cats may be happy for familiar carers to enter via the sleeping area, but not strangers – in which case an external corridor or walkway could filter visitors.

External Safety Corridor

Access to the sleep area is via a door from the exercise run, which in turn leads to the external safety corridor. An external (outside, unheated) covered safety corridor is necessary to prevent a cat escaping where there is a door to the exercise area. This also protects the exercise runs from bad weather, and separates any cats outside the cattery where mesh is used on the exercise run. The **disadvantage** is the cats' view is obscured by two layers of mesh.

Internal _and_ External Corridors

There is another option of having two corridors (adjacent to both sleeping and exercise areas) but this will obviously be more expensive and require more space to build than one – but it might provide you with the perfect layout.

The final decision comes down to personal preference, space and budget available, and how you wish to manage the cattery access for staff and visitors.

You can see drawings of different corridor options after the photographs opposite.

Corridor width of 1500mm (5ft) which feels spacious

Corridor at 900mm (3ft) wide giving more of a 'tunnel' effect

Walk-in/Full Height Style
Showing corridor options

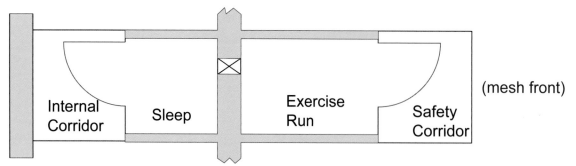

(mesh front)

INTERNAL ACCESS CORRIDOR + EXTERNAL SAFETY CORRIDOR
Internal corridor leading into sleeping area only. Safety corridor leading to
exercise area only. Cat gaining access to both sleep/exercise via a cat flap

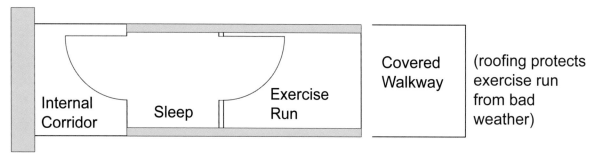

(roofing protects
exercise run
from bad
weather)

INTERNAL CORRIDOR (OPTIONAL EXTERNAL COVERED WALKWAY)
Internal corridor leading into sleeping area, with a full-height door leading
from the sleeping area to the exercise run. The public initially view the cats
from the external covered walkway. Cat flap in door or side panel.

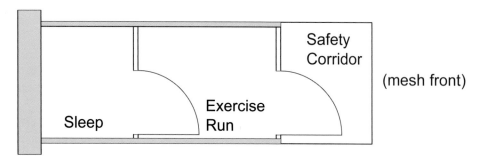

(mesh front)

EXTERNAL CORRIDOR
All access to the sleep and exercise runs is from the safety corridor.
Cat flap in door or side panel.

UNIT STYLES

Walk-in/Full-height

This is a full-height, 'walk-in' style at human height and is generally the more common design found in the UK.

Advantages of having full height units:

- Provides greater freedom and choice for the cat

- Ease of access for staff

- Allows the use of various height shelving

- Looks and feels more spacious to clients

Although it is ideal to allow cats full height, it is also worth remembering that there are practical staff issues to be considered, such as staff still being able to reach the cat if required! This style Is only marginally more expensive than the penthouse style (raised sleeping box), but **provides much more of the important vertical space cats need** to express their natural behaviour (such as being able to get to a high place for safety or a vantage point, jump, climb and have more choice about where to rest).

Penthouse

The Penthouse utilises an insulated cabin raised off the ground and accessed via a ramp.

There are disadvantages with the Penthouse design, these are primarily:

- **Limited space**
  Limited space for 2 or more cats

- **Access difficulties for cats**
  Possible access difficulties for elderly and infirm cats when using the ramp

- **Access difficulties for staff**
  Cleaning for example, we've seen owners having to **climb inside the units to clean them**, (not ideal if you are employing staff – for health and safety reasons alone)

- **Food, water and litter tray too close together**
  The litter tray and food/water areas tend to be very close together if both are situated in the heated section. **(Cats do not like to have these areas close together)**

With new construction using the Penthouses style, the UK's CIEH regulations require a minimum height of 1220 mm (4 ft). This can make cleaning difficult as the unit is often placed at of 760 mm (30") off the ground. This, combined with a unit at 1220mm/4ft high, will give an overall height of 1980mm/6'6", and although this is not as high as a walk-in unit, it will be **more difficult to clean**. Correctly sized, these units can be just as effective as full height walk-in units. **However, the greatest disadvantage is for access for elderly and infirm cats.** If you are set on having the penthouse style, it would be wise to also install a number of full-height, walk-in units for any cats that cannot cope with steps and ramps. Again, this provides a great deal of flexibility for the owner.

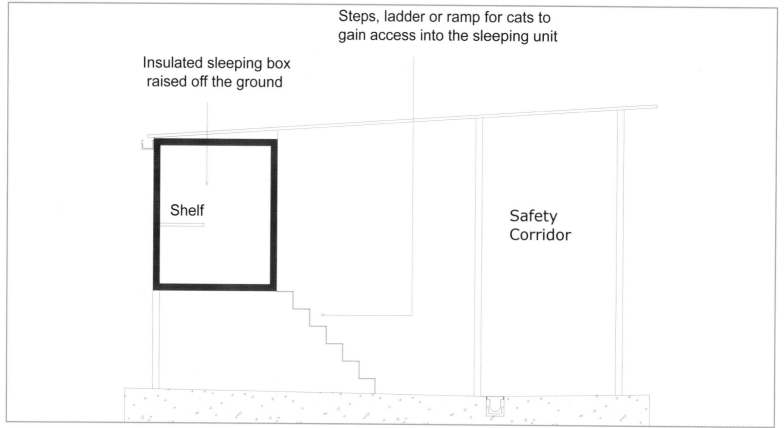

Steps, ladder or ramp for cats to gain access into the sleeping unit

Insulated sleeping box raised off the ground

Shelf

Safety Corridor

CASE STUDY:
PENTHOUSE STYLE RESCUE

Organisation:	RSPCA, Blackberry Farm
Location:	UK, Buckinghamshire
Cattery Type:	Indoor/Semi
Cattery Function:	Rescue
Number of Units:	34
Unit Size Sleep:	32" x 32" x 38"
	800 x 800 x 960mm
Date Built:	1996

www.rspca.org

A RESCUE AND REHOMING CENTRE WITH A FAST REHOMING RATE THANKS TO PLENTY OF VISITORS. QUIRKY TOUCHES, A RETAIL SHOP, AND PLENTY TO SEE AND DO HELPS KEEP CATS AND VISITORS HAPPY

RSPCA BLACKBERRY FARM

FRIENDLY, FUN & EDUCATIONAL

Sue James, Cat Supervisor for the RSPCA's Blackberry Farm rehoming centre showed us around the site. Lots of thought has gone into making the centre as friendly as possible, with plenty of signs, cat facts and humorous touches such as the realistic cat model appearing from a fake cat flap (shown below and on the large photo to the left) which has apparently fooled lots of people!

ANIMAL TRAIL & CAT FACTS

With an 'animal trail' for children to follow and important 'cat facts' on boards throughout the cattery – they are certainly getting their message across, with the cat boards providing messages such as "Cats can take a couple of months to

settle into their new home", "Long-haired cats need lots of grooming" and "Cats and dogs need to have their teeth looked after, just like we do" all making potential owners think about the responsibility of taking on a cat, and help prepare them for a little patience settling their new pet in.

ADOPT ME!

On walking through the cattery the cats certainly do their own PR! Enticing you to say hello by miaowing, rubbing against the glass or kitten antics, draws your attention to them easily.

With a high rehoming rate (which Sue puts down to the sheer number of visitors), the cats are not at Blackberry Farm for long!

What are you most pleased with?

When moving cats from the indoor-only admissions rooms (called lynx, cheetah, puma and leopard) to the semi-outdoor main cattery, after a couple of days settling down, it is obvious how much the cats enjoy being able to use the outside runs and greater space. With ducks, chickens and wildlife, there is plenty to watch too!

What would you do differently?

Cover the entire exercise area with translucent roofing. If funds permitted, it would be useful to have a dedicated mother and kitten unit, this would allow more indoor space and privacy, as even after hanging curtains over the sleeping areas, people still move them to look inside, and ideally a larger sleep area for two adult cats sharing for the short time they are here.

DUAL-ASPECT DESIGN:

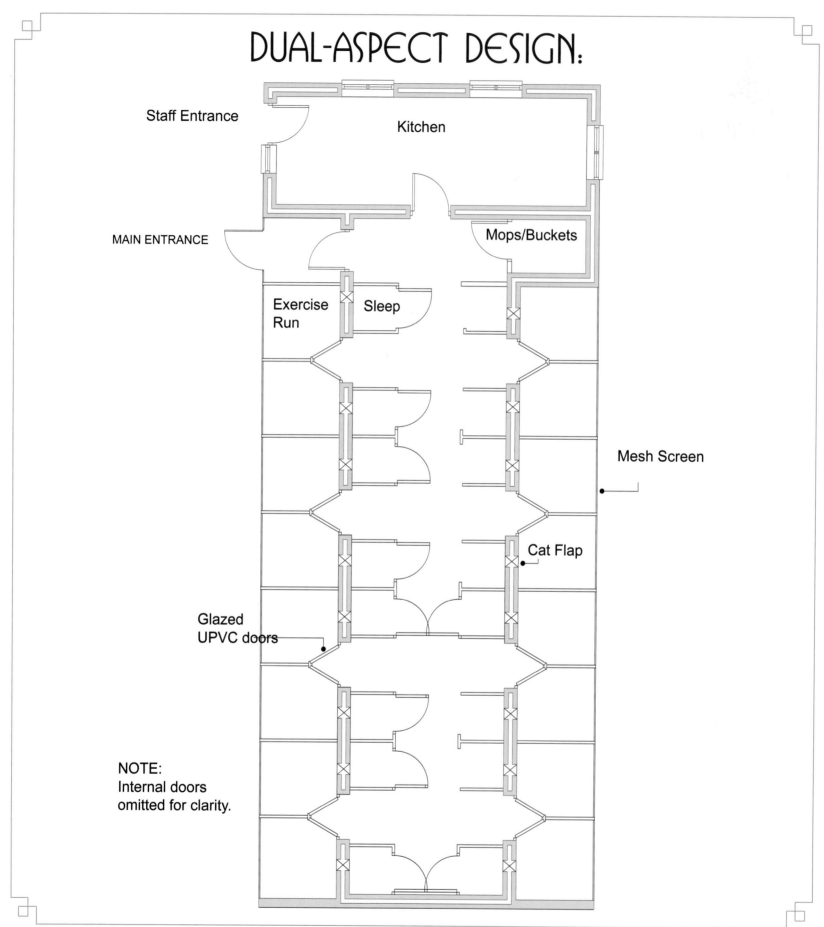

Staff Entrance

Kitchen

MAIN ENTRANCE

Mops/Buckets

Exercise Run

Sleep

Mesh Screen

Cat Flap

Glazed UPVC doors

NOTE:
Internal doors omitted for clarity.

CATTERY PHOTOS:

Above: looking back into the building from outside.

This innovative design has been used at some RSPCA centres for the past 10 years. This design allows the public to view the cats inside and outside from the central corridor.

Left: from the internal corridor visitors can view the cats in their sleeping boxes on the wall, as well as in their exercise runs

HOLDING UNITS

Both holding units and admissions units are temporary housing facilities used before moving cats into the main cattery.

The difference is that **holding units** are for short term temporary use (up to 24 hours) used during changeover times (usually at weekends for commercial catteries) whereas **admissions units** are generally larger and used for 10–14 days and used to assess the cats' health (usually rescue catteries).

Holding units have advantages to the cattery owner, however they must be used with care and not as a matter of course in order to increase the number of cats that can be held.

The UK's CIEH give the following minimum sizes:

- 1.1m²/12ft² with a minimum height of 900mm/3ft

- In general, holding units should not account for more than 25% of the total number of residential units

The cat does not
offer services.
The cat offers itself.
Of course he wants
care & shelter,
you don't buy love
for nothing

William S Burroughs

MOTHER AND KITTEN

This is a more specialised building, and in the main used by charities, sanctuaries and breeders.

Designs and layouts will vary enormously and very much depend on the scale of the operation. These buildings tend to be indoor rooms and often sited away from the main business. This is partly for safety reasons and also to minimise the risk of infection.

For charities, another reason for not having this facility open to the public is to ensure that adult cats are not overlooked in favour of kittens!

Kitten Doors

As you can see from the photograph top right, there are two doors, the lower one being kitten height!
This is an innovative design to reduce the risk of possible injury or trapping kittens when closing doors, a particular risk with litters of kittens. The lower door can stay closed, and staff can reach in or step over it when required.

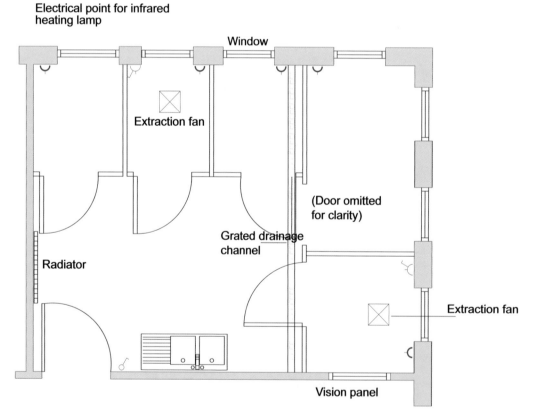

Electrical point for infrared heating lamp

Window

Extraction fan

(Door omitted for clarity)

Grated drainage channel

Radiator

Extraction fan

Vision panel

NOTE:

This indoor kitten room was a conversion of part of an existing building. The aim was to provide a quiet room away from public view for pregnant cats and litters of kittens.

The work consisted of knocking down internal walls, cutting out openings for windows to provide high levels of natural light, improved heating and ventilation.

Also installed were split "stable" type doors to provide easier access for staff when trying to gain access into the unit with large numbers of kittens.

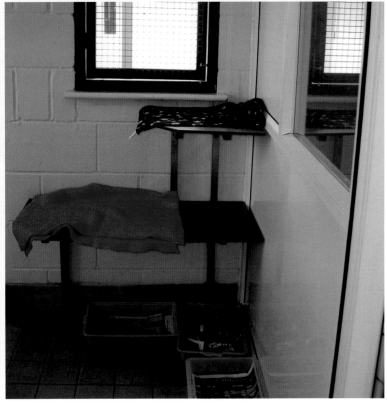

MULTI-CAT HOUSING

Multi-cat housing involves keeping many unfamiliar cats together in one area. This option is ONLY suitable for rescues, breeders and at home. Careful management and understanding is essential, as **this does not suit all cats**.

Whether in a multi-cat home environment or a rescue, there needs to be enough points for food, water, entry/exit, litter, scratching posts and beds to stop more dominant cats from monopolising these important resources. Ideally you need one item of each resource for every cat, plus one spare.

Cats become mature between the ages of 2 and 4 years. It is generally at maturity that multiple housing can become an issue. You can clearly see in the photograph opposite there are no problems with these kittens being housed together!

Boarding Catteries

Any form of multi-cat housing is against all UK CIEH standards for boarding establishments due to the risk of cross-infection, stress and problems arising. This type of housing has been used in the USA. It is not advisable for boarding (more details on the next few pages).

Rescue, Long-stay or Permanent Catteries

However, for cats that are long-stay, in a stable colony, permanent residents or related/familiar to each other, it can be a useful way to keep a larger number of cats in one area, providing them with greater levels of accommodation and stimulation, and hopefully a more pleasing, long-term environment. **That is, as long as this arrangement suits the cats** (remember that it is easier for cats to protect themselves by becoming withdrawn (becoming still and 'invisible'), cats have formidable weapons (teeth and claws) and it is sensible for them to avoid potential problems).
Obviously, for catteries that are providing permanent or long-term care, some of the issues and concerns regarding disease control are reduced, as the cats' history is a known factor.

This style of housing needs careful and knowledgeable management to ensure that the balance is correct in terms of numbers, and that the cats are not suffering from stress, bullying and other problems associated with the keeping of a large number of cats in one area. **Multi-cat owners** will benefit from and enjoy reading Vicky Halls' *Cat Detective*.

> The main success factors are: the number of cats housed, their age, and the quantity and quality of space.
> This needs to be carefully balanced and managed

Advantages of multi-cat housing:

- Cost-effective, long-term or permanent care cats get larger accommodation and more stimulation in a more 'home-like' environment

Disadvantages of multi-cat housing:

- Stress, disease, food control, hygiene control

A charity sold off a cattery in 2005, (which, when constructed in 1983 was considered to be a cutting edge design!) The building consisted of a series of rooms, each room held 10 fibreglass units, stacked two high. From these units, the cats had access to a large, shared external exercise run. This was fraught with problems. The biggest issues being the number of cats for the overall space and size of the exercise area.

In the end, the charity reduced the number of cats housed by 50% to overcome some of the behavioural problems with this design. **One of the main concerns was the levels of stress in the cats.** The stress was exacerbated by the fact that new cats were continually being brought into the buildings as cats were rehomed. Obviously, because of the constant changeover of cats, it was extremely difficult for the longer-stay cats to adapt, with the constant introduction of new cats.

As we now know, very little knowledge or research had been carried out previously on the needs of cats, and it was thought that their requirements were very simple – i.e. as cats are relatively small animals, their space requirement also must be small!

In the following pages we will hear from experts in the field of feline welfare (veterinary and behaviour) about the problems that can be caused, and followed by a case study showing how multi-cat housing can work successfully, with good management and the correct facilities.

SINGLE VERSUS GROUP HOUSING

Dr Irene Rochlitz

There has been much discussion and some research on whether cats should be housed discretely or in communal groups in shelters.

Cats entering a shelter have to cope with the stress of leaving their own familiar environment (in the case of owned cats), of entering a strange new environment, of being handled by strangers and, in most cases, undergoing a veterinary examination.

They will be also be aware that there are other unfamiliar animals nearby.

In the first few weeks following arrival, it is unlikely that they will benefit from being housed with unfamiliar cats, or in a group of cats whose composition is constantly changing.

During this period, it is preferable to house cats in discrete units, to keep them in their original groups (four or more cats from the same household can be split into smaller groups of two to three cats), rather than introduce incoming cats into groups of cats with whom they are not familiar.

This period of discrete housing will also allow caretakers to find out more about the individual cat's health, behaviour and personality, and to identify, treat and control disease.

If adoption is not imminent, or if there are constraints on space, it may then be worth considering moving the cat into communal housing providing that the group is not too large, there is plenty of space that is suitably enriched, and that there is some stability in group composition.

There will be some cats that are unable to adapt to communal housing; they should be identified and housed in pairs if possible, or singly.

COMMUNAL LIVING

Nadine Gourkow

In view of the fact that cats hunt alone, they were long believed to be asocial. However, there is much evidence to the contrary. Related or familiar cats living in colonies form strong bonds, particularly females who sometimes share the care of kittens.

Cats engage in affiliative behaviour with other cats, such as body rubbing on each other (allorubbing), grooming each other (allogrooming), nose touching (greeting behaviour) and play.

Cats show a repertoire of submissive and dominant behaviours to reduce conflict. Relative rank can vary from one pair to another, and can vary depending on context.

In a natural setting, familiar cats tend to resolve conflict by increasing space between them.

When creating communal spaces for adult cats who are not related or familiar to each other and who have various levels of socialisation to cats, it is important to organize space in a way that minimizes the possibility of on-going or repeated conflict, as this can cause high stress.

It is essential to recognize that when cats have not been exposed to other cats for their entire life, they may have little or no tolerance for other cats, and may not be well suited for communal living.

Cats that engage in aggressive behaviour, or show signs of stress should be housed singly. The use of communal enclosures can be counterproductive if not appropriately designed. Communal living must encourage social contact between cats, while meeting their need for personal space and safety.

WHAT TO PROVIDE IN A COMMUNAL

To meet the psychological needs of cats, the communal space should provide:

PERSONAL SPACE:
- More single size shelves than cats, and at least 1m/3ft between shelves
- At least one single size hiding area per cat
- Several high vantage points at different heights, and with different views
- Corner shelf viewing points from which the cat cannot be approached from behind
- Separation between feeding and elimination area
- Enough free floor space for cat-to-cat play and interaction
- At least one perching area that can fit several cats
- A scratching post and items to rub on for cat-to-cat olfactory (scent) communication

PLAY:
- Opportunity to engage in simulated hunting behaviour through play, including behaviours that simulate the hunting sequence
- Opportunity for inanimate play with rolling and batting toys
- Do not hand play with cats, it may cause some cats to develop predatory play behaviour towards humans!

ACCOMMODATION FOR DIFFERENT PERSONALITY TYPES:
- Place food/water and elimination areas in places where shy cats cannot be intimidated by more confident cats
- If the cats have access to an outdoor area through a cat flap, make sure there is more than one. Some cats may try to prevent others from entering back into the indoor area

NATURAL LIGHT:
- A source of natural light

CAT GRASS:
- Provide cat grass

HUMAN CONTACT:
- Placing a chair or seat encourages people to spend time in the communal

HOW TO INTRODUCE NEW CATS TO A COMMUNITY:
- A new cat arriving changes the dynamic between all cats, and is a known source of stress
- Introduction is a two-day process (minimum)
- Place the incoming cat in a single cage within the communal space
- Plexiglas door with several small holes to enable visual/olfactory contact between cats
- Provide a hiding area for the cat in the introduction cage
- Once the incoming and resident cats seem relaxed, let the new cat explore
- Monitor initial contact between cats
- Cats should be vaccinated at least seven days prior to entering the communal and should be spayed or neutered

Problems with Multi-cat Housing

Cats that are happy together will share resting areas, rub against and groom each other, and play and greet each other in a friendly way.

As we have already seen, cats prefer to have enough space to allow them to keep a distance and level of privacy from other cats.

If the size of the accommodation is inadequate for the number of cats housed together, or does not provide sufficient hiding places, shelving, secure areas, enough facilities for resting or litter trays, entry/exit points, food, water – you will find cats showing stress through behavioural problems.

Examples of ways cats show stress:

- Hiding
- Move to get away from another cat, or changes in behaviour when a particular cat is around
- Cat aggression, hissing
- Obstructing access to cat flaps, resting areas, litter trays, food, water (bullying)
- Inappropriate soiling
- Urine spraying
- Obesity
- Over-grooming
- Illness

"Multi-cat colonies present unique, difficult problems that can escalate into serious health or animal welfare concerns.

As lovers of these fine friends, we often fail to realize that cats do not naturally live in a close group unit. Most are loners, with males and females only coming in contact at breeding. Not being herd, or group, animals means they don't easily establish the 'pecking order' natural to wolves, deer, and others that live together in large groups.

When we force them to adapt to the communal arrangement, we cause a certain level of stress. The challenge, then, to maintain a household of felines, is to keep them healthy and happy"

Cat Fanciers' Association, USA

Outdated multi-cat accommodation – the ginger cat is trying to keep away from the others and make himself appear 'invisible' by freezing/not making any movement. He is not relaxed or happy

Cats make formidable opponents – when in doubt, it is much safer to stay out of each other's way!

CASE STUDY:
MULTI-CAT COTTAGE

Organisation: Cats Protection
Location: UK, Derby
Cattery Type: Outdoor
Cattery Function: Rescue, long-stay
Number of Units: 1
Date Built: 2000

www.cats.org.uk

THE CATS PROTECTION REHOMING
CENTRE NEAR DERBY HAS, IN ADDITION
TO ITS NORMAL REHOMING CATTERY,
CONSTRUCTED A MULTI-CAT
CHALET STYLE FACILITY

CATS PROTECTION, DERBY

Although Derby Cats Protection centre has a modern rehoming cattery building where members of the public view the majority of cats when they are considering giving a cat a new home, they also have the flexibility of the multi-cat cottage. The modern cattery design has individual sleeping boxes, which have direct access to an external exercise run and for the majority of cats this semi-outdoor design works extremely well. In addition to this, they have the benefit of a multi-cat unit (shown here) providing increased flexibility and homing options for up to fourteen cats.

CAREFUL CONTROL & MANAGEMENT

It must be stressed that only fully vaccinated cats given a clean bill of health by the vet are allowed into the cat cottage. They are all blood-tested for FIV, FeLV and are only allowed entry if they are found to be negative for both. The cats are also treated regularly for fleas and worms. For this unit to work effectively it has to be carefully managed and a close eye kept on the cats to see how they settle in and adapt, to ensure that none of the cats are stressed or bullied.

POSITIVE BENEFITS

Like most rescue and rehoming charities, the aim is to place the animals in new homes as soon as possible. Centre manager, Helen Wood explained the very positive benefits the centre has found in having this type of multi-cat cottage facility available. For certain cats that simply do not adapt to the standard cattery, or for cats that have been in for an extended period of time, the centre has the flexibility to move a cat into the 'cat cottage' in order to allow more space and freedom. The cottage is set in its own fenced, secure garden and the cats have the freedom to roam as they wish. The cottage has a wide range of sleeping beds, various height shelving, chairs and multiple cat flaps; this prevents stress being caused by any cat monopolising the beds, furniture or entry and exit points.

HOME ENVIRONMENT

The cottage provides a more natural 'home' environment compared with their normal rehoming cattery facilities. The main purpose of the cottage is to provide more space and freedom for long-stay cats. The centre sets a maximum of 14 cats at any one time in the cottage. The size of the building and its surrounding garden is the governing factor.

The cottage provides an excellent, relaxing facility for cats, staff and members of the public; it provides a degree of flexibility that cannot be found in normal rehoming catteries. Helen feels that they would find if very difficult to manage the centre without the flexibility of this type of facility.

What are you most pleased with?

Helen has found it to be highly useful for cats that have been admitted to the centre for rehoming and are struggling to cope with the standard cattery building. Moving a cat into the chalet for a short time seems to help them settle and allows adaptation to the change of environment, food, staff etc far more easily. The cat can then be re-introduced to the main cattery if s/he hasn't been reserved/adopted.

What would you do differently?

We would like to add more shelving that is fixed to the wall, rather than on supporting legs, as this will make cleaning easier.

SOCIALISATION/REHOMING AREAS AND HOMELIKE ROOMS

A great idea - the addition of at least one room providing a homelike atmosphere.

It is worth thinking about the inclusion of a homelike room in every form of cattery. These are flexible rooms that can also be used for staff/owner relaxation, talking to cat owners and taking bookings or details, interviewing and even a spare office. You will always find a use for another room! Inclusions could be anything that mimics the environment of home that cats will be used to, such as television or radio, comfy sofas to relax with humans or by themselves, plenty of choices for resting areas and being able to look out of windows, playing tapes of friendly and familiar home sounds, cat furniture and toys, homelike furnishings (e.g. pictures, paintings, ticking clocks, mirrors, ornaments etc) as well as cat-friendly furnishings such as aerobic centres/scratching posts – and of course a big benefit is the greater increase in space.

Rescues: Socialisation and Rehoming Rooms

One benefit for rescues is in providing a safe, relaxed area for potential owners to get to know a cat better, and for the cats to be able to relax and show their true personality in a familiar environment. The biggest benefit may be for quiet or more difficult-to-home cats who are finding it hard to adjust to life in a cattery, where just being able to relax with a familiar human will be highly beneficial. This type of area could be an existing room, perhaps an office or staff room with sofas and a kitchen area. Socialisation rooms are currently more common for dogs (who have shown great improvement, especially on being introduced to a carer one-to-one in this more familiar, less sterile environment). without the distraction of other animals near by, but more and more organisations are seeing the benefit of this flexible option.

Commercial: Homelike Rooms

There is no reason why homelike rooms could not be used in a commercial cattery. As with rescue, many cats will benefit from this. The licensing authority may require certain conditions to be met if this area is adjacent or open to the cat runs (cleaning/disinfection, disease risk, sneeze barriers, cat-to-cat aggression) where the other cats are present – but if this need is incorporated as a separate room, it will also be more flexible for discussions with clients.

Homelike Cat Units

In a smaller, more personal cattery environment it is easy to introduce a more homely look and feel to the cat units themselves. However, everything must still be easy to clean and it will take longer to clean and keep tidy, but this can certainly look more welcoming to cat owners and may help cats to settle in faster.

Exercise Areas and Play rooms

Large, separate external/internal exercise areas can be highly beneficial for most cats, but particularly for sanctuaries and welfare organisations where cats can be kept for longer periods of time, or permanent residents.

This type of run can also be used very successfully where pet owners or breeders want to provide access to the outside, but do not want their cat to roam free.

As will be obvious by now, even my recommended sizes for accommodation will not allow a young, fit and active cat sufficient space. One way to overcome this is to construct a 'playroom' or 'home-like' social room to the main cattery. This can be as simple or extravagant as you wish. Some USA charities have developed this idea and have provided highly exciting, stimulating and welcoming rooms for the cats and visitors.

The advantages are:

- Allows greater freedom and natural behaviour for the cats

- Allows members of the public the opportunity to sit in a room with the cat and get to know them better (this is generally not practical or feasible with standard size accommodation)

- Provides the centre with greater flexibility – an extra room, or a flexible option to reduce stress in cats

- Is excellent PR!

For boarding or rescue, some frown upon the idea of having large, open exercise areas with a meshed or anti-escape top where cats can be brought into. The advantages of this option is they can run free, climb trees and show natural behaviour. Obviously the main concern here is one of hygiene and suitable surfaces that can be disinfected. However, given the limited use of this facility (i.e. for privately owned cats, those happy in the company of other cats, or cats kept for considerable periods of time at a sanctuary) the risks are minimised, as the health background of the cat is known.

The advantages of this type of facility far outweighs the practical issues in these circumstances, and provides a far greater and more natural environment for the cats. In some parts of the USA it is not unusual to find cat owners who have provided a totally secure, fenced garden to protect their pet cat from predators, reduce the risk of traffic accidents or contact with a wild animal and provides peace of mind for the owner (more details at the end of this chapter).

A good option for rescues, sanctuaries, breeders and multi-cat owners

This is a great idea for cats from the same household, very active cats, a place for potential owners to get to know a cat without distraction, or cats who aren't settling into the standard size accommodation.

Cautionary Note:

Boarding catteries - cats from different homes sharing a communal area at the same time:
In the UK this is not allowed for boarding catteries, because of risk of disease and cross-infection, (although interestingly in the USA it is fairly common).

Cat compatibility
As you are by now well aware, it is **very** important to assess whether the individual cats get on together!

CASE STUDY:
HOMELIKE SOCIALISATION ROOM

Organisation:	The Mayhew Animal Home
Location:	UK, London, Kensal Green
Cattery Type:	Semi-outdoor
Cattery Function:	Rescue
Number of Units:	44
Unit Size Sleep:	900 x 900mm/3ft x 3ft
Unit Size Exercise:	900 x 1800mm/3ft x 6ft
Date Built:	2000

www.mayhewanimalhome.org

THIS UNIQUE ANIMAL WELFARE ORGANISATION DOES MUCH MORE THAN RESCUE AND REHOME CATS AND DOGS, (THEY RECENTLY TOOK IN 150 CATS LIVING IN ONE APARTMENT!) COMMUNITY AND INTERNATIONAL HELP IS ALSO GIVEN

MAYHEW ANIMAL HOME

THE MAGICAL MAYHEW

Step from the busy city streets of London into the reception of The Mayhew Animal Home, and it is like stepping into another world. Perhaps we have been overdosing on Harry Potter recently, but the black cat sitting on the reception desk was definitely enquiring what our business was there with just a look!

The thing that immediately strikes you is that The Mayhew is definitely a 'home'. There are rooms with televisions, clocks, carers and volunteers, a pretty garden with shelters for cats and rabbits (who get along well!).

When you visit any cattery, you pick up the tiniest things that say a lot about a place. Here, the freedom is palpable and there is even a cat door in the conference room where the board of governors meet!

Kim Pearce, the Manager of The Mayhew gave us a complete tour of the Home and discussed lots of projects (past, current and future) they are involved in, both here and on their many international projects.

With over 200 volunteers and many celebrity clients, you soon understand why so many people feel 'comfortable' and want to spend time here, and why they are so willing to help.

THE CATTERY

The main cat units have glass panels under the sleeping area so that cats can see out to the garden, underfloor heating, and there is an 'unvaccinated kitten' garden so that kittens can play outside in safety during the summer. Nothing stops the cats playing - there are even cat paw prints in the concrete path in the garden!

SOCIALISATION ROOM

Cleverly, there is a window looking into the socialisation room so you can see what the cats are doing when left to their own devices – resting. However, once you step into the room everything changes; cuddles and attention are definitely on the menu! We were given a quick look-over, but when Kim asked a member of staff, Kate, to join us – the reaction was immediate! The cats became very animated, were happy to be picked up and cuddled and started using the room more. The cats were expectantly waiting for treats, and Kate did not disappoint them! Placing some treats in bowls and some in the mesh play tunnels – the cats had great fun!

The room has a sofa, cushions, cat beds, furniture, a television, windows, shelving, murals, mobiles, lots of cat toys, scratching items and activity centres, tunnels to play in, cardboard boxes and the sofa and table have covers to hide under, as well as water, food and litter trays.

This is a great place for cats and humans to play together!

What would you do differently?

Provide more rooms like this! The Mayhew are planning further 'chill-out' rooms. These are not just used for rehoming and socialising, The Mayhew also help people with difficult domestic circumstances or hospitalisation by taking care of their cats in this homelike room until the owners are able to take their cats back home again.

INDOOR-ONLY VERSUS OUTDOOR ACCESS

Dr Irene Rochlitz

In the UK, the majority of cats are allowed access to the outdoors; it is generally considered that this is the natural thing for cats to be able to do. However, in the USA, between 50 and 60 per cent of pet cats are kept permanently indoors.

HAZARDS

It is generally assumed that cats confined indoors will be healthier and live longer as they are protected from hazards associated with the outdoors. Different hazards, however, may be present in the home, such as exposure to toxic substances, household accidents etc.

PROBLEMS WITH INDOOR-ONLY

The main concern with an indoor environment is that, compared with the outdoors, it is relatively impoverished, predictable and monotonous and may cause the cat to experience boredom and stress. While we often do not know what cats do when they are outdoors, it is generally assumed that indoor cats are less active, and that this inactivity can lead to obesity and other problems. Certain behaviours, such as scratching items and spraying urine, may be considered normal when performed by a cat outdoors, but become problematic when performed indoors.

ADAPTING

Most cats seem to be able to adapt to indoor living well, providing they have been kept in this kind of environment from an early age. Some geriatric cats, or those with disabilities, may also benefit from being confined indoors, but cats used to having outdoor access may have difficulty adapting to an entirely indoor existence when adult.

CAT POPULARITY

The recent increase in popularity of the cat as a companion animal in many countries has been partly ascribed to the fact that it requires relatively little care compared with the dog, not having to be taken out for walks or be trained. Also, it can be kept in a smaller space, such as an apartment, and will use a litter tray.

SOCIAL INTERACTION

Nevertheless, cats require a certain level of social interaction with their owners, and this requirement may be increased when their physical environment is restricted. Cats confined indoors spend proportionately more time with people than cats with access to the outdoors, which has been interpreted as cats seeking additional stimulation in an environment that is relatively less stimulating.

THE DANGER OF TRAFFIC

One reason for keeping cats indoors is to protect them from road traffic accidents. Recent studies on cats and risk factors for road accidents suggest that older, neutered female cats, possibly of a pedigree breed, who are kept in at night and live in an area with low levels of traffic, are less likely to be hit by cars.

SOLUTIONS

Solutions to enable the cat to benefit from outdoor access without risk to itself or others include:

- Restricting outdoor access to certain parts of the day when the cat can be supervised

- Creating secure, yet stimulating and complex, cat-proof enclosures within a garden, for example:

  - Walk-in cages
  - Modular structures extending through a garden
  - Secure perimeter fences
  - Training a cat to go for walks on a harness

There are a number of websites that give advice to owners on how to enrich the indoor environment for their cat, for example www.indoorcat.org.

Using Indoor-only Enrichment Ideas in the Cattery

Whatever a cat's previous experience, for the time the cat is the cattery s/he will be confined to a smaller area than usual. We can utilise many ideas for enriching the environment of indoor cats and put them into practice in the cattery. To do this, we need to understand what normal behaviour for a cat is, and create ways to include compatible activities.

- **Normal routine** – Cats may 'expect' activities at certain times (such as the owner coming home at six o'clock in the evening, and this being the time for petting and feeding). If a cattery offers this more personalised service of 'matching' the cats routine, it will help the cat to settle more quickly. *Now, imagine you always have breakfast at 8 o'clock in the morning with your partner, and you look forward to having your favourite preserve on toast with tea or coffee – how would you feel if you went on holiday and breakfast was not served until two hours earlier/later than your usual time, or you were only offered things you didn't like, or were foreign to you?*

- **Elimination areas** – Ideally, cats should have a sand-like litter and preferably made from natural products, dust-free, without chemicals or fragrances added. Cats have preferences for elimination, such as litter type (feel/smell), tray location (indoors/outdoors/safe distance from entry/exit points far enough away from food and water and not in a vulnerable place) size of tray (not big enough) or height (for geriatric or arthritic cats), privacy (open tray or covered/not having to share with another cat). *Imagine you went on holiday and found that the toilet facilities were 'holes in the ground', provided very rough tissue paper, anyone could see you, or you had to share with people in the next room – would that make you feel uncomfortable or a little stressed?*

- **Sustenance** – Food, water, grass, catnip/catmint/valerian. Searching for these things naturally would take up a big chunk of the day. Keeping these items in separate places provides more interest. Using food or treats hidden in pots or puzzle toys, hiding them in different places around the cat unit or inside a paper bag or box provides something novel, fun and rewarding for the cat to do. Some cats may be encouraged to drink more if water is kept separately from food, or provided as running water in a pet water fountain, stock-flavoured, or even rain water. *Now, imagine you were bored with nothing to do, and wanted to eat some biscuits, you could have the joy of searching through your recipe books to find something mouth-watering and tempting, spend time picking out the ingredients and then baking your own, filling your kitchen with the wonderful aroma of warm biscuits. Alternatively, you could just open a ready-made packet and eat some in a few minutes.*
Which experience would keep you busy and interested for longer, and provide the most satisfaction?

- **Resting and perching places** – A variety of different places to rest (such as places high up with vantage points, heated bed or near a radiator, sunny windowsill or underfloor heating, soft bedding). It is now possible to buy floor-to-ceiling scratching posts/cat trees for very active cats to climb. *Now imagine you are in your sitting room and have only the floor and windowsills to sit on. Wouldn't it be better for you to have choices such as a soft sofa to relax in, or an armchair or day bed for reading, or to be able to go to your own bed to sleep? You might even choose somewhere cool for the summer, do some sunbathing, or choose warm and snuggly places in the colder months*

- **Privacy and safety** – Somewhere to hide provides the cat with an 'escape' even if s/he cannot leave the area. *Imagine you don't have your private retreat such as a bedroom or bathroom, or a man without his own workshop!*

- **Scratching** - For claws and scent marking, scratching areas/posts need to be tall enough for the cat to fully stretch upwards as if scratching a tree. *Imagine how you would care for your hands/feet without scissors, nail clippers/file*

- **Playing predator** – Toys allow cats to have fun and stimulation playing predator, and they will have their own preferences (mice, birds, insects, fish). Once you know which type are favourites, you can provide more interesting toys, but you need to make sure you bring in new toys, or rotate the existing ones. Toys don't have to be expensive, paper bags, tin foil balls, cardboard boxes or scraps of wool tied together are all old favourites that work well

Compromise with Semi-outdoor Access

For cats that are confined, just as a semi-outdoor cattery provides more stimulation for a cat, at home it is also important to provide as much safe outdoor access as possible. This can easily be done by enclosing all of the garden, or a large area with an angled top for escape-proof fencing.

If you can provide extra areas to screen off, such as a porch or balcony, or perhaps even a tunnel leading to an outdoor enclosure, this provides even more choice and variation. Pet product manufacturers have realised the potential for such products, and it is now easy to purchase tunnels for indoor play (fleecy/crinkly/catnip-filled) or outdoor tunnels (modular mesh/nylon units that can be slotted together).

For further ideas, it would be well worth reading books by Vicky Halls: *Cat Confidential* and *Cat Detective,* which are extremely informative and great fun to read. You can also visit www.catterydesign.com or the Safe Cats Campaign website at www.safecats.org, the Indoor Cat Initiative www.indoorcat.org, Cats International at www.catsinternational.org or search the internet for indoor cat articles to get more ideas.

How Much is Enough?
The natural territory range of a cat will be influenced by a number of things, such as the number of cats in the area, shelter, food & prey availability, mating season, individual preferences and the activity levels and sex of the cat. In international studies, the smallest ranges were in urban areas, medium ranges in farm cats and the largest ranges were found in feral cats surviving on prey. It was also found that males had ranges three times larger than females.

Outdoor Access
Escape-proof cat fencing can easily be provided for whatever area is available, whether it is a section of a garden or a few acres. On the next few pages you will find photographs of some solutions to creating a safe, external exercise area.

How to Keep Cats Safe - Outdoors

In the USA 60% of cats are indoor-only cats, whereas in the UK this is around 10% (but increasing). However, it is much better to be able to offer cats outdoor access where available and suitable. There are several manufacturers who now specialise in different forms of safe outdoor containment products for cats, which provide a much larger exercise area.
.

There are a variety of ways of providing a large outdoor area for cats, but the ideal ones that still provide security and safety are:

- Fenced area within the garden

- Fencing around the garden boundaries

- Remember to include tunnels or places to play or hide in, and objects to perch on to provide vantage points!

"Cats don't have to be deprived of the great outdoors to stay safe. Cats can be trained to accept a harness and leash, and cat enclosures can allow them to experience all the pleasures of the great outdoors without all of the risks"

Humane Society of the United States

"A purpose-built outdoor enclosure could provide your cat with the sights & smells of the outside world and give his life some variety, without exposing him to many of the outdoor risks. Alternatively, you might consider using high fencing and Elizabethan collars on trees to keep your cat within the confines of your own garden"

Feline Advisory Bureau, UK

Reasons why some cats are kept indoors:

- Pedigree cats
- Living in high-rise apartments
- Traffic
- Disease
- Poisons
- Attacks by other animals, or mistreatment by people
- Prey on small mammals, birds, and wildlife
- Zoonotic diseases (can be transmitted to humans) such as rabies
- Defecate in or damage other people's gardens
- Accidental loss – cats can get shut in sheds/garages, and even vehicles

Reasons why some cats may prefer to be indoors:

- Stress – a timid cat may find the outdoors very stressful
- Attacks by other animals or mistreatment by people
- Elderly, or for health reasons

Balcony Enclosure
Pedigree Pens UK manufactured an unusual and innovative balcony enclosure for an apartment-living cat owner in London.

www.pedigreepens.com

Climb-proof Cat Fencing
Purr…fect Fence (UK, USA and Canada) manufactures lightweight, flexible, angled mesh that is cost-effective, easy to install and has minimal visual impact. It is worth considering for a wide range of cat-based operations.

You can read more about cat fencing on the following pages.

Mention 'Cattery Design' and save 10% on your order!

www.purrfectfence.co.uk **or**
www.purrfectfence.com

CASE STUDY:
KEEPING CATS SAFE OUTDOORS

Organisation: Purr…fect Fence
Location: USA, Canada, UK

Fencing Solution for: Cat owners who want to provide a
safe outdoor area for their cats, or catteries who want to
provide a safe outdoor exercise option for their clients.

Exercise area: Small gardens/yards to acres!

www.purrfectfence.com & .co.uk

CREATE A CAT-SAFE OUTDOOR
ENCLOSURE - WHETHER A SMALL AREA
ADJACENT TO THE HOUSE, LARGE AREAS,
OR THE PERIMETER OF YOUR LAND.
IF YOU HAVE WOODLAND, ERECTING
THE FENCE JUST INSIDE THE TREE LINE
MAKES IT VIRTUALLY DISAPPEAR!

PURR...FECT FENCE

CAT WELFARE & WELLBEING

Recent studies have proven that many cats kept exclusively indoors can understandably suffer from behavioural problems and boredom/frustration.

Cats are by nature designed to roam and explore outdoors - without this ability, many can become depressed and exhibit undesirable, problem behaviours or illness. It must be similar to how humans feel when confined indoors during the long winter months - a case of cabin fever, but one that never ends!

So, how do we allow cats freedom and the health benefits of being outdoors - but in safety?

As you will see on these pages, there are kind, humane, effective, safe systems which are virtually invisible, reliable and easy to install – such as special cat fencing. It works because the movement of the cat fencing will not appeal to cats, and even determined cats who do climb it will not be able to leave, because of the angled top which prevents cats climbing over.

Since most cats can climb or jump, an effective cat fence must be at least 6ft/2m high and have an escape-proof top. Some products can be retro-fitted to the tops of existing fences.

Garden cabins and pens offer a very limited amount of space to move about in. They are also certainly not invisible in nature, are often unattractive and can be expensive. However, pens could be used in conjunction with cat fencing to create a large open area with a shelter, or even better, attach the exercise area to your home to allow more freedom and choices.

THE IDEAL CAT FENCING

When considering an outdoor cat fence, **the true outdoor experience for your cat is best and most easily created with a large, secure, fear-free and safe play/exercise area**.

Safe, kind cat fencing advantages:

- Provides you with peace of mind & happy cats
- Increased living space helps reduce behavioural issues
- Inexpensive compared with conventional fencing
- No pre-existing fence required
- Minimal visual impact to your property

What are you most pleased with?

Purr...fect Cat Fence is the first complete, free-standing, garden or yard fence enclosure for cats. Cats can safely enjoy all the benefits of the great outdoors, without you worrying about their safety. Purr...fect Cat Fence comes in kits that are **inexpensive**, **easy to install**, **virtually invisible**, and include everything you need to turn your garden or yard into a safe and secure paradise for your cats. The cat fence enclosure material is flexible, so most cats don't like to climb it. The 'Houdini-proof' arch at the top has been so effective, no cat has been able to climb over the enclosure.

Cat safety fencing is the affordable, effective, safe and visually appealing alternative to conventional fencing.

PURR...FECT
FENCE

MANAGING BUILDING PROJECTS AND CONTRACTORS

Many cattery owners and charities/sanctuaries will at some stage in their business life have to improve, refurbish or construct new buildings.

This is either due to the need to expand, or to replace dilapidated and sub-standard premises. It can be an exciting and fulfilling time; but it can also be a difficult time. The aim of this chapter is to help you prepare, and to avoid common problems.

New premises that are tailor-made for your particular business can enhance and improve operating efficiency, reduce costs and send out the correct message to potential clients that you are taking your business seriously and are prepared to invest in its future.

Making the initial decision that purpose-built, tailor-made premises are the way you wish to move forward can be time consuming, but the end results will obviously be more satisfactory and give greater long-term benefits to your business.

There are many questions that need to be asked, an example of some are:

- How much can I afford to spend on the project?

- How will it be funded?

- What are my main goals and priorities?

- How long will the work take?

- Will I have to shut down the existing cattery to allow access?

- Do I need to construct all new buildings, or can I convert some existing ones?

- Can the work be carried out in phases?

Generally, **building from scratch** offers the best opportunity
to create facilities that match
your particular needs and aspirations

LONG-TERM COSTS

Before embarking on a new-build project, alternative options should be explored and long-term cost implications considered.

New-Build versus Conversion

Generally, new-build is more expensive than conversion, however this can depend on several factors, such as the condition of the existing premises (particularly for large cost items such as foundations and structural stability), government tax implications and possible tax savings etc.

> ## Adapting existing premises is **always** a compromise and might not be the solution for your particular site

New Build

Once you have decided that new-build is the option for your business, then some fundamental issues need to be resolved, these are:

Project Brief

Even if you choose to construct the buildings yourself, it is essential that you have a clear understanding of:

- What you are trying to achieve from the buildings
- How they will fit on your site
- The materials to be used
- The overall cost of the project

Site Survey

If you are constructing a new building, particularly on a difficult site (e.g. unusual ground conditions, sloping site etc) it is worthwhile investing in a full measured survey of your boundaries and existing buildings. A scale of either 1:500 or 1:200 is normally sufficient to show building lines etc.

UK Tip: In the UK, a simple method of obtaining fairly accurate plans showing boundary lines and footprint of existing buildings is to purchase a Superplan from UK Ordnance Survey. These come in a range of scales and can be used for planning purposes, plotting for additional buildings etc.

Ancillary Cost Items

Often these tend to be overlooked, as the main focal point tends to be toward the animal buildings only. It is essential to look at **all** areas that make up the working environment.

These can be storage buildings, drainage, adequate and safe access, demolition of redundant buildings, additional insurance and any legal conditions that might be imposed by the statutory authorities.

Choosing your Building Method

As most commercial cattery projects are (in construction terms) fairly straightforward and uncomplicated buildings, this allows the use of a wide range of building methods (procurement)
.

The following are the more common methods used by most cattery owners. There are other methods available, but they tend to be for more specialist projects:

- **Owner Self-Builds**
  The owner has the necessary skills and time to construct the buildings him/herself.
  This is obviously the cheapest method, with the owner carrying out the building works and bringing in local subcontractors for the more specialist trades as and when necessary.
  This method also means that the owner locates and purchases all of the required materials

- **Manufacturer Installs**
  To use a prefabricated (pre-manufactured) buildings system.
  If a prefabricated building is to be used, it would be sensible and generally more cost-effective, to allow the manufacturer to install it, as they are used to erecting their own product. This will also mean that you have some redress if the building develops any problems at a later date!

- **Owner Subcontracts**
  The owner employs all local subcontractors on a direct labour method.
  This is normally a mixture of the owner purchasing some of the larger items directly (such as concrete blocks, roofing materials etc). For smaller, more specialist items such as electrical and plumbing fittings, it might be preferable to let the contractor purchase these (in fact, they might insist on it!)

- **Building Contractor**
  To use a main building contractor, typically a small/medium sized, local construction firm.
  This can be either self-managed, or managed by either a surveyor/architect or project manager

- **Architect/Designer Technician**
  To employ a surveyor/architect/designer to design, project manage and issue interim payment schedules for the duration of the project.
  This is a common practice for larger scale developments and does provide an additional level of safety and comfort. However, there is an additional cost penalty attached to this!

- **Design and Build**
  This is where a main contractor designs the building for you and constructs it from day one to completion

Further Deciding Factors

Flexibility:

- Self-build

- Manufacturer installs

- Owner subcontracts

Clearly these methods allow the most flexibility, with the option for the owner to stop/start the project as funds permit, or to alter the specification, without incurring any contractor-related penalties that might be imposed when using an architect.

Design Work:

- Owner subcontracts

- Building contractor

- Architect/designer technician

With these methods it is assumed that a greater level of design work has been carried out to allow the contractor to accurately cost the project.

This normally takes the form of detailed drawings showing various elevations, setting out plans (giving the correct sizes for the building, cat units etc), section drawings (giving heights and the required pitch of the roof) and materials to be used.

All of these will normally form part of the planning application.

Any planning authority will want to see what the building will look like externally in terms of size, material choice and textures.

Common Route – Using a Main Building Contractor

Assuming that you have opted for using a main building contractor as your preferred method to construct a new cattery, and that you have had some detailed plans drawn up by another party, here are some of the things that should be considered during the construction period:

Construction Cost
The Contract Price is the lump sum given by the builder.
It is essential to establish what has been costed before the contract starts and any queries or 'grey' areas ironed out. Often it is the lack of detailed information that accounts for final increased costs

Materials
Have a clear understanding of the materials you wish to use.
Most general builders will not know **why** you want to specify a particular product, when there are many alternatives available. You do not want to have a building that cannot cope with the daily wear and tear!

Contract Documents
All documents used in conjunction with the project should be made part of the contract documentation. These might include detailed drawings, survey plans, existing services on the site, these should all be used by the builder to ensure that he/she has covered all areas of work to allow the completion of the buildings.

Start Date and Contract Period
These are mutually agreed dates between the contractor and owner.
They should be realistic and take into account weather conditions, how much access the contractor is given, any restrictions that might apply etc.

Payment
The method of payment to the builder should be agreed before the contract commences.

The three methods often used are:

1. Interim or fluctuating payments

2. Fixed or stage payments

3. Lump sum payment

Most new construction that is likely to last over four weeks, most builders will want to use either methods 1 or 2.

The advantage of fixed or stage payments is that the owner will know beforehand what the monthly costs are likely to be. Again, these would need to be discussed with the builder prior to work commencing and the amounts agreed.

Variations

All variations to the project will have a cost implication, either +/-

There is nothing unusual in varying minor items in the project; even with the most detailed schemes there are always areas of work that have to be altered.

The main point to remember is that any variation should have a cost set against it BEFORE the work commences, and this needs to be recorded by both parties and signed for. This will help prevent problems nearer the end of the project if the builder asks for additional payments for work that has not been agreed to.

Special Conditions

These might be:

- **Building Regulations/Control**
  Who is responsible for payment and co-ordination?

- **Access**
  How is the builder going to gain access to the site? Who will pay for any damage to grassed/paved areas caused by heavy machinery?

- **Contractors' Claims**
  Building is an unpredictable profession, as a client you **must** be prepared for things **not** to go to plan

- **Facilities**
  Use of your facilities (e.g. toilets, kitchen, electricity, water etc)

Additional Claims

If the builder submits a claim for additional money that has not been discussed, it is essential that you investigate the claim and do not simply reject it out of hand.

Contract

A contract document will not eliminate all of the above problems, but will provide a framework that both parties have agreed to. This provides a basis of understanding that will hopefully remove many of the problem areas and issues that so often dominate and spoil projects.

The Federation of Master Builders has a selection of easy-to-use contracts that can be downloaded from its website, or purchased. See www.fmb.org.uk

PROJECT DEVELOPMENT COSTS

Clearly, before you embark upon a project you will need to know what the final cost is going to be.

It is not uncommon for the peripheral items to be overlooked, or indeed some of the more general items such as connection to the mains sewage system, electricity upgrade, water supply etc.

The following list shows some of the main items that should be taken into account when preparing your budget for any new development. Clearly this is not exhaustive, but is merely indicative of the different areas/items that should be taken into account.

It is recommended that you obtain at least **three quotations** for your project.

The easiest way to get contractors to provide you with like-for-like quotations (rather than just making up their own minds about what you want from the project!) is to provide a 'specification' of what you want (sizes, materials, access, utilities etc).

Please see www.catterydesign.com for more detailed information on Building Specifications and Building Cost Pricing Documents.

Sample Project Development Cost Sheet

FEES	#	EXTERNAL WORKS	#
Planning Permission		Car park	
Building Regulations		Lighting	
Architect		Landscaping	
Quantity Surveyor		Fencing	
Structural Engineer		Road signage	
Mechanical/Electrical Engineer		Spoil removal	
Land Agent		Landscaping	
Land Surveyor		**Sub-total:**	
CDM Planning Officer (Construction, Design and Management)			
Infrastructure costs		**EQUIPMENT**	
Electricity		Laundry equipment	
Gas		Pressure washer/steam cleaner	
Water		Water hose/fittings	
Drainage		Fire prevention	
Specialist Contractors (e.g. asbestos removal)		Office/staff room furniture and fittings	
New buildings		Computer	
Sub-total:		Telephones & intercom	
TEMPORARY WORKS		Cattery furniture (e.g. activity & scratching posts, beds, bowls, litter trays, dishes)	
Fencing/security		Music system	
Accommodation		Safe/security box	
Services (e.g. gas)		Vehicle	
Sub-total:		**Sub-total:**	
MAIN BUILDINGS			
Reception			
Cattery			
Isolation			
Sub-total:			
PROJECT TOTAL:			

Individual Buildings – Cost Comparison

We have already looked at the overall development costs. However, it is also worth looking at the individual building costs.

If you are obtaining quotations from a builder,
(whether for a simple concrete base or a complete building)
– it is always worth breaking down the quotation into
smaller components

Breaking the quotation down will make it easier for you to see how the builder has arrived at their final figure, and also to help you compare the difference between various quotations. It will also allow you to see if they have made any major errors or omissions in their pricing structure.

A typical example of the information you should be asking for is:

REF:	ITEM	COST
\multicolumn{3}{l}{**Pricing Document**}		
1	Provisional dayworks	
2	Preliminaries	
3	Substructure	
4	Solid floor	
5	Roof construction	
6	Roof cladding	
7	External Walls	
8	Windows and doors	
9	Internal walls	
10	Wall and ceiling Finishes	
11	Plumbing services	
12	Electrical services	
13	Specialist services (e.g. galvanised metalwork)	
14	External works	
15	External services (e.g. water, drainage, electricity)	
16	Profits and Overheads	
	Total:	

Project Flow

These guidelines apply to ALL projects:

Project identified

Project scheme feasibility, preliminary costings

Client Approval to basic scheme, detailed design

Planning submission
(The client has the option to wait until planning approval is granted
before committing to further design work.
Equally, if the planning authority does not have any major objections
to the proposed scheme, detailed design work can proceed in order to save time)

Tenders invited

Tenders received

Tenders approved

Financial approval

Project phase

Other Issues to be Considered

Getting Started
At the initial meeting with the architect/surveyor/designer, the general principles of the scheme will be discussed, any cost restraints set out, and a fee agreed.

Fees
The fee can either be a fixed amount (this is more normal for **smaller contracts**) or a percentage of the total contract sum. It is normal for an architect/surveyor to outline the stage payments required, and other services that are not included in their fee (e.g. structural engineer).

Larger contracts are paid on a monthly basis; the architect issues interim certificates after consultation with the supervising officer or quantity surveyor. The certificates represent the value of the work completed to date. It is normal practice for a retention of 5% to be withheld at this stage. **At the end of the building stage (practical completion) half of the retention will be paid. At the end of the Defects Liability Period**, the contractor will have rectified any defective items. It is at this stage that the final certificate is issued; and the remaining retention is paid.

What you want
If you have thought about what you want from the buildings and layout, it can be a major saving in time and money.

Alterations
Alterations can be made at any time, but it is good policy to have ironed out any major revisions before work commences.

Services
Where refurbishment work is undertaken, there can be a significant disruption of services. These areas should have been addressed during the early discussions with the architect; indeed to comply with CDM (Construction, Design and Management) Regulations all aspects of the project will need to be taken into account. It might be necessary to provide temporary services (e.g. water, electricity, however all of these have a cost implication).

Contract
The Contract document will comprise working drawings, a specification/bill of quantities, a health and safety plan, and the signed Contract.

Site Meetings
Site meetings are normally on a monthly basis. However they can be as often or as few as required. Normal practice is for all amendments and alterations to be issued by the architect, direct to the contractor. This avoids confusion and keeps costs in order.

Neighbours
Ensure that you inform your neighbours of your plans. If planning permission is submitted, most local authorities will automatically inform them, but not all.

Whenever a new development is proposed, it is human nature to be wary of it! Therefore, it is essential to keep neighbours up-to-date with your proposals

UK Party Wall Act 1996

The Act covers England and Wales. However, there are similar issues for Scotland. One item to take into consideration when planning your site layout is how close will the development be to your neighbour's boundary? Generally, if the distance is less than 6 m/20 ft, then consideration will need to be given

The Act has implications for all building owners intending to carry out work which involves:

1. Work on an existing wall shared with a neighbour

2. Building on the boundary with a neighbouring property

3. Excavating near a neighbouring building

The basic elements of the Act requires the owner who intends to carry out the work to notify in writing all adjoining owners about the works involved. This must be done at least two months prior to any work commencing.

A useful website for further information is: www.odpm.gov.uk

Planning
Do your homework before getting the planners involved. Study the local planning policy.
If planning is granted, ensure you comply with any conditions imposed as many authorities are employing enforcement officers. The role of this officer is to ensure that developments are carried out in accordance with the planning permission granted.

End Values
It is worth considering the end value of your property before embarking on major and expensive developments!

Decision-making
Plan ahead and try not to be pushed into making decisions about the design, materials etc at the last moment.

Services
Ensure that any required services are available (e.g. water, gas, electricity and drainage) before commencing work. Also check to see what the lead-times and costs will be to bring these to your site – they can be prohibitive!

Building Materials
Ensure that you know the standard of materials to be used before any confirmed orders are placed!

Ground Conditions
Ensure you know what ground conditions you have before commencing work.
Many projects suffer additional costs and delays due to unknown ground conditions. Have trial holes dug well in advance of the development as this will allow an engineer to give guidance on suitable foundations etc. It also allows any additional costs to be factored in.

Budget

Ensure that you have sufficient budget, including a contingency.
You will need to keep a constant eye on the cost of the project to ensure that you don't have an unexpected claim at the end of the contract.

The main difficulty is one of cash flow.
It is surprising how quickly the money drains away! If you have to stop the project due to cash-flow problems, it can result in lengthy delays in getting the builders back to complete any outstanding work. A programme of works showing the various stages and potential costs at each stage is essential for large-scale projects as it allows better cash flow.

A contingency allowance will normally be around 7% – 10% of the total project cost.
(The percentage is generally higher for refurbishment work).

Key Decisions

Ensure that you have a full input to any key decisions. Even when you employ an architect/surveyor you need to ensure that the building is suitable for your requirements. You are the expert in what you want from your cattery.

Take advice – but be prepared to do your own homework!

Builders

Do not expect any reputable builder to be available immediately – most are booked for at least three months in advance. This is particularly the case for smaller companies employing a work force of 5 – 20 staff.
The larger contractors have more flexibility; however, they will be more expensive!

Grey Areas

These are items that are difficult to finalise at the early stages of the development. It is essential that you continue to carry out any necessary research and ensure that these items do not delay the project.

Insurance

Ensure that you inform your insurance company of any new development

If you have taken the responsibility for the construction, it **must** be insured as it progresses. If a main contractor has insured the project while he constructs it, you will need to notify your insurance company once the practical completion stage has been reached.

WHY PROJECTS GO WRONG!

There are numerous reasons why projects go wrong, cost more, and take longer to complete than originally envisaged.

The majority of projects are, on the whole, largely successful in terms of the completed building.

No project is 100% successful, no matter who is running it, or what the budget is!

The majority of cattery buildings work extremely well, although there might be a few teething issues, or design issues that can be improved upon.

For major companies (such as retail parks or food companies) constructing a large number of developments each year with the same materials, construction methods, design layouts etc, it is far easier for them to get it right as they have already been through their 'learning curve'.

However, for the majority of cattery owners and welfare organisations, each building is a prototype and therefore bespoke. This clearly has potential problems.

The main reasons for client dissatisfaction are:

- ### Cost
  Clearly, expenditure over and above what has been set aside for the development is a concern.
  To go into a project without any form of contingency is foolish.

  The reasons for cost increase can be minimised by doing your homework before committing to the project. The majority of additional costs are often attributed to poor ground conditions (such as collapsing trenches, contaminated ground, additional drainage, steep sites where more material is excavated than allowed for).

  The costs can also be affected by external influences that you have little control over, such as the local planning department. It might be that they insist on a certain type of material that is more expensive than you have allowed for. In most cases it is quicker and easier to accept their requirements and move the project along!

- ### Contractor
  The choice of Contractor is critical to ensure that the quality is correct, the costs given are fair and accurate, and the contractor is the correct company for your project. Too large a company and it will be more expensive, too small a company and they probably won't have the resources to cope with the project

- ### Client
  Quite often it is the client who is the worst offender!
  Simple things such as altering the specification halfway through the project, or including extra items, all have financial implications

  It is perfectly acceptable to make changes. However, you need to know the cost **before** the work is carried out, to ensure you are not presented with a substantial claim for additional costs at the very end of the project

Time
Most projects will run over the contracted time period. This is not uncommon.

However, you need to keep on top of this and find out the reasons why the contractor is behind his schedule. A small overrun for a contractor who has worked diligently and thoughtfully is something that has to be lived with. It is often a small price to pay for a completed project that has can be moved into straight away, one that you are happy with and has few snagging items (a snagging list is compiled prior to the building contractor finishing, but there are minor items of work not completed or finished to your satisfaction e.g. mastic joint not completed, area of decorating not up to standard).

The problems normally arise with smaller contractors, who have taken on too much work and are juggling several contracts at the same time without the resources to complete any one project. This can be a major issue, and particularly so for a cattery owner who has booked cats in on a set date!

The other reasons for overrunning the scheduled time are often associated with long lead times, and delivery for metalwork and specialist items. Many of the suppliers of specialist animal products tend to be individual, smaller companies who often have to quote lead-times in excess of **twelve weeks**; this can lead to major issues, particularly on smaller projects.

Utility Companies
Again, this is one area that can result in the project running over the scheduled time.

If the project requires a new utility supply (e.g. electricity) the lead times are lengthy. Quite often the contractor has little power to influence the provider and simply has to wait.

If new utilities are required, these need to be identified and requested at the earliest opportunity.

Summary for a Successful Project

The aim for the successful completion of any project is:

- Be on budget

- Be on time

- Have a building that is to the required standard and specification, and meets your expectations

- Avoid claims and legal disputes with the contractor, planning officials and neighbours.

- Be fair but firm with builders. Any claims for additional payments should be investigated to establish their validity. It might be that the claim is honest and fully justified

Avoid legal arbitration if at all possible.
The only winners from this route
will be the legal representatives!

PROFESSIONAL PROJECT MANAGEMENT

Alex Darvill, Agora Management

PROFESSIONAL PROJECT MANAGEMENT

Previously within this chapter, under the heading of "Choosing Your Building Method" you will have seen outlined various typical methods of procurement, ranging from 'Owner Self-Builds' to 'Design and Build'. **However, we cannot stress strongly enough that the building industry is complex – it is one in which we are deeply involved, and extremely experienced.**

Whilst we cannot claim it to be inevitable, the likelihood is that the unaided layman will fail to deal adequately with the procurement, management and financial rigours of his project. For example, a 'Design and Build' method will fail miserably if there is an inadequate 'Schedule of Organisation Requirements' and the absence of a skilled professional to guide the prospective building owner in all aspects of this particular method.

Time spent at the planning & design stage is never wasted!

A professional project manager will spend as long as is necessary to develop a client's initial design brief into a final concept, that will provide a pleasing, functional and robust facility.

PRACTICAL CONSTRUCTION ISSUES

Building any form of animal housing is a specialist area, and this knowledge is something that can only be obtained by continually working and developing in this sector. Mistakes are easily made due to lack of knowledge, and it is often left to the client to outline the project brief and specifications.

Ultimately, the project's success or failure always starts with the design brief

A wide and detailed knowledge of building materials and of practical design issues such as ours enables a building to be tailored to each client's needs, and to any limitations that the proposed site may place upon it.

PLANNING APPLICATIONS

There are many pitfalls in making a planning application. Again, specialist knowledge will come into its own here – as a wide and detailed knowledge of planning legislation and environmental issues is essential (it has proved vital to many of our clients), and is an area in which we have an exemplary record of dealing with such complex issues.

REHOMING

3D VISUALISATIONS
We make use of an excellent 3D (3-dimensional) imaging package to enable clients to visualise fully any aspect of their proposed building.

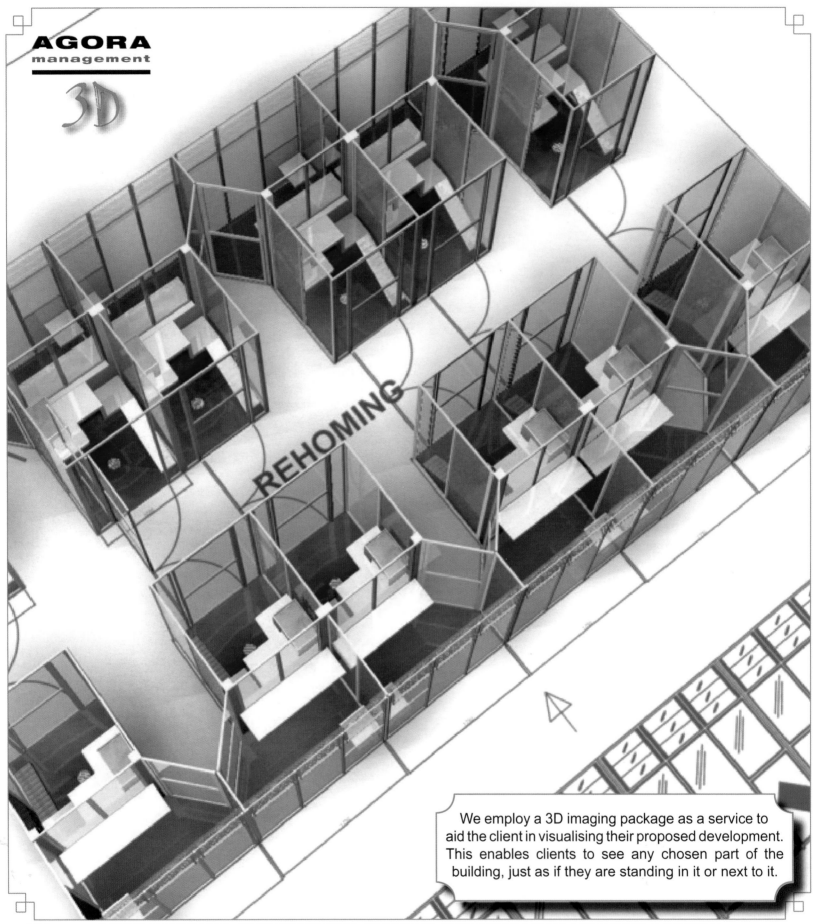

REHOMING

We employ a 3D imaging package as a service to aid the client in visualising their proposed development. This enables clients to see any chosen part of the building, just as if they are standing in it or next to it.

SPECIALIST KNOWLEDGE FOR PROJECTS

PLANNING AND ENVIRONMENTAL ISSUES

Professional project management also needs to be extremely conscious of environmental issues, particularly in respect of considerations such as planning, contaminated ground, waste disposal and the recycling of rainwater. Our policy is always to open, and to maintain, a dialogue with the relevant authorities and to work very closely with them to resolve all issues that may arise. Our record in this respect is exemplary.

ANIMAL WELFARE

At Agora Management we ensure that our knowledge of all legislation and guidelines relating to animal welfare is current, so that the facilities for which we are responsible are fully compliant.

> It is important to keep up-to-date with animal welfare regulations and issues to stay one step ahead

Our expertise extends from feline, canine and equine rehoming centres to aviaries, guide dog training centres and veterinary centres and hospitals. We are also closely involved in the development of specialist metalwork products for the kennelling aspects of such facilities.

SUITABLE MATERIALS FOR THE CATTERY

Comprehensive knowledge of suitable building materials and design considerations is vital and enables us, at an early stage, to advise on the nature and layout of a building that is likely to suit a client's brief and budget.

Whilst there may be particular reasons (perhaps related to planning or to a client's image) why a building must have a certain external style, **we remain conscious of the need to provide value for money and to strike a balance between the function of a building (which is paramount), and its form (which is an aesthetic consideration specific to each project).**

Our knowledge of materials suitable for animal welfare facilities is vast, and is constantly being updated so that we can ensure the right material is specified – not only for reasons of its initial cost, but also for its likely maintenance needs.

CLIENT ISSUES

At Agora Management, we view all projects with equal care and consideration, and are very mindful of budgetary constraints.

We provide **financial advice and control**, from initial concept design through to the settlement of the contractor's final account.

With skills in **advising and organising on behalf of a client**, we can advise on the method of building procurement best suited to the particular project under consideration.

Our **expertise in planning, programming, management and negotiation** has proved to be invaluable in ensuring that projects are completed within the contractually-dictated timescale and budgetary constraints.

We also have experience of the design and construction of multi-use sites (i.e. those with different organisations sharing the same site).

We have experience of not only putting new buildings on new sites, but also of converting and adapting existing buildings, some listed. Again, our close liaison with the relevant authorities is invaluable in this latter respect – not least where consent for a change of usage is required.

We believe very strongly that the initial design concept and budget costings we offer to our clients are of paramount importance, as they set the benchmark by which all subsequent advice may be judged and on which a client may base initial funding approval.

On the next page we have provided a typical design & development programme and initial cash flow forecast for you to show the degree of care that we take on any project from the very outset.

DESIGN DEVELOPMENT, PROCUREMENT & TENDER PROGRAMME

AGORA management

PROJECT TASKS:	WEEKS DURATION	WK 1	WK 2	WK 3	WK 4	WK 5	WK 6	WK 7	WK 8	WK 9	WK 10	WK 11	WK 12	WK 13	WK 14	WK 15	WK 16	WK 17	WK 18
DESIGN DEVELOPMENT, PROCUREMENT & TENDER PROGRAMME	**17 Weeks**																		
Client to agree appointment & procurement route	1 day																		
Client drawings for approval	15 days																		
Visit Planning Officer 2nd Consultation	1 day																		
Planners & Clients approval of draft	5 days																		
Preparation of Planning Application	8 days																		
Tender negotiations	5 weeks																		
Drawing development	5 weeks																		
Planning application & approval	1? weeks																		
Start on site																			

DESIGN DEVELOPMENT PROGRAMME

A typical design development programme:
The typical design development programme shown here turns the project from an academic concept into a reality – it is actually happening! The client can see how he fits into the design process and can consider such matters as the date from which the contractor's entitlement to periodic payments will begin.

TYPICAL LARGE PROJECT BUILD ESTIMATE

Typical Project Estimate for Client for a Large Cattery:

#	Elemental Breakdown:	Estimated Cost:	Approx. Currency Conversion:		
			EURO	USA $	CANADA $
1	Substructure	£49,500	€72,695	$86,400	$99,225
2	Frame	£10,750	€15,785	$18,765	$21,550
3	Roof	£103,500	€152,000	$180,675	$207,465
4	External walls	£49,500	€72,695	$86,400	$99,225
5	Windows and external doors	£29,500	€43,325	$51,500	$59,130
6	Internal walls	£14,250	€29,925	$24,875	$28,565
7	Internal doors	£5,000	€7,345	$8,730	$10,020
8	Wall finishes	£525	€770	$916	$1,050
9	Floor finishes	£62,500	€91,785	$109,105	$125,280
10	Ceiling finishes and supports	£10,750	€15,785	$18,765	$21,550
11	Decorations	£15,000	€22,030	$26,185	$30,070
12	Fittings (incl specialist doorsets)	£152,500	€223,965	$266,220	$305,740
13	Services	£90,000	€132,175	$157,115	$180,435
14	Site works (incl demolitions and covered way)	£80,000	€117,490	$139,655	$160,365
15	Drainage	£45,000	€66,085	$78,555	$90,205
16	External services	£34,000	€49,930	$59,353	$68,155
17	BWIC services	£9,000	€13,215	$15,710	$18,040
	(incl contractor's overheads & profit) Subtotal:	**£761,275**	**€1,127,000**	**$1,328,924**	**$1,526,070**
18	Preliminaries	£115,000	€168,890	$200,755	$230,525
	(including preliminaries) Subtotal:	**£876,275**	**€1,295,890**	**$1,529,679**	**$1,756,595**
19	Design and construction contingencies	£75,000	€110,220	$130,927	$150,340
	(Estimated Cost of Main Contract Works) TOTAL:	**£951,275**	**€1,406,110**	**$1,660,606**	**$1,906,935**

General Notes:
All figures are current and exclude tax, professional fees and planning/Building Control fees.
The estimate is based on architect's drawings e.g. A, B, C, D and E.

AGORA management

BUILD ESTIMATE

Typical larger project build estimate, as against a one-line lump estimate:
As against a one-line, lump sum estimate, an elemental estimate of the type shown here helps the client to understand how the design of each element of the project affects its estimated cost. This format is crucial in our being able to provide alternative estimates for individual elements of the project as the design is reviewed and developed.

AGORA MANAGEMENT

BACKGROUND TO THE COMPANY

Agora Management is a professional practice, formed in 1998, to provide a full range of building advisory and design services ranging from project management, architecture and quantity surveying to mechanical and electrical services and planning supervision. The various members of our practice are mature, qualified professionals with a wealth of experience in the building industry, who will take any project through from initial concept design to completion of construction on site.

Whilst we are able to provide a comprehensive service on projects of any nature, we have a particular specialisation in animal welfare facilities, be they rehoming centres, boarding kennels and catteries, veterinary centres or hospitals. There is no lower or upper limit to the value of a project with which we will assist, nor indeed any reasonable limitation as to its location.

Many of our clients have charitable status and are very pleased with the assistance we can provide for their fund raising campaigns in the form of valuing, and providing appropriate images of, individual elements of the proposed projects to enable the campaigns to be suitably focused.

Agora Management were project managers assisting in the control and design development of the projects shown in this book, including:

- **The Blue Cross Southampton** page 96 (external view)

- **The Blue Cross Cambridge** pages 244 & 253 (build), page 282 lower (external view), page 418 (kitchen)

- **Cats Protection National Cat Centre** (see next page) where we were complete project managers, planning supervisors and client representative.

Our growing list of institutional clients, with all of whom we are delighted to be associated, includes:

- Battersea Dogs and Cats Home
- The Blue Cross
- Cats Protection
- Dogs Trust
- Guide Dogs for the Blind Association
- National Animal Welfare Trust

We also provide services to individual organisations such as the Raystede Centre for Animal Welfare in Sussex, the Haven Veterinary Practice in Great Yarmouth and Northlands Veterinary Hospital in Kettering.

TO FIND OUT MORE

If you have a building need, be it a new development, the alteration of an existing facility or a change of usage to animal welfare, it is our genuine belief that we can assist you regardless of its location and project scale.

Our professional dedication and knowledge have been fundamental to our success and growth. Our current clients in the animal welfare fraternity view us as a practice able to respond to all their building needs in a timely, thoughtful and economic fashion.

We view with pleasure and anticipation the prospect of offering these same qualities to other interested organisations. Indeed, our reputation has spread across the Channel, and we now have the prospect of working in mainland Europe.

In the first instance, we invite you to contact our Managing Director, Alex Darvill (who has worked with David Key, the author of this book, for many years) to arrange an initial meeting and discussion:

Alex Darvill
Agora Management Limited
12 Kings Court, Willie Snaith Road
Newmarket, Suffolk CB8 7SG
Tel: +44 (0)1638 560343
www.agoramanagement.com

CASE STUDY:
A BIG PROJECT!

Organisation: Cats Protection National Cat Centre
Location: UK, West Sussex
Cattery Type: Indoor
Cattery Function: Rescue etc
Number of Units: 202
Unit Size Sleep: 0.7m²/7.5ft²
Unit Size Exercise: 2.94m²/31.5ft²
Date Built: 2004
www.cats.org.uk

THIS CATTERY IS CAPABLE OF HOUSING UP TO 350 CATS AND KITTENS, BUILT BY CATS PROTECTION TO ADDRESS THE NEED TO COPE WITH THE BURGEONING CAT POPULATION, AND SUBSEQUENT NEED TO CARE AND REHOME MORE CATS

CATS PROTECTION, NATIONAL CAT CENTRE

UK'S LARGEST CAT WELFARE CHARITY

Cats Protection is the UK's largest and oldest feline welfare charity, dedicated to rehoming 60,000 cats a year through its nationwide network of 29 Adoption Centres and 260 voluntary run Branches, as well as promoting responsible ownership. As a charity, they rely solely on the generosity and kindness of the public to enable them to continue caring for cats and kittens, of which there are a 7,000 in their care at any one time. Cats Protection built their National Cat Centre in 2004 for the rescue, rehabilitation and rehoming of cats from all over the country. With the capability of housing up to 350 cats and kittens within 202 pens, this was a BIG project!

The centre has state of the art veterinary facilities on site, with fully employed veterinary support team. The self-contained cabin units have underfloor heating and individual air ventilation. The total of 202 pens is broken down as follows: 52 rehoming, 30 pre homing, 32 family/multi-cat, 32 maternity, 30 admissions, and 26 for isolation. Each exercise run includes a ladder and shelving, and opaque glass screens with viewing areas into adjacent cabins.

Since opening, there has been a steady increase in homing figures. Open days and other events have raised the profile of the cattery, coupled with a carefully phased advertising programme, they are gaining more visitors.

There is still some work to do to raise public awareness of the site, and future development will include an Education and Training Centre.

No one likes to see cats penned for any length of time, and whilst it is recognised that some cats are harder to home than others, there are a number of different methods used by our centres and branches to improve rehoming opportunities, such as moving cats to different sites, publicity, advertising and providing photographs and detailed background information on the cats. No healthy cat is euthanised and we just have to work that bit harder to home some of our longer-stay cats.

THE CHANGING WORLD OF CATS

There are six million cat owning households in the UK that provide homes for 9.2 million felines. Cats are the UK's favourite pet – they fit in well with our busy lifestyles and their winning blend of independence and affection also makes them the ideal choice of pet for many older people.

The UK cat population has steadily risen – there were 4.5 million cats in the UK in 1975, rising to 9.2 million in 2004.

The existence of greater number of cats equals greater demand for feline rescue and rehoming services – and the Cats Protection National Cat Centre is a huge step forward in addressing the need to help more cats.

What are you most pleased with?

We are very happy with the design – particularly the negative air pressure system which is very effective in preventing the spread of disease. On-site veterinary facilities provide immediate treatment and care, and it also saves our cats the additional stress of transportation.

What would you do differently?

If we looked at a similar design in the future we would include more storage space, more socialisation rooms, and increase the corridor width to make it easier to move trolleys through the self-closing doors.

Photographs by David & Kay Key, and Richard Milton of Cats Protection

CATS PROTECTION:
NATIONAL CAT CENTRE

CATS PROTECTION:
NATIONAL CAT CENTRE

CONSTRUCTION MATERIALS

EXTERNAL CONSTRUCTION MATERIAL CHOICES

The construction style and choice of materials for your proposed development will depend on several issues; the location, the position of the site (e.g. on top of a hill or areas with restricted planning). All locations pose their own difficulties and restrictions, some more onerous than others.

The vernacular architecture can be broadly divided into domestic, agricultural and industrial; generally we will be interested only in domestic and agricultural.

The local planning authority will probably insist that any new development be sympathetic and in keeping with the style for that locality. All of these issues will need to be discussed with the planning authority at an early stage. It is pointless having plans drawn up for the development that will be totally unacceptable to the planners!

In areas of outstanding natural beauty or restricted planning the choice might be very limited, with the local authority insisting on the use of natural stone common to the area. The end result is higher costs for the development.

Although animal buildings tend by their very nature to be very utilitarian, it is surprising how they can be transformed and aesthetically improved with the correct choice of materials, colours and subtle architectural detail.

On the whole, it is generally only the larger charities that undertake large, architectural designed buildings with a degree of flair involved.

The costs involved with any construction project have increased considerably over the past few years, and it is not uncommon for many animal buildings constructed out of brick/block to cost similar amounts to those for domestic housing!

The nature of animal accommodation means that the rooms are generally smaller than those in houses, which has cost implications. The ground works involved for brick/block constructions are similar to those for a house; consequently the costs are similar. The roof construction, whether it is tiled or insulated steel sheeting, is also the same for a cattery building as for a house! Combine all of these factors with boiler-fired central heating systems, and it is easy to see how the costs can be greater for animal accommodation.

Many of the companies offering prefabricated systems will normally offer some level of design work as part of their package. Clearly this can be a very attractive deal.

Once the building construction method approaches the more traditional methods (i.e. brick/block), it is not unusual to find that the client has employed the services of an architect or surveyor. This can be either to design and submit plans suitable for a planning application, or to design, project manage and oversee the entire development.

Ultimately, the deciding factors are often financial, size of the development, how confident the client is in dealing with builders, and what time is available.

BUILDING CONSTRUCTION MATERIALS

Cattery construction materials fall into the following categories:

■ Timber

■ Prefabricated units of UPVC, lightweight steel frame buildings or insulated panels

■ Brick, block, stone, poured concrete

■ Conversions of existing buildings

Within the above categories there are numerous design and material options available.
Obviously, the choice of construction method is a primary and fundamental issue. The choice will have planning, cost, logistical, ease of use, and longer term issues such as maintenance and potential re-sale value if the business is sold.

All of the above materials and systems will work; however, they all have advantages and disadvantages.
Advantages and disadvantages can often be purely personal preference, and are often associated with the overall design, construction and quality of materials used.

The photographs below show some of the more common issues for each option, which we will now look at in detail for the remainder of this chapter.

TIMBER

- Cheapest of all systems

- Well-established product with several manufacturers who have developed the product over a lengthy period of time (although little advancement has been made in the basic offering)

- Easy to install

- **MUST** be clad internally to prevent cats from damaging the timber, for correct cleaning and to reduce the risk of cross-infection. As you can see in the opposite photograph, the interior of the penthouse unit is lined with a hygienic surface, but the external sections and framing are unprotected timber

- Requires insulation to prevent extremes of temperature

- Requires regular maintenance of stain coatings where it is exposed to the elements, to prevent deterioration of the timber and to keep it weatherproof

Pets

Timber is a versatile material and easy to use, hence its popularity. For pet and privately owned cats who are in a stable community and therefore have a known background – timber can be a highly useful option.

Commercial and Rescue

Warning

Just prior to the publication of this book we contacted some UK local authorities to ask them about their policy on timber boarding catteries. **Several authorities have now banned the use of timber where the cat will have contact with it.**

Disease Control

The problem with the use of timber is that it presents more risk in terms of disease control. This is more critical for charities and rescue organisations who are dealing with cats with an unknown history, but can affect commercial catteries as well.

A charity purchasing an existing boarding business in the nineteen eighties (with the view to upgrading it to a modern facility) had to continue running the boarding establishment to fulfill all the remaining bookings. The boarding cattery, which was above the kennels (hardly desirable!) admitted a cat which was later diagnosed with ringworm.
The cattery was completely emptied, all moveable items removed, disinfected or burnt, and the building was completely disinfected and fumigated. The building was then left empty for a period of five years before being demolished.
*During the demolition **five** years later, two of the builders contracted ringworm!*

This highlights how difficult it is to eradicate ringworm in old or timber buildings that cannot be adequately cleaned, and where there is a higher risk of disease due to a continual changeover of cats.

UPVC/PVCU

The use of UPVC for catteries has increased significantly over the past five years. The reasons for this are:

- Well-known and familiar product for replacement doors and windows that is quick and easy to assemble

- Easy to clean and non-porous

- Professional and clean appearance

- Is generally supplied in a white finish. Alternative colour options are available, but are more expensive (these are only used on the external face with white still being used internally).

- The product may expand slightly during periods of **prolonged heat**. Although this can be an irritation if doors/windows temporarily do not close smoothly, it does settle down again when the temperature cools

What to check:

- Check on the manufacturers warranty for discolouration – most offer a 10 year warranty for yellowing

- Costs are similar to better quality timber equivalents, or can vary up to 20% compared with poorer quality timber

- There are large variations in cost/quality between manufacturers, for what at first appear to be the same product!

- Careful consideration of the manufacturer's specification is essential to establish what the differences are to compare like-for-like. For example: compared with 25mm/1" polycarbonate opal/bronze-tinted roof sheeting, the heat-shield coating option can double the cost. This isn't noticeable when you see the products, but on a hot day you would certainly feel the difference in temperature!

- Can look more obtrusive when used as a stand-alone building in certain settings, (landscaping obviously helps any building 'settle in') but looks extremely smart in a traditional construction, or in a building conversion

The quality of the material varies **enormously** between manufacturers

Any concern about the use of this product with regard to possible extremes of temperature and ventilation issues is probably associated with poor design, poor quality roofing materials and also a possible over-use of glass.

Next we will learn more about using UPVC cat pens, followed by a case study of a rescue cattery using UPVC:
This rescue charity constructed two full-sized catteries using UPVC in the UK's hot south west and had no issues. The site in question is set in an old quarry with 30 ft/10 m cliffs on two sides. Consequently, the centre does experience extremely high temperatures, often over prolonged periods of time. It is interesting that the UPVC catteries replaced an old timber cattery. With the timber unit there were considerable problems with extremes in hot weather, with temperatures well in excess of 30°C/86°F. Even with the installation of additional insulation on the roof, the centre still had to run cooling fans during the summer months and hang blankets etc over the exercise runs. With the UPVC cattery, the centre staff do not have any concerns about heat issues or ventilation and are extremely pleased with the quality of the product.

UPVC CAT PENS

Paul Collins, Pedigree Pens

BOARDING CATTERIES

In today's discerning market there is a need for high quality, hygienic, low maintenance facilities. This strategy is important in order to market and establish your business correctly, not only because of customer demands, but also to comply with increasing local authority cattery regulation requirements. Over the last ten years we at Pedigree Pens have worked closely with our customers and built up extensive knowledge in assisting people starting up a cattery business. It is an essential part of our strategy to work closely with our customers on an ongoing basis, as this ensures our customers are happy and also provides us with a continuous programme of design and development.

We are chosen for our quality construction materials, the know-how to make this possible and we **offer a full design service**, can provide statements to assist **planning issues**, **offer advice** on advertising and marketing strategies, courses and even provide a free business support service via our website. Our website lists our customers' cattery business details, such as address, contact details, photographs and website addresses. This helps to generate new business for them, because if anyone searches the internet for a cattery in a specific county, the search engine will identify our website, through which customers can be contacted by cat owners.

We have helped over 50 boarding and rescue centres start up!

Our customers want the highest quality of boarding accommodation to provide the highest standards of comfort, hygiene and security seen in the boarding industry. Due to the emphasis on these high standards, they are able to charge higher fees for this level of service.

STARTING A NEW CATTERY

We would suggest that our boarding catteries are installed as small and exclusive developments (ideally 10 to 35 double size pens) and are focused towards the more discerning cat owner who is prepared to pay a premium for a quality service and environment. **Our pens can be installed as complete buildings, or within an existing or new cattery building**.

The cost of the pens can usually be covered by sales in the first year of trading, and possibly by the end of month eight!

SUCCESS & EXPANSION

The majority of our installations are listed on our website and each one is running very successfully, achieving repeat business year after year. Many of our customers are so successful within the first two years of opening that they contact us again looking to expand their business further!

Choosing a Pedigree Pens installation means that you will be offering a service with the highest standard of cattery, which more and more customers are demanding these days. Serious direct competition is unlikely to exist, as there are certain to be boarding catteries within your local area which offer a much lower standard of accommodation. **We can manufacture to your exact requirements, and we can supply you with:**

• Freestanding pens
• Convert existing buildings
• Fit out a new building

FREESTANDING PENS

FREESTANDING PENS

When starting a cattery, many people use the land adjoining their home. Where this is the case, we can install freestanding pens (the units are fitted to a level concrete base), e.g:

1. Patz Catz Cat Hotel: 10 double 'penthouse' style pens located in Hampshire

2. Cloughfields Cat Hotel: 'L' shape formation consisting of 15 double size pens located in Sheffield

3. Imberpark Cattery: 14 double size 'walk-in' pens located in Middlesex and 10 minutes from Heathrow

4. Templeogue Cattery: 30 double size pens this cattery is located in rural Dublin, Ireland

5. Beechcroft Cats Hotel: Cattery consisting of 30 'walk-in' style pens located rurally in Cardiff

Below:

Lowbroom Cattery: A small cattery consisting of 4 double pens, located rurally in Monmouthshire

1

2

3

4

5

CONVERSION & NEW BUILD

CONVERSION

You may have existing farm buildings or outbuildings that you wish to convert. In this case we can convert the existing building into a new cattery, requiring just the shell of a building to install under cover. Pens are installed internally and usually have a flat roof, e.g:

1. The Blue Cross Tiverton: Conversion creating 20 pens for this rescue centre located in Devon
2. Foxcombe Cats Hotel: Conversion of an existing farm building located rurally in Pembrokeshire

NEW BUILD

Pedigree Pens frequently fits out new buildings. We work closely with contractors, we provide: doors, divisions and rooms on individual requirements and our expertise, e.g:

3. Heathrow Airport (Animal Reception Centre): Kennels and cattery at for quarantine and passport pets
4. Rochdale RSPCA: 27 rescue pens at the RSPCA centre in Red Cross street Rochdale
5. The Blue Cross Lewknor: Fitted out divisions, doors and rooms to create new cattery. Located in Oxfordshire

HOLDING PENS

In addition to providing boarding facilities we also supply Holding Pens for housing cats for 24 hour periods.

PEDIGREE PENS

RESCUE CATTERIES

We will also manufacture and install high quality, insulated boarding kennels and catteries for rescue centres, examples of which can be seen at many of Britain's leading animal charities such as Cats Protection, The Blue Cross, RSPCA, and The Mayhew Animal Home.

In particular, Blue Cross and Britain's RSPCA have worked closely with us to ensure that their exact requirements for animal housing have been met fully for their long-term needs. Different styles of pens can be viewed at our Gloucestershire showroom (M5 Junction 9) – directions available from the website.

Some of our customers are in this book, including:
- Blue Cross Torbay, page 279
- Blue Cross Lewknor, 408
- Harpenden Cat Hotel, 32
- Mayhew Animal Home, 224
- Preston Hills Cat Hotel, 472
- Pyrton Cat Hotel, 88
- Templepan Cat Hotel, 286

ABOUT PEDIGREE PENS LTD

We are a BS EN ISO (Quality Assured, U.K.) registered company and specialise solely in the manufacture of PVCu animal housing and have done so since 1993. We have hundreds of installations throughout the U.K. for commercial boarders, rescue centres and private households.

Our experience in this field is second to none. We are original sponsors of the UK's CIEH (Chartered Institute of Environmental Health) Model Licence Conditions for Cat Boarding Establishments.

PRODUCT QUALITY & STANDARDS

With a clear objective: to raise standards for animal care in the private and public sectors, we have developed our exciting range of cat accommodation to address issues of hygiene, security, comfort, maintenance and longevity.

Our products are manufactured to meet increasingly high expectations and individual requirements, in addition to providing designs which have been carefully developed over the years.

All our frames are made from PVCu which is highly regarded for its self extinguishing properties. The modular design of our pens allows for installation of any number of chalets from just one or two to a hundred or more and means they can be installed at a later date to accommodate your expansion plans.

If you have any questions, please contact Paul Collins our Managing Director at:

happy cats habitats!

Pedigree Pens Ltd
A2 Northway Trading Estate
Northway, Tewkesbury
Gloucestershire GL20 8JH, UK
Phone & Fax: +44 (0)1684 299567
www.pedigreepens.com

CASE STUDY:
UPVC CONSTRUCTION

Organisation: The Blue Cross
Location: UK, Devon
Cattery Type: Semi-outdoor
Cattery Function: Rescue
Number of Units: 12
Unit Size Sleeping: 1200 x 1400mm (4ft x 4'7")
Unit Size Exercise: 1200 x 1600mm (4ft x 5'3")
Date Built: 2002

www.bluecross.org

THE BLUE CROSS REPLACED A VERY
OUTDATED TIMBER BUILDING (PREVIOUSLY A
PRIVATE BOARDING CATTERY)
WITH A BRIGHT, SPACIOUS, WELCOMING
REHOMING CATTERY

BLUE CROSS, TORBAY

In 2002, a decision was taken to replace the existing outdated timber cattery with a new UPVC prefabricated system.

The reasons for using a prefabricated system were:

- To minimise the period the centre had to work at a reduced capacity

- A compact site with restricted access meant there was limited storage space for building and construction materials and car parking

CHOOSING THE DESIGN

After some initial sketch designs it became obvious that there was only one design that offered sufficient levels of accommodation and fitted into the space available.
The final design has 12 double walk-in units (each with a width of between 1200-1400mm/4-4'6"), with attached exercise runs, a kitchen and a covered, extended canopy to allow the public to view the cats while under cover.

The aim is for the public to initially view the cats from outside the cattery. If a cat and potential owner can be matched up, the potential owner can then go inside to discuss the adoption in greater detail and be introduced to the cat.

All construction projects have their own issues and problems. Here, the main issues were:

1. Tight and restricted site with little room for storage of materials
2. Insufficient electrical supply to provide power for the new building
3. A very sheltered site (the centre is built into an old quarry) with a 10m/30ft high sandstone cliff face on two sides. Being based on the south coast, the centre experiences a warm climate. In addition, the cliff surrounding the property often means the centre experiences its own micro-climate. This can produce extremely hot days during the summer, and cold damp days in the winter

HIGH TEMPERATURES

Due to the sheltered nature of the site and in particular the location of the new building, there were concerns about possible high temperatures in the cattery during the summer months. After discussions with the manufacturer, the solution was agreed.

The main roof covering is a five-wall polycarbonate system with a heat shield reflective coating on the inner face. In addition, an insulated suspended ceiling was installed over the sleeping areas, main corridor and kitchen. (Although cats like heat they find it uncomfortable when temperatures reach 25°C/77°F or above for extended periods of time. This is particularly relevant for animals that cannot escape the heat in a cattery.

The system has proved to be extremely efficient at keeping the heat levels down to acceptable levels. The end result is that we now have a new cattery that is brighter and more welcoming for visitors, provides more space for the cats, provides prospective adopters and staff a professional, self-contained, low maintenance and hygienic building.

What are you most pleased with?

The building has high levels of natural light; each unit has shelving at various heights to allow full three- dimensional use of the sleeping and exercise areas by the cats. Each unit can accommodate three cats if required. It is surprising how many cats coming in for adoption come in as a pair!

What would you do differently?

A separate veterinary inspection room would have been ideal, but unfortunately there was not enough space for this.

LIGHTWEIGHT STEEL-FRAMED BUILDINGS

These prefabricated systems generally have similar properties to those shown for UPVC and have similar costs.

Lightweight steel-framed structures are not widely used, with only a limited number of specialist suppliers, and tend to be used by charities. They are:

- Quick and easy to assemble

- Easy to clean

- Professional and clean appearance

What to check:

- The quality of material

- That you are comparing like-for-like with alternative manufacturers

- They can look more obtrusive in certain settings

BRICK, STONE, BLOCK AND POURED CONCRETE

A traditional, solid construction method of building is always the most appealing option. The more home/house-like appearance has strong appeal for many clients.

Solid buildings are generally a bespoke option for a particular site or client requirement, and offer the most options in terms of design and architectural flair.

From marketing, business and public appeal points of view, this type of construction gives the impression of a professional, long-term commitment and feels more 'solid' and secure.

Also, bear in mind that a traditional building is a more tangible and flexible asset at a later date, should you wish to sell the property, or convert the building to another use.

The reasons for using this traditional method of construction and materials might be due to:

- Personal preference
- Design options and material choices
- Planning requirements

Certainly the design options are virtually limitless with these materials and do allow and provide for a greater degree of design flair. However, a cattery constructed using brick/block or poured concrete is the most expensive of the options to build.

CONVERSION OF EXISTING BUILDINGS

Some of the most appealing cattery buildings are often found in conversions of existing buildings.

Often there is a combination of a very old, characterful shell of a building with a modern internal cattery. If carried out correctly, this system can work extremely well, have lots of character and appeal, and provide an excellent facility.

All the points under the previous section above apply.

Clearly, there will always have to be compromise with this type of design. However, with careful consideration, this can be minimised, and can even form part of the appeal and character of the building.

On the next few pages we will see examples of new-build and conversion of traditionally constructed catteries.

A stone-built cattery

A block-built cattery

CASE STUDY: BRICK CONSTRUCTION

Organisation: Wythall Animal Sanctuary
Location: UK, Midlands
Cattery Type: Semi-outdoor
Cattery Function: Rescue
Number of Units: 26
Unit Size Sleep: 950 x 950 x 950mm (3ft x 3ft x 3ft)
Unit Size Exercise: 1000 x 1800mm (3'3" x 6ft)
Date Built: 2005

www.wythallanimalsanctuary.org.uk

A PRIVATELY RUN RESCUE CONTINUES ITS UPGRADING PROGRAMME WITH A PURPOSE BRICK BUILT CONSTRUCTION CATTERY WITH STACKED INTERNAL CAGES THAT OFFER A DEGREE OF FLEXIBILITY

WYTHALL ANIMAL SANCTUARY

The Wythall Animal Sanctuary is an independent and privately run animal rescue and rehoming charity based in the Midlands, UK. The majority of their rehoming work focuses on companion animals, mainly cats, dogs and rabbits.

UPGRADING PROGRAMME

The Charity has had an upgrading and refurbishment programme in progress for the past few years, and in that time has constructed a new purpose built rabbit unit, a kennel unit and a reception with staff facilities etc. The latest project to be completed is the cattery.

STYLE AND COST

Like all organisations, the first issue when thinking about their new cattery was what style and type would be the most suitable option, be cost-effective, give long-term durability, satisfy all of their requirements and equally important, fit on to the area of land proposed for the building and provide the necessary number of units. Wythall decided on a semi-outdoor cattery with individual sleeping units and shared exercise runs. Construction materials were brick/block with tiled and polycarbonate translucent roof construction.

The cattery has 26 sleeping units, kitchen, rehoming room, storage and a separate self-contained isolation unit.

SEMI-OUTDOOR, STACKED

After careful consideration, the sanctuary opted for a semi-outdoor design with fibreglass sleeping units internally, with direct access into external exercise runs.

The internal sleeping units are based on a hospital design, although Wythall have had them made larger than normal.

In order to provide the required number of units, Wythall designed the building with the sleeping units stacked two high. The thinking behind this design was to provide the charity with as much flexibility as possible.

FLEXIBILITY

As an independent charity they don't have the luxury of being able to move animals around to other centres if they are full. Therefore, they have opted for a design that allows them the flexibility to give a cat the choice of either sleeping unit if they have space.

If the centre is full, they still have the flexibility to provide a dedicated sleeping unit and rotate the cats to allow them into the exercise runs. The project was completed in July 2005 and the centre is extremely pleased with the finished building.

What are you most pleased with?
Easy to clean building which provides the cats with external exercise run allowing plenty of fresh air.

What would you do differently?
The only minor disappointment they have is with the floor finish. The finish is a 6mm polyurethane screed, and although this is a robust and durable surface, the finish has been left with an extremely course texture; making it very difficult to clean.

CASE STUDY:
BARN CONVERSION

Organisation:	Templepan Cattery
Location:	UK, Hertfordshire
Cattery Type:	Indoor
Cattery Function:	Boarding
Number of Units:	18
Unit Size Sleep:	1220 x 1220mm (4ft x 4ft)
Unit Size Exercise:	1220 x 1830mm (4ft x 6ft)
Date Built:	2003

www.www.templepancattery.co.uk

DESIGNER TOUCHES AND GOURMET FOOD (INDIVIDUALLY BOUGHT) ARE THE TRADEMARKS OF THIS SMALL, HOMELY BUSINESS WITH ITS INBUILT RECEPTION, KITCHEN AND BEAUTIFULLY LANDSCAPED GARDENS

TEMPLEPAN BOARDING CATTERY

THE DESIGNER TOUCH

Templepan Cattery has 18 double and family units made from UPVC and a resin floor, within a beautifully converted stable block. The location is peaceful, being situated in a private lane with perfectly maintained gardens and surroundings.

Owners Debbie and Claire Hubble are two sisters who run the cattery and provide their personal touch wherever you look. Templepan is very much a family business, as their father, Dennis, tends the beautiful and peaceful gardens.
With plug-ins oozing the feline facial pheromone that calms and helps cats to settle, planting and a water fountain, lots of toys, cat scratching posts/stands, and designer cat beds – everything is changed to match the seasons, which they obviously enjoy!

For the winter season, they have decided on rugs and lamps in the external corridor to provide a more 'home-like' environment, which is not only appealing to owners and cats, but great to work in. A nice touch is the reception area with sofa, lamp and board with photos of their boarders. Adjacent to the kitchen, the reception leads straight into the safety corridor and the cat units.

MAKING IT HAPPEN

As with many boarding facilities, 60% of their business comes through their well-designed website and they soon realised the importance of the internet to a new business!

THE WAY TO A CAT'S HEART

Debbie and Claire have a wide selection of 'gourmet' foods available and on display, and the cats get through a fair amount of tuna!

It is obviously important to help the cats settle in as soon as possible, and they find tuna does this quickly. They want their cat boarders to enjoy feeding times, and are happy to feed as they are fed at home, fussy appetites are also catered for, as are any other special feeding requirements.

CONTINUITY AND CARE

Templepan says it is one of a few catteries in the area that accepts diabetic cats needing injections.
Continuity is very important to them, and the cats certainly appreciate it, with Claire looking after the cats and Debbie taking care of the office so that everything is done thoroughly.

What are you most pleased with?

The wide safety corridor really helps to make the cattery feel welcoming and the resin floor is very easy to clean. The quality and size of the Pedigree Pens units is a benefit as they are all doubles and able to take two cats.

What would you do differently?

Ideally we would have added rooflights to increase the amount of light available inside the barn.

TEMPLEPAN BOARDING CATTERY

WELCOME TO
TEMPLEPAN CATTERY
← ENTRANCE

THERMAL INSULATION

HAVING THE
CORRECT LEVEL
OF INSULATION
HELPS KEEP YOUR
CATTERY WARM IN
WINTER AND COOL
IN SUMMER

THERMAL INSULATION – WARMTH AND COOLING

The increasing demand to conserve fuel and reduce heating bills has led to greater levels of insulation in buildings; this applies to all buildings from domestic to industrial. To provide adequate levels of thermal comfort, it is accepted that walls, floors and roof should provide resistance to excessive transfer of heat.

Thermal Transmittance – U-Values and W/m²

Thermal Transmittance is the rate at which heat is transferred through an element of a building and is called the thermal resistance or U-value. The lower the U-value, the better the insulation, and the lower the heat loss. U-values are expressed in W/m² K (watts per square metre (approx 3'3") for 1°C/33°F difference between internal and external temperatures)

The UK Building Regulations set maximum thermal resistance values for non-domestic dwellings. These are:

- Walls   0.35 W/m²
- Floors   0.25 W/m²
- Roofs   0.20 W/m²
- Windows and doors   2.0 W/m²

Helpful Hints:

- It is worth checking with Building Control to establish if any of the new buildings will be exempt from Building Regulations. The interpretation of the regulations varies with each local authority. From experience, this 'grey-area' applies to new buildings that are purely for animal use and do not contain any form of habitable rooms for humans (e.g. staff rooms or kitchens). This point is worth considering, particularly if you own a boarding cattery, as this 'grey-area' could reduce your building costs considerably by removing the inspection fees and additional legal requirements

- If your building is subject to Building Regulations or Control, it is worth noting that **many of the prefabricated systems cannot achieve the necessary U values required!** One governing factor is the level of heat that will be used in the building. If this is below 25 watts per m², it might be below the requirement for Building Regulations

- The type of construction will determine what materials can be used for insulation. The following table shows some of the more common types of insulation used in brick/block type buildings

INSULATING MATERIALS

Insulating materials keep a building warm, but also help to keep it cool!

The most common materials used to provide insulation for walls, ceilings and floors are:

MATERIAL	THERMAL CONDUCTIVITY and DENSITY	
Glass fibre	0.04 W/m°C	12 kg/m³
Perlight	0.05 W/m°C	175 kg/m³
Polyurethane	0.032 W/m°C	30 kg/m³
Polystyrene	0.037 W/m°C	15 kg/m³
Cellular glass	0.04 W/m°C	135 kg/m³
Mineral fibre		16 kg/m³

It is easy to see how polystyrene and polyurethane are highly effective insulators; this combined with their low weight, makes them highly suitable for both wall, floor and roof insulation.

Generally, because of the higher insulation qualities of polyurethane insulation products, they don't require the thickness of mineral wool to achieve the same U-values. The mineral wool and polyurethane products tend to be the more common ones used in the UK. The type of insulation used will depend on the method of construction. All of the above systems are suitable for brick and block construction, which has a cavity between the inner and outer materials. Obviously, the better the insulation, the warmer/cooler the building will be.

However, for the majority of lightweight steel framed, UPVC and timber buildings, there is a limitation on the amount of insulation that can be used. This is partly due to their method of construction, and partly cost. This is something that should be considered when looking at the various types of prefabricated catteries that are available.

Insulation products not only help to keep the building **warm** during colder periods, they also **help to keep the temperature down** during hot periods.

This is something that cannot be overlooked. When it is cold, it is easy to turn on the additional heating that should be standard in every cattery. However, in hot weather it is extremely hard, particularly over short periods, to reduce the temperature. High temperatures can be more harmful to animals than cold.

A charity that had a newly installed timber cattery in 2002 (by a well known manufacturer) had to **resort to cutting out sections of the sleeping quarters in more than 40 cat units** *to provide more ventilation and reduce the internal temperature!*
The insulation installed by the manufacturer consisted simply of 2mm insulated wall lining paper – which would obviously have little effect on temperature control or reduction!

Cautionary Note:

Vermin: most rodents will attack polyurethane and polystyrene insulation. If you live in a rural location, or suffer from rodent damage, it will be better to use fibreglass as an insulating material, as this does not seem so attractive to rodents.

11 FINISHING MATERIALS

CHOOSING THE RIGHT FINISHING MATERIALS FOR YOUR CATTERY WILL MAKE CLEANING & MAINTENANCE SO MUCH EASIER

FLOOR FINISH CONSIDERATIONS

Any form of finish used in the cattery has to start with a suitable base (e.g. concrete, screed or suitably strengthened timber for certain types of finish).

The top-wearing finish has to be resistant to water, urine, faeces, disinfectant and durable, quick drying, long lasting and tough enough to withstand everyday wear and tear.

Main criteria when specifying flooring systems are:

- Hygiene
- Safety
- Durability
- Cost

Factors to be considered when choosing flooring:

- Cleaning
- Floor Slope

Note:

The use of drainage systems will need to be discussed with your local authority. It is not acceptable to have foul drainage that simply runs into the ground, without it being collected and channelled into a recognised system.

CLEANING SYSTEM COMPATIBILITY

Before you decide on the type of floor you wish to install, it would be wise to consider your cleaning regime.

The cleaning regime, the amount of water and the disinfectant used can all have an effect on the product over a period of time. There are arguments as to the best methods for cleaning animal buildings, and whether using large amounts of water provides the best solution.

Generally, most of the following products will be suitable for the majority of catteries and, providing they have been correctly installed, should provide an easy to clean and suitable surface. For rescue catteries, this particularly applies to sanctuaries that use large amounts of water and pressure washers. For further details see the chapter on Drainage, Kitchen, Cleaning and Disinfection Systems.

Incorrectly specified, a floor finish can, at the very least be aesthetically spoilt, or at the worst, destroyed.
Liquid will rot a timber cattery and timber door frames in a VERY short time!

Below: timber door frame rotting away due to hosing and cleaning

FLOOR SLOPE

If a floor is laid with a fall, this is normally achieved using a sand and cement screed over a concrete slab base. The final wearing/finishing material then covers the screed.

For floors to be self-draining (i.e. the water runs naturally into the drainage channel without too much mopping, etc) the fall must be a minimum of 1:60, and ideally 1:50

Obviously, the fall can be increased to create a more pronounced slope to provide better water run-off. However, this has to be set against the increased material and labour costs involved. Even with a fall of 1:60, some water will remain and may need to be mopped up.

The final choice of wearing surface is normally decided by finances, type of construction, method of construction (e.g. self-build or main contractor) and the amount of use the cattery will receive.

By approaching this decision with a flexible attitude, you should be able to specify the correct product for your requirements.

Undoubtedly, a cheaper product cannot be expected to last indefinitely, but as long as this has been taken into consideration and resources and time are made available to carry out any remedial works, this should not be a problem. However, in the case of a large animal welfare charity that operates at full capacity throughout the year, it is extremely difficult and time-consuming to have to empty and close down a cattery to carry out maintenance works.

The correct choice of suitable materials for your situation is probably one of the most important decisions you will have to make.

An incorrect choice can make life extremely difficult and expensive in the long-term with unplanned remedial works, floors that are unhygienic resulting in bad odours and damp conditions

FLOORING CHOICES

The common systems used in catteries are:

- Resin floor sealers and coatings, resin screeds

- Polymer, granolithic and concrete screeds

- Vinyl sheet

- Floor tiles

We will look at these floor finishes in detail on the next few pages.

My Recommendations for High Usage Catteries

The correct floor for your situation is an important decision that needs to be taken at an early stage. Flooring can improve the aesthetics, provide a more hygienic and easy-to-clean building. As there are so many choices, it is particularly important for catteries with high usage to make the right choice of flooring, one that will be able to cope with the wear and tear of cats, staff, cleaning routines and visitors.

My first recommendation for organisations with high usage would be vitrified tiles as being the most suitable as a long-term solution to the flooring problem. They stand the test of time, and when cleaned they look like new.

On opening a technical catalogue, it can seem a little daunting at first, with all of the R and V values for industrial and barefoot areas. Obviously there is always a compromise in terms of aesthetic qualities, cost and personal preference. However, at the time of writing, a tile with a R10 rating is a good all-round tile for the cattery environment.

For two rescue catteries and a veterinary hospital constructed in 2005; the tile that has been specified for all three projects was the 'Nature' floor range manufactured by Pilkington. This tile has been used by the charity for a number of years, and at the time of writing still offers a good compromise in terms of cost, durability and slip resistance. (This is a 300 x 300 x 9mm (12" x 12" x ½") tile which has a R10 rating)

My second recommendation for organisations with high usage would be vinyl
This is far cheaper than tiles to install, quicker to lay, can be coved up walls and also used on walls as a covering material. Most commercial vinyls have a 10 year guarantee.

Resin Floor Systems

Resin Floor sealers (50-100 microns):

These systems are the **minimum** required to satisfy the UK's CIEH and provide a non-porous, washable and hygienic surface. They can be either be water or solvent based. These systems are generally applied over concrete or sand/cement screeds to harden and reduce dusting. Unlike paint systems, these products produce a chemical reaction and are **bound into the matrix of the floor surface** giving a durable, hard-wearing and dust free surface. Advantages: easy, economical to apply, retards the penetration of water, oils etc. Disadvantages: will need subsequent applications.

Resin Floor Coatings (150-300 microns):

Unlike the floor sealers, these tend to be classified as paints and **remain on the surface** of the sub-base. These paint systems can be either single or two-pack applications, and come in a range of guises and colours. However, at present, I have to say that I am still extremely wary about using this type of product as it is **prone to failure** and requires **higher levels of maintenance** than Category 1 systems.

Resin High Build Coatings (300-1000 microns):

These have similar qualities to the coatings in Category 2. Obviously, the thicker finishes at 1000 microns will be more durable than 300 microns. Again, I would be **wary of using these** for the same reasons as shown in Cat. 2.

Resin Multi-Layer Coatings (>2 mm):

These multi-layers, also known as 'sandwich' systems have good slip resistance and a matt finish. They are the minimum requirement for use in a cattery to achieve a durable surface that won't require remedial works for a number of years.

Resin Flow Applied Flooring (2–3 mm):

Flow-applied coatings, or self-smoothing coatings are generally two-part systems. Although still relatively thin, they should last approximately 10 years before remedial work is required. The inclusion of a fine aggregate into the finished surface is something to consider; it will help prevent staff and visitors slipping. The coarseness of the aggregate is a personal decision, but my general guideline is to try and achieve a finish similar to that of orange peel. Too coarse, and it will hold the dirt and be difficult to clean, too fine and it will be of little benefit.

Resin Screeds (4-6 mm)

It is normal for a polyurethane screed to be laid to an average thickness of 4mm to 6mm, applied with a steel trowel. The **cost** for this type of screed starts to become noticeably more expensive compared with a coating. However, correctly installed, a polyurethane screed will provide a durable, hygienic finish and last for many years.

Advantages:

- Gives a seamless and hygienic finish
- Semi-gloss finish
- Full range of colours
- Cost-effective
- Slip-resistance (achieved by the number of back-rollering operations carried out)
- Fast installation
- Does not require the use of sealing coats, enhancing its durability

Disadvantages:

- Can look industrial
- The quality of the system and finish is highly dependent upon the quality of contractor. Also, the finish may vary throughout the building, even using the same contractor and product
- Limited durability. This is subjective and influenced by external factors such as correct preparation, product choice, cleaning regimes, use etc
- Unevenness in the underlying layer will reflect in the coating
- Can be damaged by hot/cold pressure washer
- Discolouration e.g. disinfectants/urine

Resin Flooring Classification:

Type	Description	Notes
FeRFA 1	Floor Seal	2 coats up to 150 micron final thickness
FeRFA 2	Floor Coating	2 or more coats at 100 micron each
FeRFA 3	High-build Floor Coating	2 or more coats at 300-1000 micron final thickness
FeRFA 4	Multi-layer Flooring	Floor coating or flow-applied, multi-layers to >2mm, aggregate dressing
FeRFA 5	Flow-applied Flooring	2-3mm thickness, self-smoothing, smooth or dressed surface
FeRFA 6	Screed Flooring	>4mm thickness, heavily filled, trowel finish, usually surface-sealed
FeRFA 7	Heavy Duty Flowable Flooring	4-6mm thickness, aggregate filled
FeRFA 8	Heavy Duty Screed Flooring	>6mm thickness, aggregate filled, trowel finished, system applied, impervious throughout
Federation Resin Flooring Association, UK		

Summary of Applied Resin Floor Systems.

These systems have many good features; they have been used extensively in factories, hospitals and breweries for many years and continue to be used. They have failed in cattery environments primarily because of incorrect specification. However, the new generation of polyurethane and epoxy products offer more flexibility and improved wear quality. They also appear to give better finished results without some of the main concerns and issues often associated with the early epoxy-based systems. The matt finish of many of these products is useful when considering the anti-slip properties of the floor. I now feel more comfortable in specifying these for use in animal accommodation.

A compromise system that has greater aesthetic qualities are the epoxy quartz products at around 4mm thickness , however, instead of using a epoxy seal (this can be affected by urine and disinfectants) use a polyurethane seal.

If you choose an applied finish, whether it is a simple paint or an expensive screed, these are some of the points you should consider:

■ Use a reputable company and ensure that they make a site visit to familiarise themselves with the particular project and any problems that might occur, (e.g. epoxy screeds do not allow for any movement, while polyurethane screeds have a small amount of flexibility). This is an important point, particularly when dealing with buildings that have shown signs of movement

■ Explain fully what the product is to be used for, and how much use it will receive. Obtain a written guarantee from the manufacturers stating that the recommended product will achieve the required standard

■ Ensure that the company visits the site to check that the substrate is suitable for their product

Polymer, Granolithic and Concrete Screeds

Polymer

Polymers are based on cement and selected aggregates with a liquid copolymer additive. They are better known for their applications for industrial situations, particularly in wet areas such as breweries and fish processing, and are not particularly well known in cattery applications.

Advantages:

- Can be laid as a thin screed

- Simple installation

- Jointless in small areas

- Anti-slip aggregates can be incorporated

- Resistant to oils and acids

- Suitable for wet environments

- Suitable for steam cleaning

- Range of colours

- Cost-effective

Disadvantages:

- The quality of the finish is dependent upon the operative to ensure a uniform finish.

- The cost can be greater than that for polyurethane screed products

SUMMARY

Although not widely used for catteries, it can be used to overcome problem or damaged areas.

Polymer has been used to overlay some damaged and rough concrete exercise runs, and it has proved to be extremely durable, easy to clean and has not discoloured or stained. From my experience with this product, I would use it again. **However, there are cheaper and more aesthetically pleasing products available!**

Granolithic

This is a natural material based on cement and selected aggregates; it is normally laid with a minimum thickness of 50mm. It is a durable and long-lasting surface. However with time, some dusting may occur. To prevent this and increase its durability an application of sodium silicate hardener is normally applied. Sprinkling the surface whilst still wet, with carborundum powder will add a degree of slip resistance. Its main use today is in commercial and industrial applications.

Advantages:

- Extremely durable and does not damage easily.

Disadvantages:

- **Cost -** High initial cost

- **Aesthetics** - As this is a cement based product, it has the same dull grey/brown colour as concrete

- **Quality -** In order to provide a satisfactory finish a high level of skill and supervision is required. It also requires careful attention to detail in order to prevent cracking and crazing at a later date

- **Porous -** Will need some form of sealing agent

- **Cost -** Similar to Polymer finishes

SUMMARY

Although it is used in industry, it has **little to offer the cattery owner.**
Its poor aesthetic qualities and specialist application has meant that alternative products have superseded it.

Concrete

Concrete is often laid as the finished or wearing material. Although it is a durable product, it still needs to have a sealing coat applied to prevent water and urine from soaking into the surface. **Concrete flooring without a sealing coat is unhygienic and if used daily, the unsealed concrete will never dry out properly**.

Advantages:

- Easy to install

- Cost-effective

- Readily available

- Will withstand heavy usage

Disadvantages:

- Is liable to crack over a period of time

- Poor aesthetic qualities

Tiles

An excellent material, especially for large or rescue catteries
When talking about tiles, we are only concerned with unglazed, vitrified (non-porous) tiles with low water absorption qualities to class BI.

The choice is critical in ensuring that the product is suitable for the environment it is to be used in. All ceramic tiles are manufactured from natural sources (i.e. clay, felspar and quartz) and have been used extensively in industrial, commercial and health care applications for many years. During the nineteen eighties there was a trend to use alternative, seamless finishes to improve the hygienic qualities, hence the increase in resin based systems. However with suitable grouting and disinfectants, any concerns relating to their use in animal accommodation and harsh environments are totally unfounded. Independent research carried out by Lancashire Polytechnic, and also by Campden Food and Drink Research Association has shown that floor and wall tiled surfaces have a biological integrity at least as good as competitive materials.

The standard sizes used are:

- 150mm x 150mm   (6" x 6")
- 300mm x 300mm   (12" x 12")

Tile Advantages and Disadvantages
Advantages:

- Uniform finish

- Durable and virtually maintenance free
  (Having specified tiles for use in animal buildings for over 20 years of constant daily wear, they still look pristine and remain hygienic, and I've never had to carry out any remedial works)

- Range of colours and slip-resistance

- Resistance to most acids and alkalis (all of the units I have installed with tiles have not suffered in terms of discolouration or staining; which cannot be said for epoxy-based systems)

- Highly suitable for hot water power-washing

- They are not affected by solar radiation, which means they are fade-resistant

- Simple installation, providing that the screed has been laid to a good standard

Disadvantages:

- High initial cost – particularly with an epoxy grout (however, this is not necessary for normal commercial and charity catteries)

- Slower installation times as compared with resin based systems

- High R and V values (slip-resistance and water displacement) can be difficult to clean (you will need to find a good compromise between slip-resistance and ease of cleaning)

Slip-resistance in Tiles
Some floors have higher risks of slipping on than others.

There are a number of contributing factors:

- Type of material used

- Presence of water, fats or disinfectants

- Physical movement in confined spaces

- Type of footwear used

All these matters will influence the slip-resistance of a floor.

At present only Germany has set standards of slip-resistance for floors in commercial, industrial and barefoot areas (barefoot area is a term used to describe wet areas such as showers, changing rooms etc). It is likely that this will become the standard used by all European Union countries in the near future.

The system used by the German government to **assess and measure the level of slip-resistance is known as the 'R-value'** for commercial and industrial uses, and A, B, or C value for barefoot areas. The higher this value, the more slip-resistance the tile has. The **capacity to displace water and dirt is measured and known as the 'V-value'**. The higher the V number, the greater the space between the studs (tiles with a studded profile). The values are V4, V6, V8 and V10. Obviously the greater the space between the studs and the deeper the profile, the greater the amount of water that can be dealt with before the floor becomes dangerous.

Slip-resistance in Commercial Applications:

SLIP ANGLE°	R-VALUE
From 3° to 10°	R – 9
From 10° to 19°	R – 10
From 19° to 27°	R – 11
From 27° to 35°	R – 12
More than 35	R – 13

Barefoot (Wet) Areas:

SLIP ANGLE°	V-VALUE
Minimum slip angle – 12°	A
Minimum slip angle – 18°	B
Minimum slip angle – 24°	C

Vinyl Sheeting

For cattery owners this is an excellent material.

The commercial quality sheets available have been used extensively in canteens, kitchens and hospitals for many years – and of course privately in the home. They are available in different grades, patterns and with varying degrees of slip-resistance, this being achieved by the use of profiles, or with silicon carbide and aluminium oxide particles incorporated within the finish.

Advantages:

- Enormous range of colours and textures
- Can be coved up the wall for improved hygiene
- Joints can be heat welded to form a continuous, hygienic and watertight finish – this should *always* be specified
- Warm and quiet
- Will feel familiar to cats if they have this flooring at home

Disadvantages:

- Can be damaged by sharp objects
- It melts on contact with cigarettes – but you should obviously not be smoking in a cattery anyway!

Vinyl sheeting has many applications for the cattery owner, it is aesthetically pleasing and extremely versatile, and can be coved to form hygienic and watertight junctions.

Note:

Vinyl is totally waterproof and can be pressure washed; some are also suitable for steam cleaning.

However, the type of cleaning needs to be identified at the outset to allow for heat welding of joints, suitable silicone sealing around doors etc, to prevent water from getting under the sheet.

Covings (Required for all Flooring Types)

All catteries should have a 'sealed' junction between the wall and floor sections.

This is normally achieved in one of five ways:

1. **Tiles**
   All manufacturers have floor systems that allow for the use of a sit-on, traditional flush fitting or flush-fit coved skirting, with internal and external angles. Providing the layout has been designed to accommodate these finishing pieces, they work extremely effectively. The finishing pieces can be expensive and care should be taken to ensure that they have been included with the main floor, and not looked upon as an extra
   Helpful hint:
   Ensure that the flooring contractor allows for the necessary expansion joints between the vertical/horizontal, and also in front of floor drainage channels

2. **Polyurethane**
   This system is extremely effective; it is basically a mixture of fine aggregates and epoxy resin, which is formed into a smooth, coved skirting, normally 50mm (2") high.
   It is a quick and relatively cheap system, can be retro-fitted to any floor, it is extremely durable, jointless and gives a professional finish

3. **Vinyl Skirting**
   If vinyl flooring is fitted, the most hygienic finish is to continue the flooring material up the wall, to a height of approximately 300mm (12"). At the junction of the wall and floor a preformed plastic cove is fitted to remove the 90° junctions
   Helpful hint: An alternative is to fit a plastic skirting. However, this is normally glued on and there is always a gap between the skirting section and the floor/wall

4. **Sand/Cement**
   Sand/cement can be used in a similar fashion to that of epoxy. It is easy to install, cost-effective and can be painted to give a more professional appearance. If you opt for this system, ensure that you use fine-grained sand, and add PVA to the mixture to ensure a smooth finish that is strong and waterproof

5. **Mastic Joint**
   The cheapest and most cost-effective option is to apply a mastic joint between the two surfaces. There are a number of suitable compounds available. However, I suggest that you opt for one of the hard-setting mastics. This is harder for the cats to claw out, but it will require **maintenance**

On the next page we can see some examples of different floor types and covings.

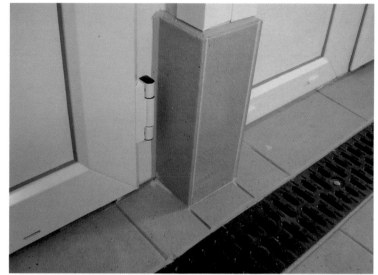

Above: tiled floors with tiled upstand and mastic joint

Above: polyurethane floor

Above: tiled floor

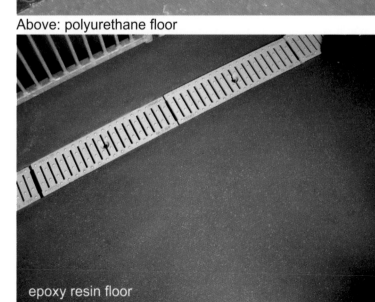

epoxy resin floor

tiled floor

Above: tiled covings to tiled floors

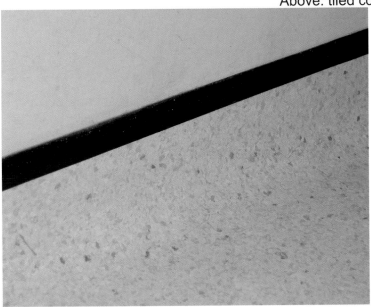

Above: vinyl sheeting

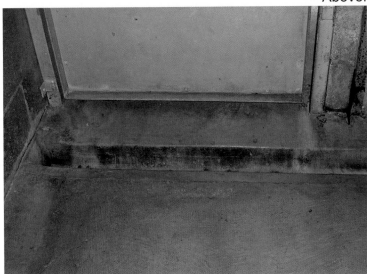

Newly laid concrete/granolithic flooring (left) and concrete flooring (right)

WHY FLOORS FAIL

The quality of the finished wearing surface is very much dependent on the quality and preparation of the sub floor and foundations. Any shortcut in these areas has the potential for failure of the building and floor system.

Failures in the foundations and floors are generally the most difficult and costly to remedy

Poor quality workmanship in floor screeds can have issues for the thinner-wearing surfaces such as vinyl. The thinner the wearing surface, the more noticeable any defects and variations will be.

Foundations

Any building requires foundations that are adequate to ensure its stability. Without suitable foundations, any building is liable to move over a period of time. It is essential for any permanent brick/block or concrete constructed building to have foundations which are suitable for the size and weight of the building and local ground conditions. It is important to take into account the amount of vegetation around the building, the proximity and type of trees, the type of soil and other issues such as old mine workings etc. Also the removal of large trees has a noticeable, long-term effect on local ground conditions.

On sites that have firm, shrinkable clay soil, it is not uncommon to find that foundations have to go down to a depth of 1 m (3'3") A local structural engineer is the best person to advise on the suitability of foundation types and depths. Any concrete slab base, even for lightweight timber units, should have a well consolidated base, and allowance made for expansion and contraction.

New concrete and screed bases

One of the main reasons for the failure of wearing finishes is moisture in the substrate. In order to prevent failure of the screed and wearing surface, it is essential that the substrate be allowed to dry out properly prior to the wearing surface being laid. The timescale required to reduce the level of humidity in the substrate will vary depending on the building design, the thickness of the slab, the ambient temperature, special concrete mixes etc.
The general guide time for drying is 1 day per millimetre of thickness of substrate.
On this basis, a concrete slab of 150mm/6" thickness with a 75mm/3" sand/cement screed could take 225 days.

Obviously, this is not practical for most construction projects. In extreme cases, the use of suppressants can be used. The general guide for the laying of finished products is to ensure that the substrate has a moisture level not exceeding 75% Relative Humidity. To ensure the RH levels, a Hygrometer should be used. The readings need to be taken over a 72-hour period to give an accurate result.

Damp proof membranes

All concrete bases should have an effective damp-proof membrane (DPM).
If you are carrying out remedial works to an older building, particularly one that has an agricultural history – check to see if it has a DPM. If in doubt, ask a local builder to carry out some investigative work to establish if one has been installed.

Movement

Any flooring product laid on a timber floor should allow for any flex or movement. A rigid screed won't allow for flex and will crack. Any limitations of a floor finish should be discussed with the manufacturer.

Contaminants

Any contamination in the substrate (this relates particularly to buildings that are being converted and adapted from previous uses) could affect the finished product. This needs to be checked with the contractor before any works commence, and the necessary corrective works employed.

Movement joints

Any movement in a building will cause the wearing finish to crack. In order to help combat this, movement joints need to be installed. The guideline is for a movement joint around the perimeter of the building and at 4500mm/15ft centres. This should be 6 mm (¼") wide and equal to the depth of the tile and bedding.

Screed thickness

The sub-screed needs to have an adequate depth and strength to support the imposed loads, and provide a suitable surface to lay tiles on.

Product not correctly specified

The correct specification for the environment the product is to be used in is essential.
This becomes critical if you need to use power washers and steam cleaning machines!

Temperature

Most of the resin-based systems require an environment that is dry, with a temperature of 15°C/59°F or above.
A reputable company will not lay these products if the environmental conditions are unsuitable.

Work quality

All of the above products require good quality workmanship to succeed.
It is essential that before the final wearing course is installed, you determine the quality of the concrete or screed sub-base. As previously mentioned, for the installation of vinyl finishes and thinner resin based systems (up to 6mm/¼") any undulations in the floor surface will show or could affect the quality or thickness of the final wearing surface. Obviously with a thicker screed finish of 12mm (½") any undulations can be disguised in the final finish.

During the installation of the sub-base,
and before the final wearing surface is laid,
use a straight edge to see how good the quality of the
workmanship is & how true and level the floor has been laid

Above: a well-laid floor (i.e.continuous fall without undulations)

Above: an incorrectly laid floor, showing a hollow in the corner of the run and consequently this is a urine/water trap

Above: the same incorrectly-laid floor as the below left photo. Water is running away from the drainage channel instead of towards it! The dry area in the foreground should be the 'lower' level and water should be draining towards you.

Time
spent
with cats
is
never
wasted

Sigmund Freud

WALLING CHOICES

Wall Finishes for Brick and Block Buildings

The range of products suitable for walls is virtually endless.

The primary aim of over-coating concrete block and cement based panel walls is to improve the hygienic qualities of the building, i.e. to prevent dirt, faeces, urine, and bacteria/viruses being ingrained in the open, porous nature of block.

The second benefit is to improve the aesthetic qualities of the building. Most concrete blocks tend to be dull grey or brown in colour, but with suitable finishes these can be dramatically improved.

Helpful Hints:

- If you are planning to apply a paint finish to concrete block work, ensure that you specify a high quality paint- grade block. A coarse, open textured block is not suitable for a paint finish; even with three or four coats, the open texture will be difficult to seal,and will not give a long lasting, pleasing appearance

- However, if you intend to apply ceramic tiles, then the cheapest block will be sufficient

The more common wall finishes are:

■ Masonry paint

■ Single or twin-pack epoxy or polyurethane systems

■ Rubber based paint

■ Standard paints

■ Plaster skim finish

■ Tiles

■ Cladding materials (e.g. vinyl sheeting or plastic boarding)

■ Engineering bricks

We will now look at these wall finishes in detail.

Masonry Paint

This is probably the cheapest system on the market that is suitable for both interior and exterior use in catteries. Most are water or acrylic based, easy to apply and can be applied during most conditions.

The large range of colours and types available enables you to choose a suitable product for either new or refurbishment work. If you opt for this system for interior use, ensure that you specify a smooth, sheen finish; this will make it far easier to clean.

Single and twin-pack epoxy/polyurethane paint

Like the floor coatings, the number of systems available in this category is immense, with a large number of companies all selling what appear to be the same product, and this is where the problems start. Most of these systems require a **higher level of application with better preparation and cleaning** than for masonry paints. Correctly specified, they provide a tough, hard wearing, chemically resistant finish. This category of finish has probably the greatest choice of colours. However, they are **more expensive** than many other paint systems.

Acrylated rubber

This product has been used extensively for industrial and commercial applications for many years. It is a single-pack system, for non-skilled application and is normally brush applied; it is **highly suitable** for damp environments and areas subject to frequent washing down. The range of colours is slightly limited, although it is sufficient for most situations. Unlike epoxy or polyurethane finishes, the surface is softer and **can be scratched** by persistent animals, although I have not found this to be of any major concern and any minor damage can easily be repaired.

It is an **expensive** product and has very **strong fumes** during application. It is not suitable for applying to a building that cannot be emptied of cats, due to the fumes. However, once dry, it is fine.

Standard decorating paints

The standard paints found in any DIY (do-it-yourself) store such as vinyl silk emulsion, eggshell and gloss are excellent products for use in the cattery. They are **easy to apply, cost-effective, and easy to maintain**.
They might not last as long as some of the more specialist paints. However, due to their relatively low cost and easy application, it is simple to redecorate when they become scuffed. Most are water-based and do not give off strong fumes during application. This makes them more suitable to apply in buildings that already have cats in them.

SUMMARY OF APPLIED WALL FINISHES
You should ensure that whatever system you choose is suitable for your requirements. I would strongly advise against using a new product from an unknown company. **Remember that when the time comes for redecorating, you need to be able to purchase the same product as you originally used.**
Most of the professional paints are based on a system of application, i.e. matching primers and undercoats with two or three topcoats; they have been designed as a system, and are therefore not suitable for mixing and matching.

Something I cannot emphasise enough,
is that whatever system you use,
always remember to keep the data sheets
or record of the product!

Single-pack epoxy/polyurethane paint

Plaster Skim Finish

This finish, which is normally seen in domestic houses can give an excellent finish to concrete block walls. This will give a uniform, home-like finish, which will need to be decorated in order to seal it and provide a finished system.

Clearly, this has a cost implication attached to it.

If you want to use pressure washers or large volumes of water; this is not a suitable finish for you.

Photograph:

The below photograph shows a plaster wall finished with emulsion paint.

Tiles

Unlike floor tiles, which are designed to withstand far higher forces and damage, wall tiles are quite fragile. Most people are aware of the standard type of wall tiles available in the DIY stores.

The most popular sizes used are:

- 150mm x 150mm   (6" x 6")
- 200mm x 100mm   (8" x 4")
- 200mm x 200mm   (8" x 8")

Wall tiles can have gloss or matt finishes.

Cladding finishes

There are some excellent materials available for cladding, e.g. vinyl sheeting, plastic cladding, resin bonded boarding. In order to prevent ingress of water and urine, these materials generally need to be professionally fixed and sealed.

Engineering bricks

This is an alternative to applied finishes. This system gives a durable finish that does not require any future maintenance. Obviously, if you opt for this system it needs to be identified at the outset of the contract. Generally, engineering bricks are used to construct division walls due to their smooth, easy to clean finish, but they can also be used throughout the entire building if required. The choice of colours in engineering bricks is limited (e.g. beige, red or blue tend to be the standard colours). This might seem rather drab, but with suitable floor and wall finishes above the engineering brick it can work extremely well. In order to prevent staining of the mortar, a waterproofing agent will need to be added during the construction stage; an alternative is to paint the joints with a clear epoxy sealer.

Cautionary Note:

If you choose this system, be aware particularly when constructing single skin walls, that **only one face will be true and smooth**. Bricks are not totally square and symmetrical, each will have small variations. Although this can be evened out by the mortar joint, the other face will be slightly more irregular.

This leaves you with two options: either you accept this, or you construct a wall two bricks deep (225mm/9") by placing bricks back-to-back (irregular sides together), giving you two even outer faces

CATTERY PARTITIONS

Metalwork

All wire caging systems used for commercial catteries and welfare centres should ideally be constructed from metal, glass or a hard plastic; the use of timber is not recommended unless some form of impervious material protects it.

General Mesh Specification

The design and specification is really your choice, but as a general guide – the recognised **standard size** is for 25mm x 25mm (1" x 1") box section with a 25mm x 25mm x 2.6mm (1" x 1" x 12 gauge) weld mesh infill. The UK's CIEH guidelines give a mesh size of 25 x 25mm x 1.60mm (1" x 1" x 16 gauge). However, this mesh gauge is **extremely thin**, and although it will keep a cat secure it will **bend and distort very easily**.

The reason for using a mesh width of 25mm/1" or less is purely for one of safety.

Kittens and very small cats can squeeze their heads through any mesh with an aperture wider than 25mm (1"). Clearly if a kitten has climbed to the top of the door and managed to squeeze its head through the mesh, it can be difficult for it to escape – and the consequences can be fatal.

Larger Mesh Specification

Some manufacturers offer a larger mesh size of 75-100mm x 25mm (3-6" x 1" x 10 gauge). **This larger size makes it easier to see into the cat unit, and does not look as heavy.** This is my preferred choice! In the photographs below, you can clearly see the difference the mesh can make.

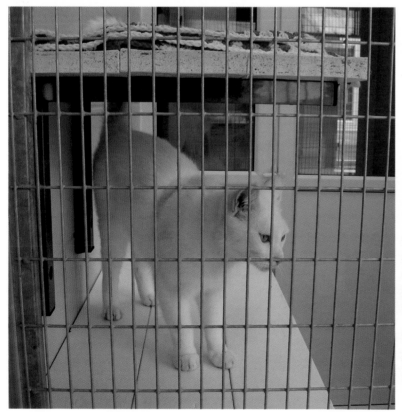

Easy to see through 75 x 25mm (3" x 1")   Not so easy to see through 25 x 25mm (1" x 1")

The systems generally used are:

- Plain metal with a paint finish
- Metal that has been hot dipped galvanised
- Stainless steel
- UPVC

Metal with paint finish, showing rust and wear

Stainless steel

Powder coated

Plain Metal with Paint Finish (shown above left)

Clearly this will be the **cheapest** system in the short term. New metal that has had a coloured paint finish looks bright, clean and gives a professional appearance – the normal paints used are Galvafroid or Hammerite. However, **once in use these finishes do not last**, particularly on the lower sections, these being the areas that receive the most damage from mops, brushes and disinfectants. After a short period of time the metal will have heavy rust deposits, be **unhygienic**, have **poor aesthetic qualities** and will **require remedial work**. This is where it becomes **expensive** in time and labour, once **rust** has taken hold, it will only be a matter of time before you need to replace it.

Stainless Steel (shown above middle)

This material is **more expensive** than galvanised systems, on average around 20% more. However, it is a **highly suitable product for catteries**. The major difference between stainless steel and galvanised steel is that there is no protective barrier to break down; stainless steel is a metal that is **resistant to rusting**. Of all the systems it is the **most expensive**, is possibly the **most hygienic**, has the **best aesthetic qualities** and does not have a coating that can break down. Stainless steel is often used in veterinary hospitals and hospital type caging systems for the doors. There are companies in the UK that use electro-polished stainless steel as their standard product for doors etc. It is well worth investigating and comparing costs against galvanised steel.

Powder Coated (shown above right)

A spray-applied finish available in any colour which looks good, but it will eventually chip and flake off in heavy duty areas. It should always be **applied over galvanised metalwork** to ensure that rusting doesn't take place.

Hot Dipped Galvanised Steel (shown opposite page, both photographs)

Galvanising is a process where all the frames and gates are dipped into a tank containing molten liquid zinc. This forms a chemical bond with the metal, which ensures a protective, durable coating. This coating, provided it is not broken, will last for many years without showing any signs of deterioration (I have seen metalwork that has been galvanised, some over 20 years old and still in perfect condition!).

It is the most cost-effective, long-term system available.

Cattery Partitions – Panels (Sneeze Barriers)

Your aim is to ensure each cat unit is totally self-contained and that there are no gaps between different units – to prevent cross-contamination.

Cattery Dividing Panels and Partitions (Sneeze Barriers)

The aim of any panel dividing cat units is to provide security, is hygienic and easy to clean – and equally important it provides the cat with an area s/he feels secure in, and not overlooked by cats in the adjoining units as this can cause a great deal of stress. These solid dividing panels not only act as the physical 'walls' that create the unit structure, but also act as sneeze barriers; (partitions are called 'sneeze barriers' because they help control minute airborne particles produced when a cat sneezes. Respiratory diseases of the cat are common, and all efforts must be made to reduce the risk).

There should be NO DIRECT CONTACT between cats from different households!
This means that PANELS BETWEEN different cat units should be SOLID (e.g. not open mesh)

The more common systems used are:

- Glass

- UPVC

- Painted brick and block

- Resin bonded plywood, faced with a GRP coating

- Plywood with vinyl sheeting

- Fireproof board (e.g. Masterboard, Fermacell which will still need to be painted to seal the porous texture)

- Plastic cladding or panelling

You can see photographs of different variations of these systems on the next few pages.

All of the above systems will provide the qualities required in a cattery. Decisions on which cattery panel options can be down to purely personal preference, the design and construction method of the building (e.g. gaining as much natural light as possible), or the business image to be portrayed. All of the systems are readily available, some are more easily fixed and make the more suitable for a competent handy person to install. The dividing panels or walls can be a mixture of solid and glass, or just solid. Panels of glass do not provide privacy.

Whatever the final solution, it should allow the cats areas of privacy, with solid panels or obscured glass

Glass

The increase in use of UPVC for catteries has lead to a greater use of glass as dividing panels, doors etc. It is also becoming more widely used in all cattery buildings including lightweight steel-framed and masonry built.
It is interesting to speak to owners who have this type of system. The general feeling is that catteries with glass partitions and doors tend to be cleaned more thoroughly and regularly than those with open mesh panels!

However, the panel should not be fully glazed, as it affords little privacy to the cats - which will be a problem for the more nervous, or those who dislike other cats.

Helpful Hints:

- Cattery doors – Most doors are approximately 760mm/30" wide and open outwards. This provides ease of access without being too large, and allows easy access into the sleeping and exercise areas

- Ensure a small gap is left under the front door panel, approximately 5mm (3/16ths") so that wash-down water can run freely into the drainage channel

- When fixing doorframes into brickwork, particularly at 100mm/4" thick, ensure the frame is measured to fix into the centre of the wall to prevent crumbling or damage to the bricks

- If you use one of the cement-based boards, it will need to be decorated with the minimum of a vinyl silk emulsion paint to seal the material

UPVC (Unplasticised Polyvinyl Chloride)

The use of this product has risen noticeably over recent years, particularly for commercial catteries and charities. Its uses are pretty much limitless, ranging from doors and partitions, right through to complete catteries. The doors and partitions can have a mix of infill types such as glass, mesh or combinations of both.
However, the size of any mesh infill should be the same as previously mentioned in the metalwork section.

Unit using glass and UPVC

Above: steel and glass panels/partitions/doors

Cats will be less stressed if there is privacy and somewhere they can hide from a neighbouring cat if required

Above: Trespa Meteon board and glass

Privacy

The above photograph show a mixture of glass and solid panels to provide a more private area for the cats.

Left: dividing block wall with obscure glass window to allow more natural light to pass between adjoining pens

Above: blue engineering brick with plastic screen

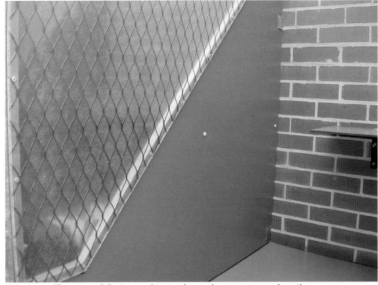

Above: Trespa Meteon board and opaque plastic

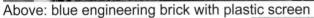

There should be
NO DIRECT CONTACT
between
cats from different
households!

ROOF COVERINGS

Natural daylight, heating, artificial lighting and ventilation are all an integral part of any building design, each dependent upon the other.

Generally, in catteries the light comes through roof lights and mid to high level windows.

The advantage of economy from natural lighting
(e.g. roof lights) has to be balanced against
the disadvantages of poor thermal and sound insulation, solar
heat gain and fire hazard associated with the materials

However, the glazing should be of sufficient area to provide suitable and adequate daylight to give uniformity to the working area.

Animal buildings with excessive areas of single glazed roof lighting can give rise to higher levels of solar gain during the summer months; this can be a major concern for any cattery owner. Obviously, having a dark building is not the answer!

UK Tip:

The CIEH suggest that the temperature should be a minimum of 10°C/50°F and a maximum of 26°C/79°F. In the UK over the past few years we have experienced **temperatures exceeding the maximum for prolonged periods** during the summer months.

Cautionary Note:

Once the ambient temperature reaches these high levels, older, poorly insulated, badly ventilated buildings with large areas of single glazed roof lights will be noticeably affected by solar gain
(like leaving a car with all windows closed in strong sunlight),
often resulting in highly distressed cats... or even worse

Roof Materials

The type of material used will depend on the construction method and cattery style and type.

In addition, if the building is subject to Building Regulations/Control, you will have to prove that the materials used reach the criteria for U-values (the rate at which heat is transferred through an element of a building).

If the building does not have to comply with Building Regulations/Control, there are more options available. However, it must be remembered that insulation works both for cold climates in retaining heat, and also in hot climates to prevent an excess of heat build-up.

Two main types of roofing for traditional type construction are:

■ Slate and tiles

■ Profiled sheet coverings

We will look at these in detail below and on the next page.

Slate and Tiles

Traditionally, roofs on smaller buildings were constructed using either slate or concrete tiles. The coverings are fixed to timber roof trusses or purlins (roof structure), with pitches of at least 22°. For aesthetic qualities, and areas with particular planning restraints, these materials are still used for traditionally constructed buildings.

The covering materials are generally poor insulators against transfer of heat. This problem has been overcome by the use of insulating materials such as glass-fibre matting and expanded PVC, the insulation is laid between the ceiling joists.

This insulating layer will act to reduce the heat loss from the building to the roof space, and also reduce the heat gain from the roof space into the building. These finishes are normally associated with traditionally constructed buildings.

Profiled Sheet Coverings

The advantage of steel as a material for roof covering is its favourable strength-to-weight ratio and ductility, make it both practical and economic to use. The other main advantage of this type of covering is the lower pitches that it can be laid at, e.g. 5°. The roof is normally a sandwich construction, with the insulating material between the outer top sheet and an inner lining sheet. The insulation thickness ranges from 40mm/1½" to 100mm/4".

The sheets come in many styles, profiles, materials and most importantly, colours. Most have a lifespan in excess of 40 years, with the major manufacturers giving a 30 year guarantee.

Note:

Any 'sandwich' roofing system should be certificated to its fire safety properties. Many of the larger UK companies will provide roofing systems that come with a Loss Prevention Certification Board (LPCB) LSP1181 test certificate

Profiled Sheet Materials

- **Hot-dipped galvanised**
  This is a method of applying a coating of zinc to the sheet as a protective barrier against the elements. The disadvantage of this sheet is that it is only available in one finished colour, silver/grey, which tones down over a period of time to a dark grey

- **Plastic coated steel sheets**
  Most plastic coated steel sheets look very much the same. However, the quality of the coating and the types of coating vary enormously, and this results in varying lifespans and costs. It is important to realise the type of coating the sheet has. The coating serves two purposes; it provides an additional protective barrier, and also introduces a wide range of colours to the standard sheets. The effects of ultra-violet radiation will gradually bleach the pigment in the coating over a period of years

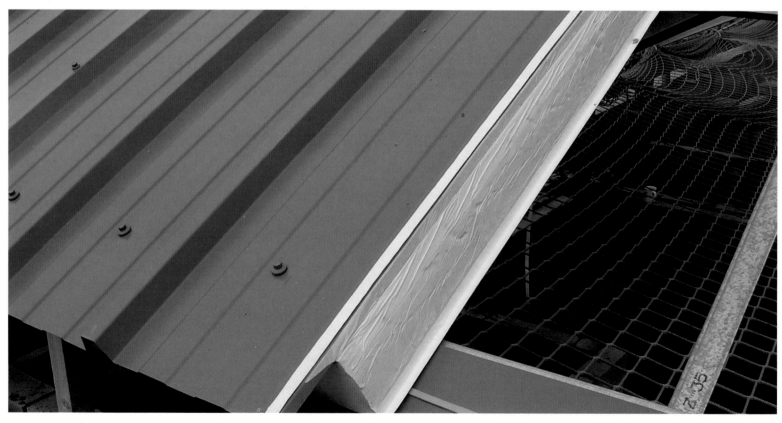

Cement sheets

Often incorrectly referred to as asbestos roof sheeting.

The sheets are made from a mixture of natural fibres with alternating layers of cement and water. The wet mixture is then rolled flat or formed into corrugated sheets and steam cured to harden it. These cement sheets are used extensively for agricultural, storage and industrial buildings.

During recent years, the introduction of colour coatings has improved the aesthetic quality of this system and made it more acceptable as a form of roof covering for smaller buildings.

Note:

Cement sheets once contained asbestos fibres. However, since March 1998, all new, British made roofing sheets are asbestos-free. The use of asbestos is now illegal. Sheets manufactured before this date will contain approximately 12% of white asbestos. This point should be taken into consideration if demolitions have to be undertaken.

If asbestos is discovered, then expert advice should be sought, this will take into account the Health and Safety aspect and the legal requirement for the removal and disposal.

Generally, the only time problems arise with asbestos sheeting is either when demolition is considered, or repairs are to be carried out. If the sheeting is secure and in good condition, it can be left in place.

Warning:

- If you use a single sheet system, without any form of insulation, be prepared for both hot and cold temperatures in the cattery

- Single skin metal roofing is extremely noisy when it rains or hailstones!

- Beware of using suspended ceiling tiles in a grid system to any indoor section of the cattery. Even with the tiles clipped in place, a nervous cat can always squeeze under the tile and into the roof void!

Exercise Run Coverings

All materials are used to obtain the maximum transmission of light (e.g. glass, and flat or profiled transparent or translucent sheets) but offer little resistance to the transmission of sound or heat.

The main systems used for prefabricated roof lights to the exercise runs are:

Glass

- This is the traditional material for roof lights. If you look at most old industrial buildings, it is almost certain that glass sheet fixed in metal frames was the system used

- Glass has poor mechanical strength and therefore requires the strength of metal glazing bars, set comparatively close together. Today, the main use of glass is for smaller, preformed dormer type double glazed window units. These provide excellent light and ventilation levels

Profiled sheeting

- **UPVC**
  This is one of the **cheapest** of the translucent plastic materials used for roof lights. It has **reasonable light transmission** (77%), **reasonable impact and scratch resistance**. On exposure to solar gain, it has a useful life expectancy of around 25 years

  However, it will **discolour with age** to give a yellow/brown colour. Over this period the **light transmission will be markedly reduced**. It tends to become very **brittle** after a short period and can **crack** very easily if walked on to carry out maintenance

- **GRP**
  Glass reinforced plastic – similar to UPVC in terms of appearance, impact resistance and strength, however it **does not have the light transmittance of UPVC**, with only 50%-70%

- **Polycarbonate**
  Is generally manufactured as double, triple or five-walled systems. It has **good light transmittance** (88%), is **extremely strong and durable** and has **good weathering qualities**. It is the **most expensive** of the plastic materials used, and is often used in situations where glass would be damaged

  Its main use is in domestic conservatories and is available in either **clear or bronzed** tint finish. The installation of a twin/triple wall system with a bronze tint or heat shield coating will help reduce solar gain, and provide a more controllable working environment. **It is highly useful as a covering over exercise runs**

Obviously the roof structure to the main sleeping area needs to be fully insulated, to prevent condensation/heat loss during the winter & solar gain during the summer

The roof structures of most animal buildings consist mainly of solid roof materials, e.g. tiles, high performance boarded roofing membranes or profiled sheet with the inclusion of a few rooflights to allow some natural light in.

However, it is the exercise run roof covering (whether this is an integral part of the building as used by most charities, or a freestanding structure as is the norm for most boarding catteries) that tends to be the area of concern to most owners.

Because of the general use of single skin products, the extremes of weather are most noticeable in the exercise runs, i.e. too hot during the summer months. Generally the problems associated with high temperatures are more difficult to correct than those with low temperatures.

Note:

The UK's CIEH guidelines state that all exercise runs must have a welded mesh under-covering to the translucent sheet for safety reasons. This should be discussed before carrying out this work. The reasoning behind this guideline is one of security. However, with suitable roof covering products that have a lifespan in excess of 10 years, this is not necessary. The wire mesh makes it impossible to clean, is an additional expense, and does not look aesthetically pleasing.

Cats Protection, National Cat Centre

Many older timber cattery manufacturers installed very cheap roof sheeting that became brittle after a period of two to three years, hence this requirement.

The methods commonly used are:

- Single solid sheet material, e.g. metal/cement roof sheet

- Single skin transparent GRP

- Part solid and part translucent single sheeting

- Multi-wall polycarbonate system

- Twin sheet system with the inclusion of insulation

Single Solid Sheet

Advantages

- Cost-effective and easy installation

Disadvantages

- Can be affected by extremes of temperature in certain locations

- Metal sheeting increases noise reverberation

- Can make the building dark in certain locations

Single sheet translucent sheeting

Advantages

- Cost-effective and easy installation

Disadvantages

- Can be affected by extremes of temperature in certain locations

- Does not provide areas of shade for the cat

Part solid – part translucent (single)

Advantages

- Cost-effective

- Easy installation

- Provides shade for the cat

- Is generally an acceptable form of covering for most situations

Disadvantages

- Can be affected by extremes of temperature in certain locations

- Can be noisy when it rains or with hailstones

Polycarbonate Multi-wall System

Advantages

■ Relatively easy installation

■ Excellent insulator and will provide protection from solar gain, particularly sheeting with a heat shield or bronzed tint finish

■ Extremely strong and durable

■ Has a smooth finish that makes it easy to clean

Disadvantages

■ More expensive than single sheet systems, however, the long-term cost benefits are considerable

Twin sheet system with insulation

Advantages

■ Excellent insulator providing protection from solar gain

■ The lining sheet can be a waterproof board, i.e. master board with the insulation sandwiched between the lining and top sheet, or an acoustic board/tile forming a false ceiling. This will provide a smooth, easy-to-clean finish within the exercise runs, as well as providing protection from solar gain

Disadvantages

■ Expensive to install

Helpful Hints:

If you have an existing cattery with large areas of translucent sheeting, and experience problems with excessive heat during the summer months – then you need to take action.

The normal method is to paint over some of the roof lights with a white or solar reflective paint.

Although this is only a temporary measure, it will rectify a major problem for a while. A more expensive measure is either to replace some of the sheeting with solid/insulated boarding, or to spray/paint one of the specialist solar reflective coating products over the top.

Summary

The multi-wall polycarbonate coverings offer the most long-term advantages for the cattery owner

ENVIRONMENT CONTROL

LIGHTING, HEATING, COOLING AND FRESH AIR PROVIDE SIGNIFICANT BENEFITS TO CATS, STAFF & CLIENTS

ENVIRONMENT CONTROL

In this chapter, we look at the environment within the cattery building, using:

- ◼ Lighting

- ◼ Heating and cooling systems

- ◼ Ventilation

- ◼ Risk of disease (increasing/reducing factors)

- ◼ Condensation/dehumidification

LIGHTING

A cattery with lots of natural daylight and sunlight will always feel more inviting.

Lighting is a major use of electricity, second only to water and space heating. Therefore consideration should be given to the type and amount installed with provision for flexibility.

Daylight & Sunlight

Clearly, the amount of natural daylight entering the building will have a marked effect on the amount of artificial lighting required. Whatever form of lighting is provided, it has to be adequate for safe and effective working at any time of the day or night. Recent advances in lighting technology can give energy savings of approximately 30%, especially when compared with installations over 10 years old. Sunlight is also a natural killer of viruses and bacteria.

Internal Lighting

Consideration should be given to ensure that you have suitable working light for cleaning, disinfecting and daily routines. Of all systems available, fluorescent tubes are regarded as being the most suitable for the majority of animal accommodation. They range from 1200mm/4ft to 2400mm/8ft and come in either single or double fittings, are low maintenance, cost-effective and with an operating life of 5,000-15,000 hours. The fittings can have integral emergency lighting if required. Fluorescent fittings with 2D fittings (low energy) provide supplementary lighting and offer the most flexible of systems. The 2D fittings are generally of the 'bulkhead' type and are often used in individual cat units, or as illumination for open walkways.

Helpful Hints:

- If you specify fluorescent tubular lighting, it is well worth spending a little extra to purchase the dust/vapour proof enclosed unit. Apart from being easier to clean, this type of unit will withstand being splashed by over-enthusiastic staff using hose-pipes!

- Change to the new smaller 26mm/1½" diameter tubes. The older 38mm/1" are approximately 8% more expensive to run. The new 26mm tubes will fit into your existing holders without modification

- Replace existing starters with new electronic units to ensure a flicker-free start-up, and reduce wear

- Fluorescent fittings with high frequency ballast are the most efficient. Although more expensive to buy, they have energy cost savings of around 15%

External Lighting

There should be suitable amenity lighting for external walkways, car parking etc.

HEATING AND TEMPERATURE

The key word is 'flexibility'- choose the system that is right for your requirements and level of use.

The CIEH recommend a cattery temperature of between 10°C/50°F to 26°C/79°F. Depending on the size of the building, its insulation qualities and the time of the year it is in use, all of these factors will affect the type of heating system you install.

Temperature regulations for other countries:

- UK Quarantine   7°C   (44° F – No maximum given)
- Missouri, USA   10–29.5°C   (50–85° F)
- Colorado, USA   10–32.2° C   (50–90° F)
- Australia   15–27°C   (59–80° F)
- New Zealand   15°–22° C   (59–72° F)

The decision on what type of heating system to install in the cattery needs to be taken at an early date. It is often dictated by the services available locally, (e.g. mains gas) the type and design of the building (e.g. outdoor or indoor cattery). In older properties, the heating is often one of the last items to be upgraded, frequently relying on infrared heat lamps, or the occasional floor-standing electric fan heater. It is not always the cost of upgrading these systems that prevents the work from being carried out; often it can be the problem of choosing the most suitable system.

Whichever system is used, it must be convenient, have a suitable service back-up, be adequate for the purpose it is intended for, and easy to use. It is pointless having a complicated system that the staff are afraid of, or do not understand.

It is also worth considering the amount of use the heaters will receive. If for an isolated building that is only used for a few weeks a year, then an expensive boiler-fired heating system will not be the most cost-effective or suitable.

Heating systems commonly in use:

- Infrared heat lamps

- Electric fan heaters

- Quartz halogen heaters

- Night storage heaters

- Boiler-fired high level fan convectors

- Domestic radiators or tubular heating pipes

- Underfloor heating (electric and wet system)

- Solar energy

- Air conditioning

- Heat recovery

We will look at these in detail on the next few pages.

Infrared Heat Lamps

This system uses several types of bulb, such as red heat bulbs, ceramic heat lamps and dull emitter bulbs. Since the heat is radiant, the animals feel the warmth immediately. All have been around for a long time and are still commonly used for cats, dogs, poultry and particularly pigs. The infrared rays given off are similar to those given off by the sun.

The **advantages** of this system are that it is relatively cheap to install, simple to use, and cost-effective when used in small numbers. The lamps are designed to provide a direct heat over the animal, they do not provide an effective level of warmth to the building or room. Most charities tend to use them for young or frail cats as a backup to the main heating system.

If you choose to install this system, ensure you use the ceramic or dull emitters, they are far safer and stronger than the red bulb variety, which tend to explode when splashed with water. All electrically operated equipment needs to be correctly installed at high level, out of the animal's reach and to have a suitably protected electrical supply.

The disadvantages of using heat lamps are:

- They do not provide the 'luxury' image that today's market is demanding

- They make for buildings that are cold to work in (it is only the cat that receives the warmth in the sleeping area)

- There is a danger of scalding the cat if the lamp is too close. This is the reason why heat lamps cannot be used in penthouse style units - the lamp needs to be at least 1m/3ft higher than the cats

Electric Fan Heaters

Unlike infrared heaters, an electric fan convector is suitable for room heating, particularly for large areas. The industrial varieties come in a range of powers from 2kw to 25kw. They are usually wall or ceiling mounted, simple to use, normally with a built-in thermostat and provide instant heat.
The **disadvantage of these units is the cost of running them**; four heaters at 6kw each are extremely expensive to run. However, for buildings that are used only intermittently, they are highly suitable.

Quartz Halogen Heaters

These units are often specified where there is a need for localised heat or immediate warmth. They are commonly used in industrial and commercial applications in premises that are lightly constructed, naturally cold and have poor insulation. They are also used in large buildings, which need to have only a small area heated. They normally come in 1.5kw-4.5kw loading per unit.

The same warnings apply to all forms of electric heating used in a potentially wet or damp environment; they must be correctly installed by a qualified electrician and have suitably protected circuits.

Night Storage Heaters

A modern night storage heater is slim at not more than 170mm/7" deep, and an efficient form of room heating. These appliances are cost-effective, being charged during the night on cheaper electricity; controllable and correctly sized they can give off high levels of heat. For certain applications, they are highly recommended, **advantages** are when used in staff rooms, and rooms that house perishable goods that need to be kept damp free. They can be used in the cattery environment **providing** you can raise them off the floor by approximately 300mm/12", to prevent water and urine from corroding them. The **disadvantages** associated with them in a cattery environment are that during the early evening when it starts to get cold the heaters are losing their heating capacity; they will not be recharged until after 12.30 am. Without any additional form of heating, this could lead to the **building being too cold** for a period of time. For this system to work cost-effectively, you will need an 'off-peak' (white meter) electricity supply.

Boiler-fired High Level Fan Convectors

These units are normally found in industrial units, warehouses and large areas that require a good level of heating. Unlike electrical fan convectors, these units require a boiler, either gas or oil fired as they operate on high temperature hot water. They have a finned tubular heating element, with a fan to improve the circulation of warm air. In addition to providing heat, they can also be used during the summer months as a cooling fan. The important point to remember when specifying such units is to **check the level of noise** they produce when working; you need the quietest unit available. Some people are concerned about the possibility of dust, germs, air-borne viruses etc being blown through the building with this type of system. I have to say that I haven't found this to be problem. However, it is far more suspect as a source of **possible disease spread** than a still air system.

Domestic Radiators

Most modern panel radiators are constructed using light gauge steel, pressing-welded together. Heavy cast iron units are also available and are used extensively in homes and offices. Radiators, like boiler-fired fan convectors, require some form of boiler to provide the necessary hot water for them to operate. An alternative to radiators is tubular heating pipes. These are normally 50mm/2" diameter and extremely durable. However, they have the disadvantage of not being aesthetically pleasing. The other concern is if they are mounted at low level, there is a risk of cats, particularly small kittens and nervous cats trapping their legs behind the pipes if they do not have a protective cage over them.

It is normal practice to install radiators at low level, as in a domestic house.

For a cattery, the radiators should be lifted slightly higher above the floor than normal (approx 400mm/16-18") to prevent the base from rusting from urine or cleaning/disinfection.

The advantages of radiant heat are:

- Gives a greater feeling of warmth with a lower air temperature; this achieves about a 15% saving in fuel costs

- A system that any heating engineer is familiar with

- It warms the whole area of the building where used, making it more pleasant to work in and visit

Underfloor Heating (Electric and Wet System)

There has been a significant increase in the use of underfloor heating (UFH) in recent years. This is because of cost, easier installation, improved product quality, aesthetic qualities (it is hidden) and cheaper running costs. It is not a new technology, as the Romans pioneered its use!

There are two main types of system, either warm water flowing through pipes, or electric cables. Underfloor heating can be used throughout the entire building, or be a hybrid system using underfloor and radiators or electric heating in less frequently used buildings.

Electric

Underfloor heating has a higher capital cost than most other forms of electric heating; however correctly installed, it should last for many years without requiring maintenance. This system normally comes as sealed pads of varying sizes or lengths of insulated cable in a mesh mat, laid to the required areas. The low running costs make them highly cost-effective, with the added flexibility to select small areas where the heat is required.

Wet system

It was during the 1960's that underfloor heating became popular for a short while using copper and steel pipes with hot water running through them, from an oil/gas fired boiler. This system did not last for long; it proved to be unreliable, difficult to maintain and had to be run at extremely high temperatures, particularly with poorly insulated buildings.
Since then it has evolved considerably with the use of polyethylene and aluminium pipes and better-insulated homes.

Advantages:

- Aesthetically pleasing, with no obvious source of heat

- Low running costs, with savings of over 15% compared with radiator systems

- The heat is distributed evenly across the floor, this helps to dry the floor extremely quickly

- No moving parts

- The electric systems are easy to install and are suitable for a competent handyman/do-it-yourself enthusiast

- No air being moved or pushed around by fan convectors; some consider this the most beneficial advantage (e.g. less risk from airborne diseases such as cat flu)

Disadvantages:

- Higher capital costs to install

- The floor needs to be well insulated to provide an effective output

- The system is less responsive to changes in ambient temperature. For buildings that are in constant use throughout the winter months, this is not an issue. However, it takes longer to bring the room up to the required temperature, and, consequently it takes longer to cool down. This is because it heats up the concrete base, which has a dense thermal mass

- Most of the electric systems cannot be run on cheap off-peak electricity

Helpful hints for underfloor heating:

- Leave approximately 30% of the sleeping area free of heating. This allows the cat some freedom to choose either a warm or slightly cooler area

- Ensure that you have detailed drawings of the areas covered by the cables or pads. This might be extremely useful for the any future works that might be carried out, particularly if fixing new metalwork to the floor

- Check with the manufacturer that it is suitable for the wearing surface you plan to lay (e.g. vinyl)

- If installed with a tiled finish, ensure that the adhesive and grout are compatible

- Check on the guarantee of the pipe if you install a wet system. Most of the reputable companies offer a 50 year guarantee, however this needs to be in writing!

- Use the manufacturer's design service. This is normally part of the package if you purchase a wet system

- The wet systems work best with modern, condensing boilers

Solar Energy

Although this has been used in larger-scale catteries, there is no reason why it should not be used anywhere. It has certainly gained prominence for the domestic market, and is normally associated with providing hot water. Like all things, the cost of installation has to be weighed against the time it takes to pay back the initial costs. It is worth looking at what government grants are available. A conventional system uses solar collectors, through which water is circulated, heated and then piped to a well-insulated storage tank. The solar panels are normally sited on the roof of the building, although they can be mounted in any convenient location.

Mechanical Ventilation with Heat Recovery (MVHR)

With the ever-increasing costs of fuel, there has been a push to use less energy and equally to use more cost-effective and efficient heating and ventilation systems. Heat recovery is one option available. A heat recovery system attached to a mechanical, whole-building ventilation system can recover approximately 60% of the heat that would otherwise be wasted. The basic operation of the system is to use fresh air that is brought into the building; this passes through an heat exchanger and picks up the heat recovered from the stale air. The warmed air is then ducted to other parts of the building. These systems are generally modular and can incorporate other elements such as: comfort cooling, air conditioning, air filtering and dehumidification. In order for these systems to work properly they need to be fully designed by a competent company, and take into account the special requirements of animal buildings (which might not be fully apparent).

The critical points outside the normal design issues are:

- Separating the intake and exhaust terminals to ensure that there is no crossover of contaminated air

- Ensure that the units have accessible and easy-to-clean filters. Cat hairs are very fine and can cause significant maintenance issues if the filters are not cleaned regularly

- Ensure you know the operating noise levels of the system

If installed correctly, these systems can provide a fully controllable environment covering humidity, warmth, cooling and ventilation. However, they are more expensive to install and do require a greater level of maintenance than standard boiler-operated heating and ventilation systems.

For smaller boarding catteries and rescue organisations in temperate climates (particularly those using semi-outdoor designs), it would not be ideal, and a better option would be to look at some of the simpler systems mentioned earlier.

COOLING SYSTEMS (AIR CONDITIONING)

The aim of air conditioning is to control and maintain a building's environment. This covers all aspects from heating, cooling and ventilation to humidity control.

There are two basic types of air conditioning, either single zone packaged units or complete systems.

Single Zone Packaged Units
Single zone packaged units are used for single rooms through to complete building systems.

Complete Systems
Complete systems are normally fitted during the construction stage. They are an integral part of the design, and design parameters are calculated on the location of the building, its size, insulation values etc. Retro-fitting (installing at a later date) a full building system does not generally work as well.

The aim of any system is to ensure that it is designed for your particular situation, building size and location. All of these things should be discussed with your design company or heating/cooling engineer or consultant. These tend to be used for indoor-only designs or for consistently hot climates. The issues are exactly the same as with MVHR.

VENTILATION

The need for adequate ventilation to any cattery is paramount.

The primary aims are:

- Removal and dilution of airborne animal diseases such as cat flu

- Reduction in humidity levels

- Removal of carbon monoxide

- Removal of odours and smells

- Not to create excessive draughts

It is generally recognised that any system utilised in animal accommodation has to be supplemented by mechanical means to ensure control.

We will now look at what is meant by 'air changes per hour' and different ventilation systems.

AIR CHANGES PER HOUR

The number of air changes per hour is the rate at which the air in the building is expelled, and replaced with fresh air from outside.

The general guide used is approximately 4 – 6 changes per hour, with the option to boost to around 8 if required during a period of disease outbreak.

Under normal operating conditions we have found that the 4 – 6 changes per hour is sufficient for usual conditions. As most of the disease problems occur during the warmer summer months, the capacity to boost the ventilation rate is a desirable option.

What must also be taken into consideration is the style and design of the buildings, the number of visitors who have access into the animal units (which increases the risk of disease transfer), the type of cats being admitted (e.g. strays or fully vaccinated pets), and the number of cats housed.

All of these factors will have a significant effect on the incidence of disease outbreak, frequency and severity.

The following examples are design and performance criteria set by some of the leading animal welfare organisations:

   ▪ **Universities Federation for Animal Welfare**
   Recommend a minimum ventilation rate of 10 – 12 air changes per hour.
   It also recommends the use of negative pressure systems, with fan speeds maintained below 0.25 m/s to avoid discomfort from draughts

   ▪ **The Humane Society of the United States**
   Recommend a rate of between 8 – 15 air changes per hour

   ▪ **Feline Advisory Bureau**
   Recommend a rate of between 4 – 8 air changes per hour

Practical Issues

In reality, the majority of domestic cattery owners and animal welfare organisations operating rehoming centres will choose a basic ventilation system.

The great difficulty in attempting to achieve the higher levels of ventilation (i.e. 10 – 12+ per hour in normal animal welfare environments) that have only basic heat producing equipment, is the difficulty in maintaining the required temperature within the building.

To maintain the required temperature within the building that has high levels of extraction, the heat producing equipment has to be increased in size, capacity and sophistication to balance these two opposing requirements. The costs involved in trying to balance these requirements can be considerable, and need to be fully designed and engineered to achieve a balanced system.

VENTILATION SYSTEMS

Ventilation systems in use:

- Natural ventilation

- Natural inlet with mechanical extract

- Mechanical inlet with natural extract

- Mechanical inlet with mechanical extract

- Heat recovery units

- Multi-port extraction system

The design, type of system and your own particular requirements and will vary enormously. Often the determining factors will be cost, amount of use, building type and construction method.

Natural Ventilation

This is the simplest and cheapest method available to the cattery owner.
Natural ventilation is often described as either cross ventilation or passive ventilation (stack effect).

- **Cross Ventilation**
  This utilises openable windows, doors and cat flaps etc, which transfer laterally across the building.

- **Stack Effect**
  This utilises the principle that as hot air rises and warms, it becomes less dense than the surrounding air, (this is know as convection). It is dependent on the wind and air temperature (warm air rises) which creates a stack effect. If there is no wind and the temperature inside the building is at the same temperature as the outside, natural ventilation will be non-existent.

  The utilisation of the 'stack effect' is well known and is exploited in operations that generally have consistently high internal temperatures such as poultry houses and foundries.
  However, because of the relative low ceiling height of most commercial catteries, the small amount of heat given off by cats (as compared with large poultry houses and large animals such as cattle) and its lack of controllability, I believe that it has little to offer cattery owners that have semi-outdoor or indoor catteries.

Natural inlet with single fan mechanical extract

This is the most common type of system and is generally used in domestic kitchens, veterinary room and public conveniences etc.
The extractor fan creates negative pressure on its inlet side, this causes the air inside the room to move toward the fan, which is then displaced by fresh air coming from outside.
This is **probably the most widely-used system in animal accommodation**; it is cost-effective, simple to use, can be controlled and will remove odours and condensation. Its main use is in single rooms.

Mechanical inlet and natural extract

Fresh air is impelled into the building, thereby creating a positive pressure; the contaminated air is expelled by natural seepage through windows, cat flaps etc. In its basic form, this system uses warmed air in the roof space, this applies only to buildings with a 'cold roof' design. If the building has a 'warm roof' design (as is common with a lot of animal buildings using composite steel sheeted roof systems) then consideration needs to be given to ensure that cold air is not forced into the building. This has further complications in locations with freezing, cold weather conditions.

Mechanical Inlet and Extract

This system offers the greatest degree of control; it is the most expensive and is used in cinemas, offices and particularly operating theatres. The air is normally filtered and the warm extracted air can be recirculated to save fuel costs. For offices, etc a slight pressurisation of the air inside the building is achieved by using an extract fan smaller than the inlet fan. However in most animal accommodations **this system does not work particularly efficiently** because of the cat flaps and doors being open for extended periods. The other concern is one of **recirculating contaminated air**.

Heat Recovery Units

These simple units, while providing excellent ventilation rates, also recover some of the removed heat from the room/building. The design of the system ensures there is no cross-contamination of extracted stale or contaminated air, with fresh incoming air. **These units have their limitations** and need frequent servicing, particularly in catteries, to ensure that the filters are clean to allow the unit to function to its maximum capacity.

Multi-Port Extraction System:

This is basically a natural inlet with mechanical extract, which uses a multi-port outlet system.

My Preferred System:

Having tried many systems, I have to say that in terms of cost-effectiveness, ease of servicing and maintenance, ease of installation and proven benefit, the following is still my preferred choice:

The preferred ventilation method is the use of a ducted system connected to multi-port, ceiling-mounted extraction grills, all connected to high performance acoustic fan. The flow is provided by gaps around the cat flaps etc and door trickle ventilation. This type of system has proven to be **extremely beneficial in reducing the overall incidence of disease outbreak** and also a **reduction in the severity of the outbreak**. The system allows for uniform extraction over the entire area of the building. The mechanical systems are more expensive to install, but offer more controllability over natural systems.

Consideration Points:

- Use manual time clocks and control systems. The fully electronic humidity switches do not allow staff the desired flexibility to easily override and boost the system

- The extraction fan should not have an in-line filter (built-in), as this only increases the maintenance

- Any extraction port in hospital type cages should have a fully adjustable cover grill to allow some control over the extraction levels

- Fit trickle ventilators at high level (1.75m/6ft) above the floor. This will allow some movement of air within the cat unit. This also allows a supply of replacement air. If the system has a particularly high extraction rate, this will need to be catered for in the design to ensure a free flow of air

- Ensure that expelled air is not forced into, or on to, other catteries or cats

SUMMARY:
There is a commonly-held belief that simply increasing the number of air changes will prevent the risk or spread of disease in a cattery environment. This is simply not the case. There are many other contributing factors that can help reduce and equally increase the incidence of disease outbreak.

With the need for welfare organisations to allow the public to view their animals, and with the continuing influx of new animals, it is inevitable that there will be periods when the building has to be closed down to control the disease risk.

Non-airborne Diseases

It must be remembered that ventilation will not provide protection from the other diseases that are not airborne. Reducing the risk of direct contact diseases such as FeLV and FIV, or the indirect contact diseases such as enteritis, is equally important.

The ventilation aspect cannot be considered as a stand-alone aspect of the building design. It has to be an integral part of the overall building design, cleaning routine and the management control system at the centre.

It is pointless spending excessively, purely to achieve the higher rates of ventilation/exchange. The costs of installing expensive, high maintenance and oversized heat-producing equipment (for what could be very limited use) could be considerable.

This factor becomes more noticeable given that the vast majority of disease incidence tends to occur during the summer months when the heating is normally switched off.

RISK OF DISEASE – INCREASING AND REDUCING FACTORS

To minimise the risk of disease outbreak and spread, some other factors have to be taken into consideration, as ventilation alone will not prevent disease outbreaks.

Factors affecting the risk of disease:

RISK-INCREASING FACTORS:

- Large numbers of animals housed in one area
- Dark, damp buildings
- Public access to all areas
- Poor quality and unhygienic surfaces and finishes
- Stressed and bored animals, lack of environmental enrichment
- Poor cleaning regimes
- Poor staff management and control systems
- Draughty buildings
- Buildings that are subject to extremes of temperature

RISK-REDUCING FACTORS:

- Happy, relaxed cats having lots of human contact with plenty of options to play, climb, scratch, things to watch
- Good management
- Buildings that have natural cross ventilation
- Animals have access to natural daylight/sunlight (sunlight is a natural killer of viruses and bacteria)
- Reducing the amount of shared air
- Providing a stimulating environment
- Ventilation systems designed to provide the correct number of air changes covering all the building, and not just isolated pockets near windows etc
- Quality finishes that allow the building to dry quickly, thus ensuring that the building environment is dry
- Type of cleaning regime (excessive use of water can create additional problems)
- Type of heating system (having used several methods I am convinced that either underfloor or radiant heating types are the most convenient and suitable for animal accommodation)
- Good staff awareness and training
- Smaller, more individual buildings
- Providing public zones to restrict access to some areas

CONDENSATION (DEHUMIDIFICATION)

Many catteries are too wet or damp. The reasons for this are obvious: water from over-zealous cleaning processes, damp bedding, uncovered exercise runs etc.

All of these factors contribute to a poor environment in which to house cats; a damp environment is a breeding place for viruses and germs.

Condensation is a problem that affects many buildings, not just catteries. It is particularly noticeable during the winter months, and at night, when the temperature falls, the humidity rises and condensation forms.

Your bathroom window is a good indicator of the problem!
If you run a hot bath on a cold day, it will not be long before the inside of the window is heavy with running water. The air we breathe is like a big sponge; the warmer the air, the more water in the form of vapour it can absorb. As soon as the air is cooled for any reason it contracts and has to unload its absorbed water on to the cold surface, this is condensation (dew).

The materials used in modern catteries are not the most beneficial to counter this problem; the cold, hard finishes of tiles or sealed block work readily show the problem. In older buildings constructed of timber, the problem was not so noticeable; timber being warmer to the touch and therefore able to hold more vapour.
The vapour was still there and became absorbed into the timber; an ideal place for germs and bacteria to breed.
The fundamental principle of minimising condensation as a result of high humidity is to maintain a balance between the ventilation, the heating and thermal properties of the building.

To combat the problems associated with condensation often requires taking various levels of action; each stage has to be carried out separately, this allows you to measure how effective it has been.
Heating, ventilation and humidity should be looked at as a whole and not as isolated problems; approaching the problem in this manner should give excellent results.

If heating and ventilation alone do not correct the problem of condensation, you are then faced with two choices. These are:

■ Dehumidification
These simple units can be of great advantage to any property owner and are used extensively for drying new houses, basement cellars and for keeping document stores dry. They come in a range of sizes and extraction levels, they are cost-effective, give excellent results and are simple to operate and maintain

The basic principle of the system is that moist air within the building is drawn over a heater coil, ensuring it deposits its condensed water, which is then drained away. During this process the latent energy of the water vapour is recovered and is recycled back into the air as it leaves the unit. This warmed air can be a useful source of heating for the building.
Correctly sized, a dehumidifier will reduce your heating and ventilation costs and at the same time improve the cattery environment by removing excess moisture from the air

■ Building Construction and Management Technique
Look at the construction method and fabric of the building (e.g. old, outdated building, rising damp etc), and also your management techniques (e.g. cleaning, amount of water used etc)

ENVIRONMENT ENRICHMENT ENRICHMENT

Soldiers
like
dogs;
artists
like
cats

Desmond Morris

WHY ENRICH THE ENVIRONMENT

A cattery is an unnatural environment, and therefore the more that can be done to 'enrich' and improve the environment to help cats adapt, the more they will be able to express natural behaviour.

'Enriching' the environment can be done by providing for the following needs:

Hiding – somewhere to feel safe
Cats entering a new environment will need time to adapt and settle in. A cat's natural response to this change of environment is to 'hide'. This requirement can easily be provided with anything from a cardboard box to a luxury cat igloo. Once the cat is feeling safe and more confident, s/he will start to explore the new surroundings. Where no hiding space is provided, cats will try and create somewhere to feel safe by hiding in a cat flap tunnel, behind other items such as beds, a litter tray or may resort to staying very still in a corner if there is nowhere else. It is so easy to provide somewhere to hide, but not seen often enough!

Somewhere to hide: ensure you include this fundamental requirement for cats to help them settle in quickly

Being up high – provides a safe vantage point
Climbing, jumping and being high up (for safety and the best view) are fundamental parts of natural cat behaviour. Resting places above ground level allow cats to relax and rest comfortably in safety. Again, allowing the cats to express their natural behaviour is all part of reducing their stress levels. Vertical space can easily be provided by ramps, steps, 'suite' type rooms with plenty of walkways and shelving. It is interesting to see that, even in small confined hospital type cages, cats will use any shelving provided for a greater percentage of the time than at 'ground' level. Elevated platforms provide somewhere to observe the surroundings and this can be provided easily with shelving.

Choices
Having the freedom to 'make choices' about where to rest or what to play with should be provided to further help reduce stress. The aim is to make the best use of the space available, introduce different toys or equipment to provide novelty for long stay cats.

Plenty of human contact with familiar faces
Catteries worldwide have stated that maintaining continuity of staff has a noticeable and positive effect on the cats. This can be provided by playing, grooming, stroking & just spending time together.

Encouraging and allowing cats to 'think' or solve problems
In a natural environment cats would be able to show natural behaviour such as searching for food, hunting, exploring, survey surroundings.

Encouraging and allowing cats to use all their senses
The design and style of building, cleaning/disinfection methods used, using ingenuity to provide novel ways to encourage cats to think and become more active by using all their senses (sight, smell, sound, taste, touch).

This chapter is dedicated to providing you with some ideas on how to put all of these essential requirements into practice daily.

ENVIRONMENT ENRICHMENT

Dr Irene Rochlitz

HOUSING REQUIREMENTS:

QUALITY OF SPACE

Beyond a certain minimum size of enclosure, it is the quality rather than the quantity of space that is most important.

CLIMBING, JUMPING, BEING UP HIGH

Most cats enjoy climbing and jumping and, as much of their time is spent off the floor; they use elevated areas as vantage points from which to survey their surroundings.

There should, therefore, be structures within the enclosure that enable cats to use the vertical dimension, such as shelves, climbing posts, walkways, windowsills and platforms

RESTING AND SLEEPING

Cats spend a large portion of their day either resting or sleeping, so it is important that the rest areas have comfortable surfaces such as pillows.

BEDDING

One study found that cats preferred polyester fleece to cotton-looped towel, woven rush-matting and corrugated cardboard for lying on. Another study found that cats preferred wood as a substrate to plastic, and also liked materials that maintain a constant temperature such as straw, hay, wood shavings and fabric. As cats are more likely to rest alone than with others, there should be a sufficient number of comfortable resting areas for all cats in the enclosure.

LITTER AND TRAYS

Since cats can have individual preferences for litter and tray characteristics, a range of litter types and designs of litter trays (covered or open) should be available. There should be at least one litter tray per two cats and preferably one per cat, sited away from feeding and resting areas.

HIDING

Hiding is a behaviour that cats often show in response to stressful situations or changes in their environment, for example when they want to avoid being with other cats or people.

If hiding places are not provided, cats may use the litter tray for this purpose. Therefore, in addition to open resting areas (such as shelves) there should be resting areas where cats can retreat to and be concealed, such as high-sided cat beds, 'igloo' beds and boxes.

Photograph courtesy of Dr Cerian Webb

BARRIERS AND DIVIDERS

Visual barriers such as vertical panels, curtains and other room divisions, can also be useful.

We will now look at more ways of improving the environment for cats:

- Social environment
- Sensory environment
- Occupational environment
- Nutritional environment

SOCIAL ENVIRONMENT

OTHER CATS

In multi-cat households and some animal sanctuaries, cats are expected to spend most of their lives together.

The majority of cats can be housed in groups providing that they are well socialized to other cats, and that there is sufficient good-quality space, easy access to feeding and elimination areas and plenty of concealed retreats and resting places.

Ideally, the composition of the group should be stable, with minimal additions or losses of cats.

Cats entering catteries and shelters should not be mixed with unfamiliar cats except in exceptional circumstances (for example, healthy long-stay shelter cats in small stable groups).

Cats that fail to adapt to living in groups should be identified and housed in pairs or singly.

HUMANS

The caregiver, whether a member of shelter staff, an animal technician, an owner or a veterinary nurse, has a huge influence on the cat's welfare, and the best housing conditions cannot substitute for the caregiver's compassionate care and attention.

Unfortunately, it is often this direct involvement of staff in animal care that is curtailed, especially in situations where there are limits on financial resources, shortage of time or high work demands.

Care-givers

Periods of time, which are not part of routine care-taking procedures (such as feeding or cleaning), should be available every day for cats to interact with their caregiver.

In order to care for them properly, the care-giver should like cats and be knowledgeable about them.

This knowledge can be acquired from many sources, such as books and other printed information, internet sites, veterinary practices, animal behaviour courses, animal behaviourists, animal rescue charities, and from mentoring and supervision by peers.

Because some information may be controversial, contradictory or wrong, inexperienced caregivers will require guidance from reputable sources.

Allowing care-givers to enrich the environment of cats under their care can also enrich their own lives.

This involvement introduces variation in their work, provides them with opportunities to learn about the species, to devise the enrichment and to observe its effects, and, by improving the cats' welfare, makes their work more rewarding.

SENSORY ENVIRONMENT

USING THE SENSES

The quality of the external environment is very important to cats, whose senses are highly developed.

SIGHT

Cats spend a lot of time observing the environment immediately outside their enclosure; they will often settle on windowsills if they are wide and comfortable enough, but other suitable vantage points, such as climbing platforms and shelves placed near windows can be used.

Outdoor Access

If cats do not have free access to the outdoors they should have access to enclosed outdoor runs or, if this is not possible, their enclosure should have windows so that they can look outside.

Attracting Wildlife

Plants that attract butterflies, and other items such as bird-tables or water fountains can be placed outside the enclosures to provide points of interest for the cats to watch.

SMELL

Cats have an excellent sense of smell and they use this sense to communicate. Sebaceous glands are located throughout the body, especially on the head and the peri-anal area (around the anus), and between the toes (digits).

Scratching, which causes scent to be deposited from the inter-digital glands, is frequently observed in cats; this marking behaviour also leaves visual signals (lines or striations) and helps to maintain the claws in good shape Surfaces for the deposition of these olfactory and visual signals and for claw abrasion, such as scratch posts, rush matting, pieces of carpet and wood, should be provided.

Enrichment using the cat's sense of smell is not used very often, perhaps because of the relatively poor sense of smell of humans compared with cats.

Catnip is well known as a stimulant for cats, though not all cats are affected by it. It is usually supplied as a dried herb or in toys, and can be grown as a fresh plant in pots.

SOUND

In some animal houses auditory enrichment (using the sense of sound) using a radio, to provide music and human conversation, is thought to prevent animals from being startled by sudden noises and help them to get used to human voices, and to provide a degree of continuity in the environment. Video recordings of images and sounds that are thought to appeal to cats are available, though their effectiveness has not been evaluated.

TOUCH

Cats enjoy the sun, often seeking out warm, sunny spots to lie in, so housing should be constructed, if possible, to include a western, southern or eastern aspect, depending on the climate.

TASTE Continues on the next page…

using the senses

NUTRITIONAL ENVIRONMENT

Domestic cats are usually offered two or three meals a day, although their preferred pattern of feeding is one of frequent small meals.

Frequent feeding may not always be possible and ad libitum feeding may lead to obesity.

HUNTING & FEEDING BEHAVIOUR

Another environmental enrichment technique is to increase the time animals spend in pseudo-predatory (hunting) and feeding behaviour.

Dry food can be put into containers with holes through which the cat has to extract individual pieces.

For the cat that is food-orientated, small amounts of dry food can be hidden in the environment to make it more interesting to explore.

Toy-like objects that are destructible and have nutritional value may be of interest to cats, but there are few such items available commercially.

SEPARATE WATER FROM FOOD

Cats often prefer to drink away from the feeding area, so bowls of water should be placed in a number of locations, both indoors and outdoors.

GRASS

Grass grown in containers can be provided for indoor-only cats; some cats like to chew it and it is thought that this can help with the elimination of furballs (trichobezoars).

OCCUPATIONAL ENVIRONMENT

Many cats play alone or with their owners, rather than with other cats, so there should be enough space for them to play without disturbing others.

There should be a variety of toys and they should be replaced regularly, as cats like exploring new things.

TOYS

Many toys are made to resemble mice and other small animals and to look attractive to humans, but they are often not very effective for the cat. If the toys move, have a lot of surface texture and 'behave' like prey, they are most likely to be used, but ping-pong balls, pieces of string, balls of tin foil etc. can also be effective.

EXPLORING

Cats enjoy exploring, so new objects such as boxes, large paper bags and other structures can be placed into their environment every so often.

HIDING

Ideas for places to hide:

- Cardboard boxes with 'doors' cut out
- Beds with hoods
- Activity centres with hideaways, tunnels or hammocks
- Tunnels (fleece, crinkly paper, nylon or tunnels with pockets for catnip pouches)
- Beds or boxes on high shelves
- Blankets draped over shelves, secured firmly with clips
- Washable/steamable household items such as trugs/baskets/bowls for cats to snuggle in
- Hammocks
- Hanging flower baskets with bedding inside
- Plastic/disposable cat play centres (castles/boats etc)
- Beds with high sides

HIDING PLACES PROVIDE SAFETY

PERCHING/UP HIGH/VANTAGE POINTS

Ideas for places to perch up high:

- Shelving at various levels
- Floor-to-ceiling scratching posts/activity centres
- Wall boxes
- Walkways and ramps
- Seats/chairs
- Activity centres/scratching posts with platforms
- Short cat ladders (many have sisal/carpet treads)
- Tall ladders (stable or fixed)
- Travel baskets/carriers
- Plastic/disposable cat play centres (castles/boats etc)
- Spiral staircases leading to shelving
- Series of shelves to jump to various heights
- Lower shelving for kittens and elderly/arthritic cats

BEING UP HIGH PROVIDES A SAFE & INTERESTING VANTAGE POINT

CLIMBING AND JUMPING

When cats feel unsafe or stressed and they can't 'escape' from the real or perceived danger, their natural inclination is to move upwards to get away. As we have already seen, it is important for cats to have high vantage points, and therefore they will need something to climb on to get to the high places. At home you may well find your cat on top of the wardrobe, cupboards and chests, fridge or freezer, using windowsills, book shelves and mantelpieces - possibly even doing a circuit around the room without even touching the floor!

In the cattery we can provide for this need with things to climb and jump on to get up high, having a choice of levels by providing shelving, activity centres and by using boxes or even the cat's travel carrier. For the kitten, elderly or arthritic cat, the option of lower shelving still provides them with a choice of levels. Even in a veterinary/medical cage or penthouse 'box' at 1m/3ft high, cats will still prefer to use shelving!

On the next few pages we will look at examples of how we can provide for the cats' need to climb and get up high, or to a different level - off the floor, by using fixed and moveable cat furniture.

CAT FURNITURE

Fixed Cat Furniture

Cat flaps

There is a wide range of cat flaps on the market. I would suggest that you install one of the larger styles (see photo top right) as this makes it easier for the cat to use and tend to be less prone to damage. The flap needs to allow the cats to 'step down' when using it. If the bottom of the flap is flush with the unit/shelf floor, there is a chance that the cat can get his/her paws stuck when trying to retreat backwards.

Shelving, Ramps and Walkways

Whatever shelving is installed, it should be easy to clean and non-absorbent, have adequate width to fit a basket or bedding on and have a **lightly textured surface to prevent cats slipping when jumping on and off** – particularly if bedding is placed on the shelving.

Note: Some catteries still use timber ramps as this provides a warm finish. In the event of a disease outbreak it is accepted that they will need to be disposed of.

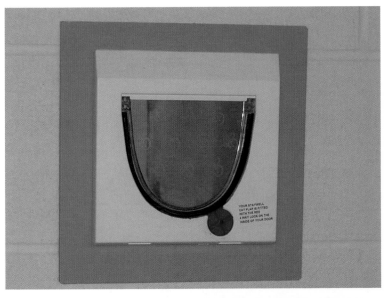

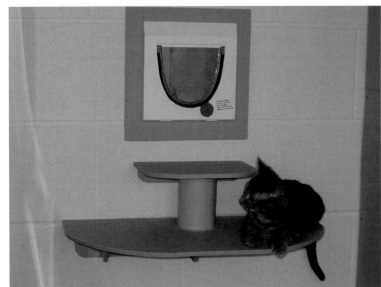

 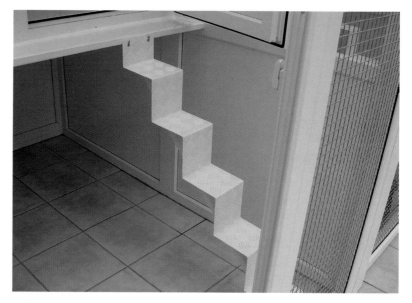

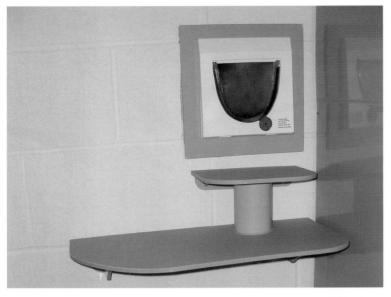

Moveable Cat Furniture

Ideas for moveable cat furniture:

- Cardboard boxes - cats love to get in them, sit on them, play with toys inside them!

- Cat climbing posts

- Cat stands/aerobic/activity centres

- Scratching posts with platforms

- Canvas/fabric hammocks

- Fleecy/furry radiator hammocks for the winter

- Window seats or perches that clip on

- Novelty or themed furniture (zen/japanese/feng-shui style, fabric trees, logs fixed together to provide a frame)

- Cat ladders for activity centres

- Tunnels

- Furniture with dangling toys to bat (mice, spiders, balls, feathers)

- Catnip scented furniture

- Modular/tubular shelving that slots together to form different platforms and heights (do-it-yourself stores are a cheap source, or there are configurable systems using multiple cat activity centres)

- Off-the-floor bedding such as sofas or beds to step into, useful for kittens, elderly or arthritic cats

- Toy centres such as castles, boats, cottages (available commercially, or make your own with cardboard boxes)

- Circular, high-sided or doughnut-shaped beds to climb into

- Plastic or rubber beds with high sides to place bedding in

- Stable/fixed, human ladders for very active cats! These could lead to shelving

- Travel carriers, can be sat on or hidden in

- Human seats or chairs

- Child/canine/equestrian items may be used indoors or outdoors for an element of fun and shelter (such as plastic play equipment, jumps, play-houses, seats and tables)

- Make cat-sized spiral staircases as a special feature

- Human-sized spiral staircases look impressive in a larger socialisation room, or suite

Photograph courtesy Kitty Hill Resort for Cats

INTERACTION WITH FAMILIAR FACES

Developing a relationship with the same person or people is important. Consistency in the relationship is vital to cats – new people are a source of anxiety or stress.

The experiences cats have previously had of people, their confidence/extrovert/introvert nature, whether they have been in a cattery before, and whether they have indoor-only or outdoor access will all be factors in how quickly they settle in, and what sort of relationship you will have with them.

Owners form a strong bond with their cats. They can also get over-attached to their cats, and cats can get over-attached to their owners. Some cats will be very independent, and others will have a much more dependent relationship. If the owner is upset at leaving the cat, it may cause extra stress in the cat, over and above being 'moved' to the new environment of the cattery. You should **never** force a cat into doing anything - it is much better to let him/her come to you of their own accord to help establish trust. Cattery owners can help both cats and their owners in a variety of ways, all of which are about establishing trust.

Kittens should be socialised from a very early age, part of which is introducing them to being 'handled' by humans and to be able to cope with the 'staring' that humans often direct at them (cats stare to threaten (so blink and look away!).

Feeding a cat helps establish a relationship with the carer, therefore we can use this knowledge in the cattery by providing treats, talking to the cat in a high-pitched and soft voice whilst providing food, and generally 'making a meal of it' (!) by spending more time with cats in their first few feeding times, when it is crucial to get them to start eating away from home.

The amount of care and attention shown to the cats in person, how proud the owner is of their facility, what supportive and enriching elements the cattery owner has to help the cats settle in, knowledge and experience, a kind and empathetic nature and of course the image the cattery building presents and promotional material such as the website.

Some ideas for human interaction:

- Keep the same carers looking after the same cats, continuity is important
- Ensure the longer-term carer provides the first few meals, it helps to develop a relationship quickly
- Provide treats on the first few visits to help establish a positive relationship
- Talk in a high-pitched, soft voice
- Always use the cat's name
- For cuddling cats, use a towel and have a backup, both should have your scent, as well as the cat's scent
- Allow time to play with the cats, using favourite toys
- Allow time to stroke and groom the cats, for well-being
- Find out as much as you can about the cat's temperament, likes and dislikes (cat profile), this will help ensure you do positive things for the cat that don't cause stress
- Spend as much time with the cats as you are able to, this will help the cat place his/her trust in you

In the rest of this chapter we will look at how we can stimulate all the cat senses in the cattery to provide a fuller life while they are with you, and help them settle in as quickly as possible.

EVEN THE BEST
HOUSING CONDITIONS
CANNOT BE A
SUBSTITUTE FOR
COMPASSIONATE LOVE,
CARE & ATTENTION
~
IN AN IDEAL WORLD
OF COURSE, YOU
WOULD HAVE BOTH!

A happy
arrangement: many
people prefer cats to
other people,
and many
cats prefer people
to other cats

Mason Cooley

SIGHT

Cats see colour toned down (imagine turning the colour down on a TV until it is barely noticeable) so that anything moving immediately stands out.

Cats are far-sighted and cannot see individual items in front of them clearly (they would not be able to see the big 'A' at the top of a sight chart) but the second anything moves — they focus on it. If something is static, it will not awaken the cats interest as much as something that moves or changes (or appears to).

Cats have superb night vision thanks to a mirror-like surface at the back of the eye which reflects light back to the retina (you will see this at night, or when taking a photograph) and in dim light the pupil opens wide to allow in as much light as possible.

You can see from this toned-down world just how important movement is to a cat. Perfect vision for a predator!

Ideas for including things to watch:

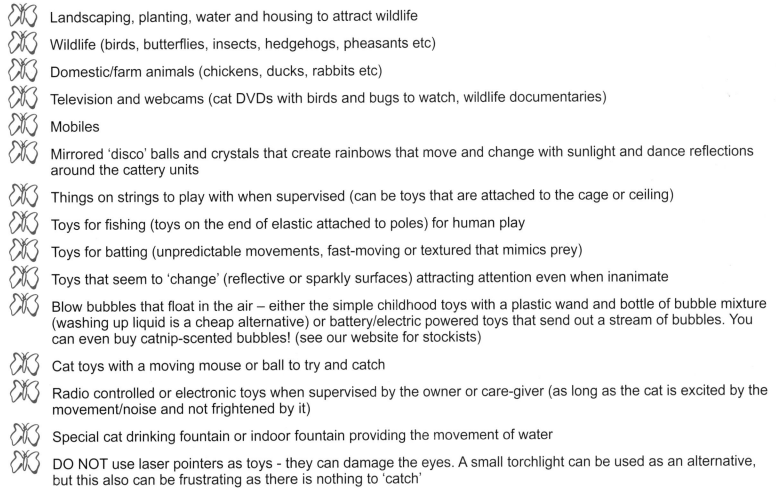

- Landscaping, planting, water and housing to attract wildlife

- Wildlife (birds, butterflies, insects, hedgehogs, pheasants etc)

- Domestic/farm animals (chickens, ducks, rabbits etc)

- Television and webcams (cat DVDs with birds and bugs to watch, wildlife documentaries)

- Mobiles

- Mirrored 'disco' balls and crystals that create rainbows that move and change with sunlight and dance reflections around the cattery units

- Things on strings to play with when supervised (can be toys that are attached to the cage or ceiling)

- Toys for fishing (toys on the end of elastic attached to poles) for human play

- Toys for batting (unpredictable movements, fast-moving or textured that mimics prey)

- Toys that seem to 'change' (reflective or sparkly surfaces) attracting attention even when inanimate

- Blow bubbles that float in the air – either the simple childhood toys with a plastic wand and bottle of bubble mixture (washing up liquid is a cheap alternative) or battery/electric powered toys that send out a stream of bubbles. You can even buy catnip-scented bubbles! (see our website for stockists)

- Cat toys with a moving mouse or ball to try and catch

- Radio controlled or electronic toys when supervised by the owner or care-giver (as long as the cat is excited by the movement/noise and not frightened by it)

- Special cat drinking fountain or indoor fountain providing the movement of water

- DO NOT use laser pointers as toys - they can damage the eyes. A small torchlight can be used as an alternative, but this also can be frustrating as there is nothing to 'catch'

Imagine having this
as your
only outlook
every day!

SOUND

Cats can move their ears independently of each other, providing the perfect equipment for listening to various sounds at once, and in different locations at once, even if in another direction to where the cat is heading.

Cats and humans have a similar range of hearing at the low end of the scale, but cats are able to hear much higher-pitched sounds (even better than dogs) which is ideal for locating the exciting high-pitched squeaking of prey. Cats can judge the location of a sound to within 3"/7.5cm being made 1m/3ft away.

Ideas for providing sounds:

- Classical music (remember not to leave it on all the time)

- 'New Age' type music with natural sounds such as birdsong, insects, water and gentle weather such as rain or the wind blowing softly (again, not all the time)

- Toys with a high-pitched squeak to mimic prey

- Talk to cats in a high-pitched, soft voice

- Use clicker-training to interact with cats and get them thinking about how to earn treats etc

- Crinkle play bags/tunnels provide a satisfying crunchy texture/noise and can contain removable catnip sachets

- Television, if they are used to having one at home (but not to be left on all the time)

- **Always use the cat's name**, ask him/her to come to you (you may need to teach this if the owner hasn't bothered!)

SMELL

Cats have a sense of smell that is much sharper than humans, about fourteen times greater!

Ideas for providing scents:

- Keeping litter and food/water well apart from each other

- Use feline facial pheromone to comfort and soothe cats. A spray can be used in the car, carrier or cat unit, and a plug-in diffuser in the cattery. You will need to ensure that this is done at least 15 minutes before cat use

- Hiding titbits to 'sniff out', or using strong-smelling food such as tuna or ham

- Feathers (will smell of prey)

- Garden items, twigs, flowers – something different to investigate (non-poisonous of course)

- Catnip if suitable (fresh, dried, and you can even purchase catnip-scented blow bubbles)

- DO NOT use the household fragrance plug-in/spray fresheners (a clean cattery will not smell!)

- Use cotton gloves (from the pharmacy, supermarket or superstore) to rub on the cats cheeks to capture his/her own scent. This will be useful when adopting a cat, making the home smell familiar to help settle him/her in quickly, or in the cattery if the owner is prepared to do this. Alternatively, rotating towels that have the cats scent on so you always smell 'familiar' when you approach the cat

- Items that smell of the cat, owner or home – familiar smells are comforting in new situations

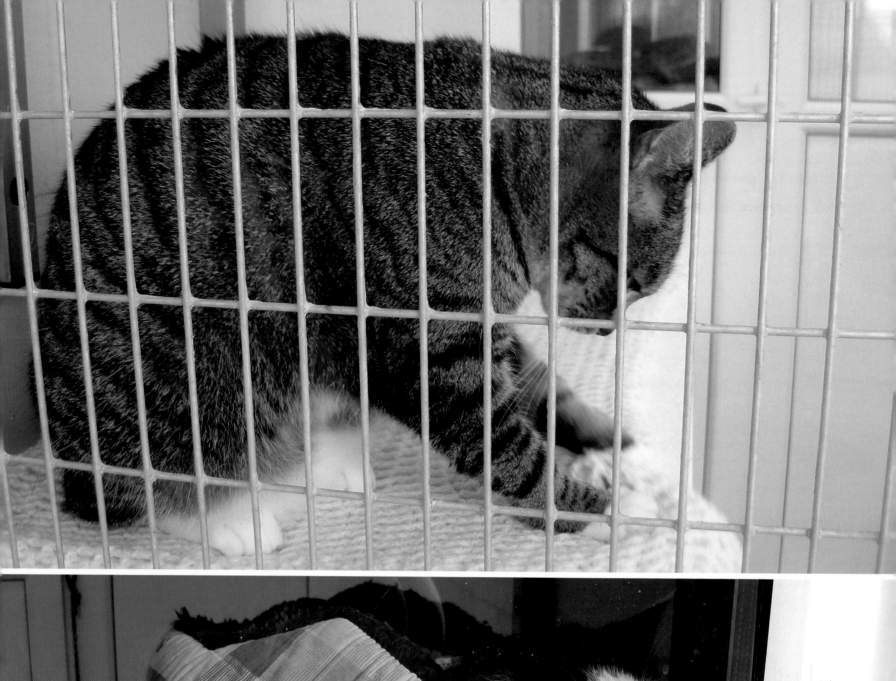

TOUCH

Cats investigate with their paws, mouths and whiskers, which also helps them judge distances, and objects in the dark.

Ideas for using touch and texture:

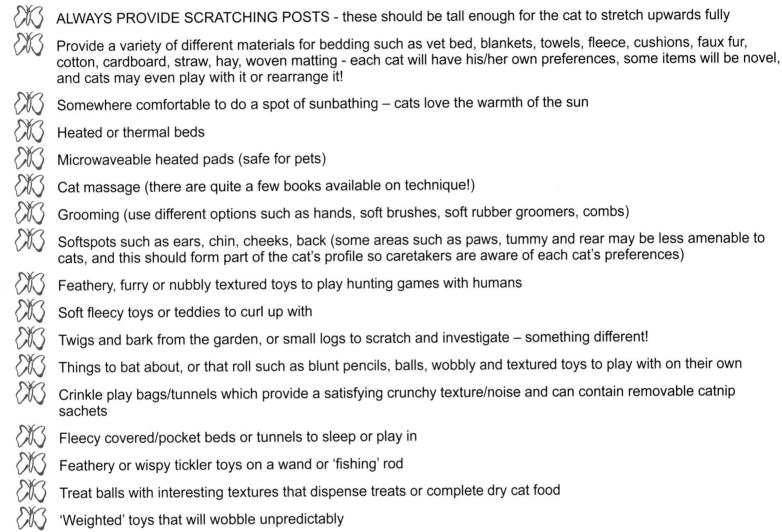

- ALWAYS PROVIDE SCRATCHING POSTS - these should be tall enough for the cat to stretch upwards fully

- Provide a variety of different materials for bedding such as vet bed, blankets, towels, fleece, cushions, faux fur, cotton, cardboard, straw, hay, woven matting - each cat will have his/her own preferences, some items will be novel, and cats may even play with it or rearrange it!

- Somewhere comfortable to do a spot of sunbathing – cats love the warmth of the sun

- Heated or thermal beds

- Microwaveable heated pads (safe for pets)

- Cat massage (there are quite a few books available on technique!)

- Grooming (use different options such as hands, soft brushes, soft rubber groomers, combs)

- Softspots such as ears, chin, cheeks, back (some areas such as paws, tummy and rear may be less amenable to cats, and this should form part of the cat's profile so caretakers are aware of each cat's preferences)

- Feathery, furry or nubbly textured toys to play hunting games with humans

- Soft fleecy toys or teddies to curl up with

- Twigs and bark from the garden, or small logs to scratch and investigate – something different!

- Things to bat about, or that roll such as blunt pencils, balls, wobbly and textured toys to play with on their own

- Crinkle play bags/tunnels which provide a satisfying crunchy texture/noise and can contain removable catnip sachets

- Fleecy covered/pocket beds or tunnels to sleep or play in

- Feathery or wispy tickler toys on a wand or 'fishing' rod

- Treat balls with interesting textures that dispense treats or complete dry cat food

- 'Weighted' toys that will wobble unpredictably

TASTE

Most owners feed their cat at regular times, and/or leave complete dry food available all day. This may be easy for owners, but it is certainly predictable for cats! Naturally, cats would spend six or more hours a day searching and hunting for food, using all their senses and focusing completely on the outdoor stimuli around them. A far cry from being confined and fed at the same time twice a day!

Make life more interesting by dividing up food portions into several smaller ones, positioned in various locations and heights such as multiple shelves/activity centres, hide or place dry food into puzzle toys (either bought, or make your own from cardboard tubes or yogurt pots or clear plastic bottles/containers with holes in) – cats are natural snackers! Cats can detect bitter/acidic/salty tastes but not sweet. Try leaving a trail of strong-smelling cheese on surfaces leading to a treat or toy.

Cats would naturally seek out water in a different place and time from food, so you can simulate this by placing water in a different location from food. **It would be well worth trying this out at home, not just in the cattery!**

Ideas for food and nutrition:

- Always keep litter well apart from food and water
- Puzzle toys (bought or made)
- Hide tidbits to hunt, place food in several locations
- Warm food slightly as this may be more appealing
- Provide cat grass
- Multiple feed-spots are ideal for more than one cat
- Try offering tuna if the cat hasn't eaten anything

Ideas for water:

- Always keep water separate from food
- Try flavouring water with a tiny amount of fish or chicken stock
- Water Fountains (pet fountains or home use) especially for cats that should be encouraged to drink more (kidney problems or diabetes)
- Provide large bowls of water for those cats that love to 'play' with it!

Grass and Catnip/Catmint

Cat Grass:

- Helps cats bring up furballs and adds roughage
- Buy in pots, ready to grow indoors or sow seeds and grow them yourself
- Do not use chemicals or fertilisers when growing cat grass
- Germinates quickly (within two days) and grows to about 6"/15cm within 5 days
- Very easy to grow and care for
- Lasts between 2–3 weeks, then starts to wither and turn yellow
- When it reaches 2"/5cm start sowing seeds in the next pot
- Can be grown indoors at home, or for the cattery
- DO NOT use grass from your lawn, it may well have contaminants, fertiliser or pesticide residues

CAT GRASS

CATNIP/CATMINT
NEPETA CATARIA

Catnip/Catmint

- Harmless, non-addictive perennial herb from the mint family
- Buy from garden centres or sow direct from seed
- Plant in the garden in full sun for a constant source of fresh catnip
- Dry for use in toys, or purchase dried catnip
- Do not use chemicals or fertilisers when growing catnip
- Affects 80% of cats (both male and female) young or elderly cats may not show a response.
- Catnip entices the cat to roll around on it and induces a 'high' in cats (but not all, and it can make some cats aggressive)
- Cats may sniff, play with or even eat catnip
- Only a little is required
- Hide catnip toys in various places
- Buy, or grow and dry catnip for replacing toy scent
- Use sparingly – do not leave catnip scented items out all the time or they will lose their novelty factor
- Can be used as therapy for depressed cats

PREDATORY BEHAVIOUR

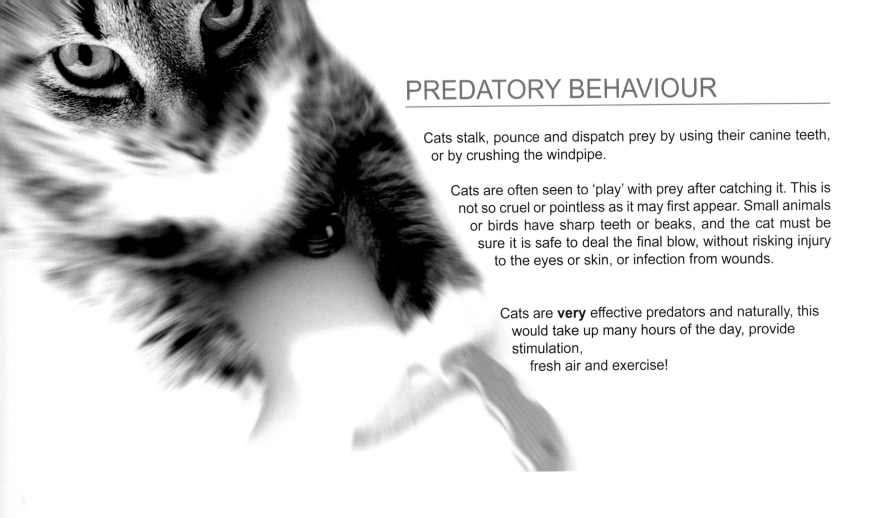

Cats stalk, pounce and dispatch prey by using their canine teeth, or by crushing the windpipe.

Cats are often seen to 'play' with prey after catching it. This is not so cruel or pointless as it may first appear. Small animals or birds have sharp teeth or beaks, and the cat must be sure it is safe to deal the final blow, without risking injury to the eyes or skin, or infection from wounds.

Cats are **very** effective predators and naturally, this would take up many hours of the day, provide stimulation,
fresh air and exercise!

We can use the predatory instincts of cats to make life more exciting and stimulating in the cattery, some ideas are:

- Wind-up or battery operated toys to chase

- Toys with a high-pitched squeak

- Erratic and unpredictable movement in toys and games provides the most excitement

- Watch wildlife, domestic or farm animals

- You can find out a cat's preference for prey easily with toys (furry, buggy, bouncy, string, fluidity)

- A small toy in a paper bag, cardboard box or pot

- Catnip toys

- Fishing/wand toys to catch and chase

- Circular toys with balls or mice to chase around

- Toys with paw-sized holes in (puzzles) to catch toys or treats (can be created from a flat box)

- Gloves with very long, dangly fingers with puppet toys or bobbles at the end

- String, yarn and balls of wool can be chased, but must not be left alone with the cat (in case of digestion or strangulation)

- Tin foil balls, cotton reels, ping-pong balls, cat toys can all be pounced on and chased

After
dark
all
cats
are
leopards

Native American Proverb

Purring would seem
to be an automatic
safety device
for dealing with
happiness
overflow

Monica Edwards

PURRING

With all these incredible senses, cats may have yet another 'trick up their sleeve'.

For centuries, humans have wondered why cats purr.

We believe they purr when content or happy. However, cats are also known to purr when they are injured, frightened or giving birth, so there must surely be other reasons to purr, especially if they purr (requires expending energy) at a time when they need energy most to recover.

When cats may purr:

- When happy, friendy or in contentment (cats purr when being stroked so we love to hear a purring cat!)

- When uncomfortable or in great pain, for comfort

- When wanting or receiving attention

- When a mother cat calls her kittens to be nursed (when they are too young to see, hear or smell her they will be able to feel the vibrations of the purr) and kittens may purr to let mum know 'all is well'

Many big cats also purr, and as cats have purred for generations, there must be a good reason for the purr's survival.

There may well be another important reason. A recent study of domestic cats, cheetahs, ocelots, pumas and servals was done to measure the cats' purring by microphone. Every cat generated strong frequencies between 25–150 Hz.

This fascinating study found that domestic cats, servals, ocelots, and pumas produced frequencies of 25 Hz and 50 Hz, which happen to be the two lowest frequencies that best promote bone growth/fracture healing. The interesting thing is that these frequencies are already used in treatment for bone growth/fractures, pain, oedema (accumulation of fluid in tissue spaces/body cavity), muscle growth/strain, joint flexibility, difficulty in breathing, and wounds!

- Purring may reduce pain, help heal wounds, or even help keep a cat's bones strong

The cat already has incredible senses (sight, sound, smell, taste, touch) and formidable weapons (teeth and claws). A further advantage of an internal healing mechanism that would speed up recovery time and help keep muscles and bone strong when sedentary would indeed be a blessing!

If we needed another reason to make a cat purr – surely this is the purrfect one?!

The Felid Purr: A bio-mechanical healing mechanism: you can read more about this fascinating study at:
www.animalvoice.com/catpur.htm

SETTLING IN

Do you know how to help a cat settle in as soon as possible?

Ideas for how to help cats settle in quickly:

- Clients can cause the cat stress inadvertently by being upset at leaving him/her – inform them!

- Once you know the cat, could anything be done to settle the cat in more quickly next time? Make notes!

- Provide somewhere for the cat to hide (e.g. a box, or leave the cat in its basket with the door open) to feel safe

- Spray corners of the travel carrier/unit with feline facial pheromone (15 minutes **before** placing the cat into it)

- Play classical music quietly in the background

- Allow the cat to settle in the unit, allowing him/her to decide whether it was time to make friends with you yet

- Increase your knowledge of cat behaviour (e.g. staring at cats makes them uncomfortable)

- Use the cat's name at every opportunity

- Pay particular attention to being there for the first few meal times when settling the cat in

- Use treats and toys to help make friends with the cat

- Place a towel with the cat's own familiar scent on your shoulder if the cat is happy to be picked up, or you can use cotton gloves to stroke the cat around the face and chin, leaving the cat's own scent on the gloves (also useful for introducing a cat to a new home by placing his/her own scent there in advance)

- Thoroughly understand how to recognise normal behaviour (eating, grooming, eliminating) and abnormal behaviour (pacing, circling, self mutilation, excessive vocalisation, defensive aggression) and the signs of anxiety, fear, frustration, depression and stress (see Chapter 5 Cat Welfare)

- Provide 'try-it' days and weekends and create special 'settling-in' programs for different cat needs – cats who have experience of catteries settle in faster

Cat Profile

A 'Cat Profile' will be extremely important to help you understand each cat's individual requirements, character, needs and normal environment at home. This information will not only be important for the cat's welfare, but the owners will be reassured that you will be caring for their pet in the best manner.

If you take the time to look after a smaller number of cats extremely well, and equally take the time to discuss their stay with the owner – a reputation as a caring and quality cattery will be yours.

Clients will respect the professionalism of your care, be happy to leave their cat with you more often than they might otherwise, and recommend you to all their cat-loving friends.

Just think about how many of your friends also have cats. Don't you discuss catteries, groomers, breeders, rescues, cat books and magazines, veterinary appointments etc with them? So will your customers, they are the best way of gaining new interest!

CASE STUDY:
MAKING A DIFFERENCE

Organisation: The Blue Cross, Lewknor
Location: UK, Oxfordshire
Cattery Type: Semi-outdoor
Cattery Function: Rescue & rehoming
Number of Units: 36
Unit Size Sleep: 4' x 4' or 5' x 4'
Unit Size Exercise: 4' x 6' or 5' x 6'
Date Built: 2005

www.bluecross.org.uk

TWO NEW CATTERIES BUILT ON A NEWLY
PURCHASED SITE TO PROVIDE CAT
ACCOMMODATION THAT IS FULL OF LIGHT,
NATURAL VENTILATION AND A WELCOMING
FEEL APPRECIATED BY ALL WHO VISIT AND
WORK AT THE CENTRE

BLUE CROSS, LEWKNOR

THE NEED TO UPGRADE

As part of its upgrading and development programme in 2004, The Blue Cross Animal Welfare Charity wanted to relocate its old and outdated cat centre in Chalfont St Peter in Buckinghamshire. **The decision to relocate the centre was taken on several issues:**

- To replace an old and outdated cattery
- Limited space on site meant expansion and space for fundraising events was impractical
- The centre could not provide facilities for dogs because of the close proximity of neighbours

After a short search, the Charity found and made an offer to purchase an existing dog welfare centre in Oxfordshire that was being sold. The offer was made on the basis that full planning permission could be obtained from the local authority to construct two cattery buildings. Fortunately, planning permission was granted with a limited number of conditions only.

EXISTING INFRASTRUCTURE

With an existing site that has buildings and infrastructure, this can limit the potential design layout of the site. However, in this case, the charity was fortunate that the buildings were generally in the right location for its needs.

CATTERY DESIGNS

The design and layout for the new catteries took on board many considerations. Some of these were planning related and some were animal welfare issues. The planning requirements meant that the buildings had to have low profile roofing, had to blend in with the local architecture and be sympathetic to the existing buildings on the site.

Following my initial three suggested schemes, the decision was taken to construct two 'U' shaped buildings to form a double courtyard setting.

From a purely financial point, it would have been more cost-effective to construct one large building. However this would have looked too imposing. It would also have meant that the cats on one side of the building had little environment enrichment, and been unable to watch day-to-day activities.

ENVIRONMENT ENRICHMENT

For some locations and sites it is impossible to give every cat unit an aspect that has good levels of stimulation and an interesting outlook. However, when the option is available to enable a better outlook for the cats – it should be taken.

Having recently rebuilt an old centre that had little stimulation and outlook, the Charity is very aware of just how much a poor environment can affect the cat's health.

This is particularly important for cats, which, by their nature are not normally taken out for exercise in the way dogs are.

The Charity is delighted with the design, the public impression of the site, the ease of working for staff and the size of cat units, providing cat-friendly accommodation to a high animal welfare standard.

The Centre Manager explains how the centre works for her and her staff (continued...)

What are you most pleased with?

All of it! How it works, how if feels, the location and views, how easy it is to clean, the public perception of the charity especially if they are expecting to find a rescue centre that isn't as bright, open and cheerful as this one! Julie's next project is to plant a flower meadow which will attract lots of dragonflies, butterflies and insects for the cats to watch.

What would you do differently?

A separate 'playroom' for socialising cats and getting to know their new owners would have been icing on the cake. It is fine when there are only a few people at the centre, but when it gets busy it would be nice to have a separate area.

Semi-outdoor Style
Cattery Building with Courtyard Garden

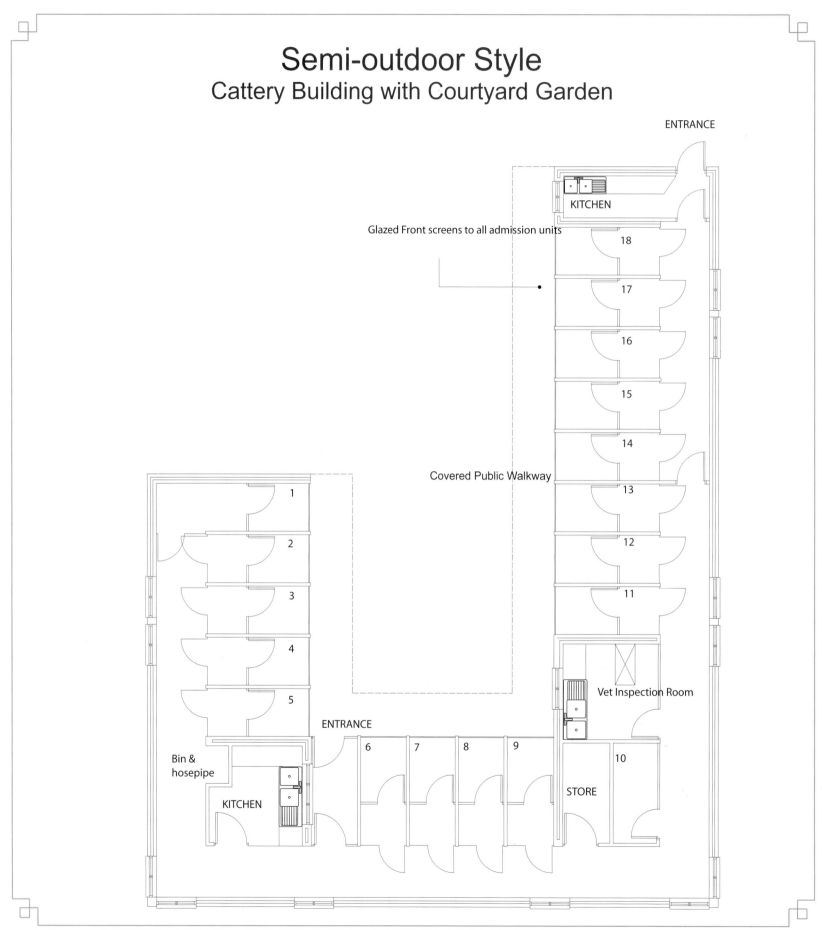

ENTRANCE

KITCHEN

Glazed Front screens to all admission units

18

17

16

15

14

Covered Public Walkway

13

12

11

Vet Inspection Room

1

2

3

4

5

ENTRANCE

Bin & hosepipe

KITCHEN

6

7

8

9

10

STORE

CENTRE MANAGER:

Julie Stone, the Manager of The Blue Cross Centre at Lewknor shares her thoughts about the centre:

The spacious cattery units at the Lewknor Centre enable the cats to exhibit more natural behaviour. Cats can move freely between an inside heated area, through a cat flap and into a light and airy exercise area. The outside world provides visual stimulation, without putting the cats under the added pressure of being able to see other neighbouring cats.

MAXIMISING VERTICAL SPACE

The provision of multi-level shelving enables cats to climb, which is vitally important in sedentary animals when in a rescue centre for a long time. Overweight cats are more difficult to rehome, and are prone to a variety of illnesses, so providing them with opportunities to move about and explore is vital.

CHOICES FOR CATS

Giving the resident cats choices enables them to settle in more quickly. They can choose to interact, or to move away and hide if they feel the need. Observations of interactions between cats and visitors are always interesting to watch. Each day could be a boring experience for many cats, especially if staff are very busy attending to the multiple daily tasks that are necessary.

However, here visitors can walk freely around the outside of the catteries, and the cats can choose to watch or interact with visitors. This is especially important for younger cats that are at the critical stage of their development.

The floor area in each cat unit is large enough to allow for several litter trays to be placed. Cats that normally toilet outside are still able to walk through a cat flap and use the litter trays in the external exercise area. Some cats prefer to be more private and therefore in some cases 'covered' litter trays are used.

QUALITY OF STAFF IS VITAL

The quality of staff is vitally important in a cattery such as this. Staff could avoid handling difficult cats, which would lead to some not getting the interaction they need to improve their behaviour.

Although we do inevitably encounter some aggressive cats, the vast majority settle in quickly and are handleable. Some of the shelves are quite high, and this can cause a problem with very aggressive cats when entering and leaving the units. However, the units are big enough for both staff and volunteers to walk inside, and the provision of a secure corridor enables free exercise for kittens and very energetic cats to burn off their excess energy!

CATTERY BUILDING 1

CATTERY BUILDING 2

THE BLUE CROSS CENTRE AT LEWKNOR

14 DRAINAGE, KITCHEN, CLEANING

CATTERY DRAINAGE SYSTEMS

The scale of development, the design of cattery and the type of cats that are going to be housed, any company policy, the number of visitors the cattery receives will all help determine the type of system installed.

All animal buildings should have efficient drainage systems if the cleaning policy is based on using hose-pipes and large volumes of water. This should include both the internal sleeping area and the external exercise area.

In the UK, USA and Canada all foul and surface water discharges are controlled by their Environment Agency (full details of the requirement are shown under site drainage and disposal systems).

Generally local authorities and the Environmental Agency will not allow any form of wash-down water to seep naturally into the ground; it must be channelled into an approved drainage collection system.

The type of system needs to be identified early in your design.

Equally important is the cleaning regime that will be used

As previously mentioned, many animal buildings are much too wet, simply because of the amount of water used in the cleaning process.

The more common drainage systems used are:

- Preformed channels (trench drains)
- Ceramic dished channel
- Self-constructed/manufactured system
- Single outlet gullies

We will look at these drainage systems in more detail on the opposite page.

Preformed Channels (Trench Drains)

The benefit of using a complete drainage system is that it makes for an easy, trouble-free system. **The most commonly used material is polymer concrete** – this is light in weight, and has a smooth internal surface (helping to prevent a build-up of sediment). It is available in pre-sloped sections, and is resistant to most acids and dilute alkalis.

The more popular ranges come with a variety of suitable gratings, from pedestrian weights right up to units suitable for airports. They are inherently safe, with secure, lockable gratings if required, and will handle a large volume of water without it splashing and swilling all over the floor (this system is often used by larger organisations).

The only disadvantage with a grated system is that some people are concerned it is a potential area for germs/bacteria to build up. However, with correct cleaning management and hygiene controls, this should not be a problem; it is however slightly more time-consuming to lift and clean the gratings.

Note for pre-sloped channels:

if the floor is level, you will need to use a pre-sloped channel system. This will ensure that the water in the channel is self-draining and prevent foul, stagnant water settling in the channel, which would be an area for germs and bacteria to build up.

Ceramic Dished Channel

Clearly if you have a tiled floor, the obvious answer is to install a complementary channel tiled system. The major manufacturers all provide suitable systems with the necessary sections (ie. stopends, corners etc). The range of colours does tend to be limited.

The system, when correctly installed, is extremely durable, aesthetically pleasing and hygienic. The only problem I have found with these channel tiles is the shallowness of the dish; it is only 20mm deep.

However, this system works extremely well for the small volumes of water generally used in catteries.

Self-constructed/Manufactured Systems

Many methods are used to provide adequate drainage, and most work extremely well. The two favoured methods used are half-round polyester-coated metal, or ceramic tiles used to form a square channel. Both systems will work extremely efficiently – when correctly installed.

As mentioned earlier, if you choose an open channel system it will be better to install twin channels; this will prevent the dilemma of trying to walk down the corridor and constantly crossing over the channel. **The important point to remember when installing any form of channel is to ensure it has an adequate slope so the water runs naturally into the drainage outlet.**

Single Outlet Gullies

These come in a range of sizes and are highly suitable for single rooms where the floor is laid in a four-way fall into the centre of the room. They are also useful for draining buckets of dirty water, rather than trying to lift into a high sink.

KITCHEN FACILITIES

The size and fitting-out of a cattery kitchen can be as simple or as elaborate as you want it to be. It is highly dependent on your preference, the type of food used, and the number of cats housed.

However, it should have the following basic elements:

- **Food preparation sink _and_ litter tray cleaning sink** (twin bowls allow one each for clean and dirty work)
  A separate litter tray washing facility allows the two processes (i.e. washing dishes and trays) to be kept totally separate to reduce the risk of infection and disease. It also allows two members of staff to work at the same time

- Adequate hot water

- Storage

- Staff hand-washing facility

It may also be desirable to consider the following items, which some may consider a luxury and extravagant; however, times and demands are changing, and time spent washing dishes is often considered to be wasted time.

- Dishwasher

- Sluice

FOOD PREPARATION, LITTER TRAY CLEANING AND SINK UNITS

In large welfare centres it has been common policy to install catering type stainless steel kitchen equipment. It has proved to be cost-effective, easy to maintain and hygienic.

Ten years ago the cost of stainless steel was prohibitive; it was a regular occurrence for me to visit industrial, hotel/catering auctions to try to purchase second-hand equipment!

However, more recently the cost of new equipment has plummeted and is now at a level where it can be purchased new for the same price as second-hand. This provides the added benefit of being able to purchase the correct size and specification for the particular application.

Because of the increased use of dried cat food, the amount of working space required has been reduced.

However, consideration should be given to the provision of adequate storage for dirty dishes and more particularly washing and drying cat litter trays – these take up a considerable amount of space.

HOT WATER

A good supply of hot water is essential for all establishments.

Apart from washing dishes and general cleaning, some organisations have installed pressurised systems to enable hosepipes to be connected to the hot water system for daily washing down of the cattery.

The type of system used to provide the water will depend on the volume required and the mains utilities available.

The main hot water systems available are:

◼ Centralised boiler system

◼ Gas multi-point heaters

◼ Electric

A centralised boiler system

This can be either gas, oil or solid fuel. However, I would not recommend the use of solid fuel because of the storage and manual handling problems

A cattery boiler system is exactly the same as installed in a domestic home; the only difference is that the size may be larger to provide a greater heat output and the volume of hot water required. Clearly, it makes sense to combine and utilise the boiler for the cattery heating as well

Boilers come in two system types:

◼ **A conventional system** – this requires the installation of a hot water storage cylinder, a cold-water storage tank and a feed/expansion tank for the central heating

◼ **A combi-system** – this heats water directly from the cold mains, as you require it. There is no hot water storage; consequently you will require an incoming cold water main with a reliable and constant pressure to enable these units to works efficiently. They do have limitations for use on large-scale projects with multiple hot water points

Gas Multi-point Heaters

For large scale developments that require large volumes of hot water, these units are extremely beneficial. They will provide unlimited amounts of hot water with fast recovery rates; they can be linked to several outlets

Electric

Generally, the cost for heating water electrically is more than by gas or oil. It also has the disadvantage of taking longer to recover the required temperature.

The types of electric water heaters available are:

■ **Pressure**
This is probably the most suitable system for the cattery owner, it is basically a large hot water cylinder with storage capacities for 50 to 450 litres. The larger units normally have two heating elements, one in the bottom and the other at the top of the cylinder. The lower element will heat the entire contents of the cylinder and is often used on 'off-peak' electricity, whilst the top is used as a boost.
This system will require the installation of a cold water storage tank at high level

■ **Cistern**
These operate on the same principle as the pressure cylinder, but they have their own built-in cold-water storage tank.
As the hot water is used, the cold water from the cistern replaces it. As a rule, they tend to be extremely limited in their use and capacities, normally with storage for around 25 to 135 litres

■ **Open**
These units are often installed over hand basins in toilets, staff rooms, etc. and are classified as 'point of use' heaters. They range in size from 6 to 136 litres and normally have a single heating element. They can be either mains-supplied or connected to a storage cistern

■ **Instantaneous heaters**
These are designed for direct connection to the cold water mains. They operate on exactly the same principle as a domestic electric shower, i.e. a heating coil heats the water as it flows over it. They have limited benefit to the cattery owner. However, for buildings that only receive occasional use, they are an effective provider of hot water

Note for off-peak electricity (white meter):

If you decide to use electricity as your main source for central heating and water heating, you should consider installing an 'off-peak' meter. This will be supplied by your electricity company and operates between 11pm and 7am. The unit rate for this electricity is normally about a third of the daytime rate.

SUMMARY OF HOT WATER HEATING SYSTEMS

Fired boiler:

■ Provides large bulk storage/volume, is cost-effective, one boiler can serve several buildings, they have quick heat recovery times. Professional installation is required

Electrical:

■ Ideal for isolated rooms/buildings requiring only a small amount of water

■ Extended recovery times

■ High revenue costs

■ Simple installation

Washing Facilities

Staff Hand-washing

With the ever-increasing legislation regarding health and safety, it is becoming more important to provide suitable staff washing facilities that are separate from those used for animal-related work.

Dishwasher

This might seem a luxury, even extravagant, but it is not as frivolous as it sounds. A large cattery with 50 cats will generate 100 dishes per day to wash and approximately 50 – 100 litter trays if standard cat litter is used; this will take a member of staff 1-2 hours to complete. An alternative is to use disposable cardboard food dishes as some larger welfare organisations do. **Remember this is a daily routine, which quickly becomes extremely boring and tedious!**
The installation of a dishwasher will release the staff member to carry out other duties and also give far more hygienic results due to the far higher temperatures of water used. The greater temperatures involved will destroy most bacteria/ viruses and the inclusion of disinfectants will destroy any remaining. These machines can be purchased second-hand through auctions, e.g. hotels, hospitals and catering equipment dealers. Before purchasing, you must ensure that you have the necessary infrastructure to enable the equipment to be installed.

Sluice or Bucket Sink

Generally most soiled cat litter is taken away as dry waste. If you install a sluice or bucket sink, the following should be taken in to consideration.

- If your drainage system is suitable for faecal matter, you will need some form of receptacle for it to be tipped or flushed into. If you do not have a suitable manhole that has a hinged or liftable lid, you will need a sluice; these are either ceramic or stainless steel. The basic principle is exactly the same as a domestic toilet, although most systems use larger diameter pipe-work

- If you propose to install such a unit in or near the kitchen, it is aesthetically better and more hygienic to provide a dedicated room; this can also be used to store disinfectants, buckets etc. In addition, you will also need to install a water supply/hose-pipe to enable the utensils to be cleaned

An alternative to the standard type of sluice is to install one of the proprietary macerator systems on the market. These consist of a sluice combined with an electric macerator pump; they normally operate from a 13amp socket and are plumbed into the drainage system. However, it would be worth checking with the manufacturers of the pump to ensure it is suitable and can cope with cat litter.

Kitchen Storage

The amount of space required in the kitchen is often overlooked, resulting in inadequate provision.

Ideally all sites require some form of central bulk storage facility; this combined with storage close to the centre of activity makes life far easier. The ideal place for your daily working storage is close to the kitchen.

Remember that to stock the store room, adequate
and easy access is a major consideration

THE DIFFERENCE BETWEEN CLEANING AND DISINFECTION

The level and standard required will vary with each owner, the construction type and materials used, and the function of the cattery. **However, whatever the type of facility you have, there will be times when a large part of the daily routine will involve a considerable amount of cleaning.** Obviously, for large-scale developments, sanctuaries and charities with a continual turnover of cats, this process becomes extremely important. The cleaning method and disinfection policy will depend on the type of cattery (e.g.boarding/rescue etc)

Daily Disinfection (Medical Model)

In the medical model, every wall, floor, item of bedding etc is cleaned daily and the building flooded with water and disinfected. This model will be more important where a high turnover of cats from unknown backgrounds is present and/or no environment enrichment is provided, as these cats will already be stressed and have little resistance to pathogens. (Also see Admissions in Chapter 4 Ancillary Buildings)

Spot Cleaning (Ethological Model)

In the ethological model (scientific study of animal behavior, especially as it occurs in a natural environment), the medical model is regarded as contributing to disease risk by increasing the level of stress in cats (as all familiar scents are removed from the pen and replaced with scent the cat finds overwhelming, especially when there is no option to escape from it). However, when spot cleaning, cats can remain in their enriched pen during cleaning and can hide if they wish. The walls can be spot cleaned with a clean cloth (change cloth between cages) and litter and bowls can be changed. **This method is only recommended for catteries where environmental enrichment (hiding, perching, etc) is provided.** I have seen many catteries using this cleaning policy. Instead of using hose-pipes to clean the building, they simply use dampened cloths and mops, dustpan and brush (one per unit) for litter spills. Clearly, this has many **advantages** such as cost, reducing the amount of water used, reducing the amount of stress in the cats and therefore they will be less prone to disease or illness. There are also less environmental implications using this method.

The spot-cleaning method has also been known to REDUCE illness and disease, which is quite the opposite to what you might think. The reasoning behind this method is simple: where is the benefit in removing the bedding etc, using strong-smelling chemicals (to which cats are very sensitive) simply to put the same healthy cat back into the unit shortly afterwards? The cat has lost its own scent from the unit and bedding (his/her safe and familiar area), and has to start all over again to place their scent back in the unit. **Obviously, if the unit is soiled it must be cleaned.** However, for the majority of cats, (especially those vaccinated and with a known background, or for rescue environments with the luxury of a separate admissions building) a daily clean or tidy up is fine and total disinfection is unnecessary under everyday conditions.

One analogy I can think of is to compare it to the veterinary surgery. When an animal has been examined and is leaving, the staff will disinfect the table before the next animal is brought in. This is sensible and totally logical.
However, I have never met a vet who removes the animal from the table halfway through the examination, simply to disinfect the table and then place the same animal straight back on!

Nadine Gourkow, the Animal Welfare Manager for the BCSPCA in Canada recommends that catteries wanting to experiment with different cleaning methods do so. She says:

"Try it for yourself, use the medical model in one area and the ethological model in another, and compare your disease rate and the stress of your cats. We know that stress is such an important factor in many diseases affecting shelter cats. We should reduce any and every source of stress to prevent disease and promote good welfare.

The other thing to change is not taking the towel away. Staff had been disinfecting the towels every day, but instead, we implemented a rotation of towels so the cat always has two, and there's one that's always saturated with the cat's smell. And what we found is that the disease rate actually went down when we weren't disinfecting daily"

Nadine Gourkow – Animal Welfare Manager BCSPCA

Obviously, between cats, or if the cat has been ill, then full and suitable cleaning and disinfection should be carried out.

It is interesting to watch staff who have managed old, outdated catteries with lots of gaps, nooks and crannies that were potential areas for the accumulation of litter, hair, urine etc to move over into brand new facilities. On the whole, they continue to use the same cleaning routine and regime as they have always done and no account is taken of the improved surfaces, finishes, sealed junctions, and easy-to-wipe wall surfaces!

Clearly you need to minimise the risk of disease as much as possible. Simple things such as having individual dustpan/brushes and cleaning cloths for each individual unit, washing your hands between each unit etc make a difference.

However, the biggest single route for disease transmission is either by direct contact (cat to cat), cat to food dish, or via staff. Clearly it is impractical to change your clothing between each cat in the cattery!

How to Try the Spot Cleaning Method

SAME CAT daily routine : cleaning and tidying

- This will just be a question of 'tidying up' odd bits of cat litter and cat hair (eg dustpan and brush) or 'freshening up' a unit. Cats have very sensitive noses and build up their own scents in a territory to settle themselves

- Cleaning up after any specific problems

- Cleaning corridors, especially if the public have access, or in wet weather

BETWEEN CATS routine : disinfection

- **Mop and bucket**

- **Flooding with water (hose-pipes or pressure washers)**
  Obviously not an option for timber buildings or cages as they won't have drainage, and the water will soon rot the timber. This method is more usual in large catteries or shelters where correct drainage channels have been installed. The use of hose-pipes in catteries is a quick way of cleaning, but it does have many disadvantages. It is not unusual for charities and sanctuaries to install fully grated drainage systems in their buildings to provide an outlet for wash-down water. Clearly, this suggests that they have a policy of using hose-pipes rather than mops and buckets. If linear drainage is installed, then it makes sense to lay the floor with a slope in order that any water can run into the drainage system

- **Wet and dry vacuum cleaners**

- **Steam cleaning**

Cleaning Systems

There are many options available to help with the cleaning routine. With all disinfectants, you should be sure that they are safe for use in the cattery environment.

Hose-pipes

It is far easier to install points for hose connections around the building, rather than relying on one long length of pipe. These can be either permanently fixed, or simple snap-on connections that can be moved around the building. (See more information in the chapter on Environmental Legislation.)

Mop/sponge and Bucket

For catteries that have good floor finishes (e.g. smooth, easy-to-wipe surfaces) a mop and bucket is still regarded as being the easiest and quickest method for daily cleaning.

Disposable Disinfectant Wipes

Another alternative, either in lieu of a sponge and bucket or to complement other systems. Again, the aim is to reduce the risk of cross-infection.

Pressure washer

The process of cleaning by the use of hot pressure washer is an extremely effective method. These systems can be either mobile or permanently fixed; the mobile system tends to be the more common option used. However, the majority of catteries simply do not lend themselves to this type of cleaning.

Mobile system

These units normally have a working pressure of approximately 1500psi, this being adequate for most cleaning situations. The nozzle can be changed to suit the type of work required, from a fine spray to a jet of water; your requirement should be discussed with the sales representative. Most units are suitable for connection to a domestic 13-amp socket outlet and require only a domestic water supply. The majority of hot cleaners use diesel fuel to fire the built-in boiler, which heats the water. A suitable machine will have a working life of around 15 years. If you use a mobile hot pressure washer, ensure that you purchase additional lengths of lance hose. This will allow the machine to be left outside while the building is being cleaned. The noise, fumes and manual handling problems associated with these large, heavy machines can be a major problem.

Wet and Dry Vacuum Cleaners

These inexpensive cleaners have many uses for the cattery owner. The machines (which are also used for cleaning carpets and have a spray facility) can also be used to apply disinfectants and also to vacuum up any excess water etc. Because they produce a fine mist spray (compared to a pressure washer) this makes it much more controllable, reduces the amount of water, and also clears it on completion.

Another option is the battery-operated hand vacuum cleaner. These lightweight, inexpensive machines are ideal for general day-to-day cleaning of the cat unit, particularly if the only mess to be removed is a small amount of spilled cat litter and cat hair!

Central Vacuum Cleaning

Although I haven't seen this system installed into a cattery, there is no reason why it shouldn't be used. The main advantage with a central vacuum system is that only a short section of hose-pipe has to be moved around and simply plugged into a suitable outlet point close to the working area. The noise of the motor is some distance away, again, this removes a potentially stressful activity for the cats.

Fixed system

The principle for fixed systems is exactly the same as that used on mobile systems; on the whole fixed systems tend to be larger and require three phase electrical supplies. The advantage of this system over the mobile unit is that it is permanent, utilising fixed pipework in the building. All that is required is for the staff to connect a short length of hose into one of the outlets provided, ensure the machine is switched on, and start to clean. This system is particularly suited to large buildings or multi-storey complexes.

Disinfection Systems

Disinfection is either physical or chemical; most catteries will use chemical means, being the most convenient.

Physical methods involve the use of heat, sunlight and electricity, while chemical use involves liquids, gases and steam. Whatever method you use must be capable of destroying the virus/bacteria; it is no good using a sweet-smelling compound that masks any odour, but does not act upon the bacteria/virus.

- Chemical disinfection systems

- Physical disinfection systems

Details of both types of system follow on the next page.

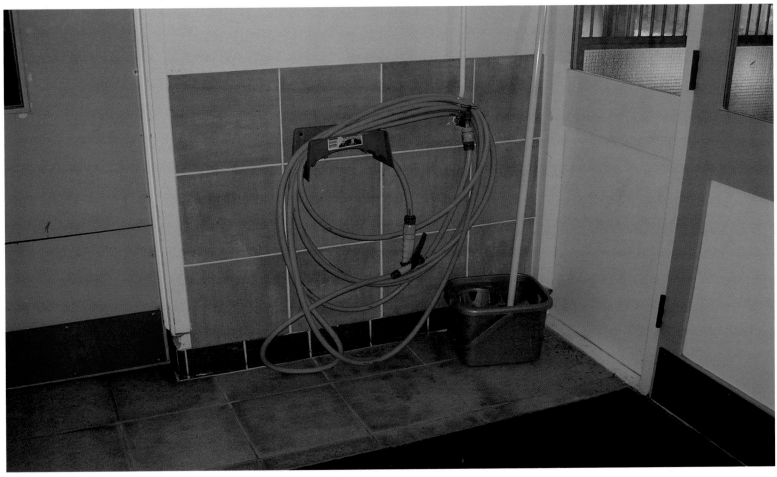

Chemical Systems

Chemical disinfectants act in one of three ways:

- Oxidising agents, or as reducing agents

- Corrosives or coagulants, acting upon the bacteria

- Bacterial poisons

Most chemical disinfectants are supplied in concentrated forms and require diluting with clean water before they can be used. It is accepted that warm water (not hot) is more beneficial during the mixing stage, as it increases the efficiency of the disinfectant.

Once the solution has been applied, it requires a 'contact time' to ensure that the bacteria/virus has been killed; this is normally between 10-30 minutes; after this time it can be washed/rinsed away with clean water.

Notes:

- For any disinfectant to work efficiently and correctly to destroy the bacteria, the building will need to be cleaned beforehand to remove faecal matter, bedding, etc

- Ensure that you mix the disinfectant to the correct strength as recommended by the manufacturer – too strong a mixture will NOT improve the efficiency of the product!

- Do not use or mix disinfectants from different manufacturers – this can result in both compounds working against each other

- Ensure all your staff know the correct dilution rates and how to mix them correctly. The reasons for this are twofold: first, extra strong mixtures are generally not any more effective than the recommend strength, and second, it is a waste of money!

- There are many disinfectants available to the cattery owner and these are constantly changing. Government/ environmental agencies may issue a list of approved disinfectants. However, these tend to have an agricultural predisposition and many will not be suitable for the cattery environment

- It would be wise to seek advice from your veterinary surgeon or local animal welfare charity to see what they advise

Physical Disinfection Systems

- Steam cleaning
  Heat from the steam naturally kills off bugs and viruses. This could be an excellent option for cleaning sisal/ scratching posts rather than with chemicals (which can stain and look unsightly).

Use feline facial
pheromone spray
in the unit corners
'between' cats
(at least 15 minutes beforehand)
to help them settle
in & feel safe

Summary for a Modern Cattery

By now, you will have a good indication of what are modern, efficient cattery buildings that not only take into account the needs of the staff, but also the cats' needs and requirements.

To summarise, the guiding principles for a modern cattery are:

- **Security**
  This is paramount for any animal-related business. There should always be a minimum of 2 safety doors, and ideally 3. For boarding cattery owners, **the loss of a cat can be extremely damaging to their business**

- **Plan ahead**
  It is not always cost-effective to refurbish existing buildings, you may not achieve the desired result with a design and layout that is second best. **Purpose-designed and constructed facilities are hard to beat!**

- **Design for the future**
  A green field next to you at the present might be a housing estate in 10 years; check potential land use with the local authority and find out who owns the land

- **Have a professional land survey carried out**
  This is the **only** way to plan a large site

- **Build to the highest standard you can afford**
  Experience proves that well-constructed catteries are easier to maintain, clean and offer better disease control

- **A well-designed cattery will be less labour intensive**
  This is a hidden cost that is not immediately apparent

- **Design the cattery to ensure the public does not have total freedom to view all the building**
  The cats need to have an inner sanctum free from disturbance; this is particularly relevant to rescue centres. This can be achieved by visitors and the public having access only to the outer exercise run, leaving the central corridor as a quiet area for the cats and staff to carry out daily routines, and by providing extra places to hide

- **Install light coloured floor/wall finishes**
  This reflects light, immediately removes the 'prison' like appearance that has been associated with animal buildings and also shows up areas that might not be as clean as they could be!

- **Install play equipment into exercise runs**
  Something for the cats to jump on, run through or climb; it all helps to enhance and enrich their environment and is something that visitors/owners will like to see

- **Design floors to ensure they drain adequately** to avoiding the problem of standing water.
  A dry building presents a better image, it is safer as there is less chance of slipping, and it also reduces the risks of some viruses (a damp warm environment is a potential breeding ground for disease)

- **Provide soft landscaping to the site**
  This will help soften the hard lines of the buildings and give a far more aesthetically pleasing site

- **Unusual features**
  If you want to install a particular feature and it is not readily available, speak to a specialist company about your idea – it is surprising how willing to find a solution for you most companies are!

The designs mentioned represent some of the latest thinking and advances for catteries.

Everyone involved with cats will have their own ideas on the best way to house them; there is no single way that is correct; different methods work for different people, locations, types of cat, etc.

One thing is certain, although some of the latest catteries have come a long way and are a great improvement over catteries built 10 years ago, they are still evolving and will continue to do so for many years. The improvements and modifications might be only minor, but added to some basic well-proven systems and designs, things can only improve.

Moreover, everyone can learn something new, whether it is a system, method or procedure to improve, enhance or make easier.

Cattery requirements are the same worldwide, so it makes sense to incorporate good ideas to make life in the cattery as pleasant and happy as possible.

Ideas can be taken from other countries, welfare research, or from other cattery functions (boarding/rescue/show etc) where there is always something new to learn, an improvement to find, or a problem to avoid!

You should always be on the lookout for an idea that will improve your cattery and raise standards

To sum up, the following four points should always be borne in mind when building catteries:

- Think ahead by planning for the future
- Think daylight
- Think calm, colourful finishes
- Think quality, it will pay in the long term

UTILITY AND SERVICE SUPPLIES

MAIN UTILITY AND SERVICE SUPPLIES

These hidden supplies are the lifeblood of any building, whether it is a cattery, a domestic house or a high-rise block of flats; a modern building cannot function without them! Whatever system you have installed, it needs to be effective, trouble-free and readily available.

All catteries will require the following:

- Heating

- Electricity for lighting

- Clean drinking water

HEATING

As previously discussed, the type of heating has to be decided early in the project. Often the choice will be limited, (usually because the utility company does not have a mains supply in your area). It is probably what will dictate the fuel you will use.

The main fuels are:

- Mains Gas

- Bulk Bottled Gas (LPG)

- Oil

- Electricity

- Solid Fuel

Mains Gas

This is the most convenient and cost-effective method for the provision of heating and hot water available. Where possible you should have a mains supply brought to your site. The problem for an isolated, rural centre is that the mains supply might be several miles away, and the cost of providing a service for a single property would be prohibitive. However, it is worth checking with the supply companies to see what their plans are for your particular location, and obtaining a quotation for the necessary works.

Bulk Bottled Gas (LPG)

For most rural locations without the luxury of mains supplies, this is one option available.
Once installed, the boilers require only minor adjustment to enable them to run on **liquid petroleum gas** (LPG). This system varies from a mains supply in that you will have a tank/s installed on your land; these tanks remain the property of the supply company, and you will pay a quarterly rental for each tank. Although this system works extremely efficiently, on the whole this type of gas is more expensive than mains supplied and at the time of writing more expensive than oil.

The size of tanks required will depend on the usage, the size of the boilers and the number of boilers on the site. An average tank capable of running a large boiler will measure 2m x 1m/6ft x 3ft, the delivery driver will need reasonable access to fill it, and it must be sited at least 3m/10ft off your boundary, and at least 6m/20ft away from a residential building.

Oil

You will need to install a suitable tank; the minimum capacity should be 1,000 litres. The larger tanks are suitable for large commercial boilers with high outputs (BTU), a central storage system serving several boilers, or a site with potential access problems, particularly during the winter months. Unlike gas, which is distributed under pressure, most oil systems work on gravity (i.e. the tank has to be at the same height as the boiler) which might require the tank to be raised on blocks.
Oil comes in two grades for domestic use – 28 second (kerosene) and 35 second (gas oil).
When ordering oil or replacement/additional boilers, this must be borne in mind and compatible units installed.
A boiler designed and set to run on one grade and as such will not run on any other grade without some modification to the burner. Kerosene is the cleaner of the two fuels, and therefore is slightly more expensive.
Most tanks for commercial operations will need to have a bunded or double-wall system. This ensures that in the event of the tank leaking, the oil is contained and cannot pollute the environment by seeping into the ground.

Solid Fuel

This is another option available. However, it does have many disadvantages, such as the storage of fuels, the considerable time and effort required to top-up the boiler (even with a modern hopper feed system), is a major consideration.
It involves considerable manual handling, compared with the alternatives available; it has little to offer a large, busy cattery complex, which would not generally have the dedicated staff to look after such systems.

ELECTRICITY

A site can be powered entirely by electricity; it will be relatively cheap to install, but the running costs will be extremely high. It has **several other disadvantages**; it is not as flexible as gas or oil when dealing with large volumes of hot water; it is extremely limited when looking at large commercial laundry equipment, it does not have the flexibility of many of the other systems available, and is more likely to be affected by adverse weather or interruptions to the supply.

For a large all-electric site, the incoming cable will probably be three-phase; usually on a commercial tariff and billed monthly. The choice of whether electricity is to be used for heating is highly dependent on the construction and design of cattery, and whether you are heating individual units or much larger spaces.

On the whole, I would not recommend a large site being powered entirely by electricity.

The nature of animal work means it is common to find the majority of electrical appliances, lighting etc will be switched on during the working day, especially during the winter months. If the heating is by electricity, this has a tremendous draw on the available supply. Therefore, the incoming supply needs to be adequate to provide all your power requirements, whatever the situation.

Note: When electricity loading-supply calculations are made for most domestic situations, there is an element of 'diversity' allowed within the calculation. This means an assumption is made that all the electrical loading will NOT be required at the same time. However, in a large, busy cattery it is often the case that all of the electrical loading WILL be required at the same time, and this high demand should be discussed with the engineer.

WATER SUPPLY

All cattery buildings will require a water supply. The supply size and capacity will depend largely on the scale of the development. Clearly a large site with many staff all requiring water at the same time could result in a lack of supply when required; this can be very irritating for staff and become a considerable waste of time in the long term.

In order to make this daily process as easy as possible, some thought should be given to the following:

Cold water supply

Whatever system you use will require a good supply of cold water.
Before embarking on a large construction programme, thought should be given to ensure that the main supply is of sufficient capacity to enable the site to function all year round. It is also essential to check the local water authority requirements, which varies with each authority. Generally there are two distinct systems, direct and indirect.
More information on the issues affecting water supplies can be found in the chapter on Environmental Legislation.

Direct water supply

This system has large, high level reservoirs providing a good level of mains pressure, the main principle being that the incoming mains water supply will serve all of the sanitary fittings, cold taps and cold-water storage cistern.
As the hose supply points are fed directly off the main supply, the pressure tends to be more than adequate for the purposes of hosing and washing down the cat units.
However, it is essential to establish if direct connection to the mains is legal; most water authorities will not allow this type of system where animals are housed, because of concerns about contamination of their supply.

Indirect water supply

In this system, all sanitary fittings, sinks (except one drinking supply, normally the kitchen sink) are supplied from the cold-water storage cistern. Commonly, this is the system stipulated by water companies.
As the system feeds all the sinks and hose points, the cold-water supply cistern requires to be much larger to cope with the demands of several hose points possibly being used at the same time.
At the early stages of development it is not always possible to know the exact number of people and animals that will occupy the centre and more importantly the amount of water that will be used. All of these factors will determine what size of storage tank/s is required.

Water usage

As a general guide, the amount of water larger centres use on a daily basis (e.g. 40 dog kennels and 30 cat units + laundry, etc is approximately 4,000 litres per day (880 gallons per day).
See the chapter on Environmental Legislation for further information on hose-pipes.

Water for buildings with inadequate mains pressure

For high-rise buildings, those constructed on high ground, or where an indirect system is required, it is unlikely that the mains pressure will be adequate for the purposes of providing sufficient pressure to enable the development to be washed down quickly and efficiently, as well as for washing machines to work correctly.

Remember that this is a **daily process** and any wasted time can quickly become a major irritation.

To overcome this problem you have several choices, these are:

■ Direct pumping from the main supply

■ Indirect pumping from the main supply

■ Private water supply

■ Water meter

We will now look at how to overcome these problems in more detail.

Direct pumping from the main supply

Generally, most water authorities do not allow this method to increase the water pressure to the site. This is because of the risks of contamination to the main supply. The basic principle is that a booster pump is fitted on the incoming main supply, thus enabling the cold water outlets to have good pressure.

Indirect pumping from the main supply

This system is probably the more common one used for animal buildings, it being accepted by most water authorities. The basic principle is for the incoming mains supply to run into a reservoir or cistern; this provides the 'break' between the mains supply and the outlets. A booster pump is installed on the draw-off pipe from the cistern. It is normal practice for a low-level switch to be fitted on the cistern to protect the pump in case the water supply is used at a faster rate than which it can be supplied.

The size of the cistern and pump will depend on the amount of outlets, the size of the property, the length of pipe run, and the pressure of the incoming supply (a supply with a greater pressure will fill the storage tanks more quickly than a supply with poor pressure; consequently this can help reduce the amount of water storage required). Thought should be given to the number of staff who will be working in the building at the same time using hose-pipes; the more staff, the larger the capacities the pumps and cisterns will require for washing machines etc.

For smaller sites, it is generally cheaper and more efficient to install booster pumps where they are required, rather than installing a centralised system. However, not all of the buildings will require good pressure hose outlets. A typical booster pump will operate at a pressure of around 3 – 5 bars/43 psi.

A typical mains supply coming from one of the water companies will be in three parts:

■ Water company service main

■ A service pipe which is the property of the Water Company.
The pipe runs from the service main to the boundary of your property, where it is terminated by a stopcock.
The size of the incoming service pipe will be determined by the amount of water that will be used; for a larger site either a 32mm or a 50mm service pipe would be suitable; the larger the pipe the higher the standing charge will be

■ The supply pipe from the stopcock into the property, which is the responsibility of the consumer

Private water supply

Many isolated sites do not have the luxury of a utility company supply. For these properties, it is not uncommon to find the property being supplied from bore well or aquifer (underground bed or layer yielding ground water for wells and springs etc). Whichever system you have must be capable of supplying all your requirements, all year round. It is pointless having a private supply that is incapable of providing water all year, the problems with private supplies are generally more pronounced during the summer months. If your supply is from a private source it must be tested to ensure it is safe to drink.

Water Meter

Within the next few years all commercial companies will have water meters; some areas have already started a compulsory programme of installing them. Meters, where fitted, are read on a quarterly basis by the water company; the water used is charged for as measured by the meter.

If you have a large development and are starting from scratch, it would be worth considering water-saving measures such as the installation of tanks to hold and recycle rainwater etc.

Photograph courtesy of the Mayhew Animal Home

ENVIRONMENTAL LEGISLATION

All businesses have been affected by increased environmental legislation in recent years. This has been particularly noticeable for owners of animal-related businesses, including catteries, kennels, stables and farms.

It must be stressed that the scale of the development has the greatest effect on the level of environmental legislation you will need to comply with, and therefore the possible cost implications. The larger the project, the more closely the legislative bodies will look it at and state what is required.

The main areas that cause the most issues and problems are:

- Sewage disposal (Foul Water)
- Groundwater Regulations 1999
- Faeces disposal
- Surface water drainage
- Water supply regulations
- Laundry
- Hose-pipes

In this chapter we will look at these environmental issues/problems.

SEWAGE DISPOSAL

The legal requirements for the discharge of sewage are covered by building regulations and the environmental protection agencies.

The safe and efficient disposal of foul and surface water is taken as a 'right' in developed countries, and should be considered of major importance to the health and welfare of staff/visitors and animals on the site.

Any poorly-constructed system will not only affect your site; but could have far-reaching consequences with pollution to water supplies/courses and contamination to other land, resulting in prosecution.

In the UK for example, the standard response from the Environment Agency to any planning application for the construction of any form of animal establishment (primarily kennels, catteries and stables) where mains drainage is not available, is to install a sealed cesspool.

A cattery owner has several choices available for the proper disposal of foul/waste and surface water. Even though catteries by their nature are not as high a risk as kennels, they are still put in the same risk category!

The main systems are:

- Sewer (public and private)
- Pumped sewage system
- Cesspool
- Septic or settlement tank
- Biological filter or treatment plant
- Filtration mound
- Reed bed

We will look at sewage disposal systems in detail on the next few pages.

Sewer

A sewer can be either private or public.

Most sewers built on private land since 1937 are private, but not all. The local authority should be able to give advice and guidance on this, as they are required to keep detailed maps. A private sewer is the responsibility of the owners of the buildings that it serves, and all costs are shared unless there has been a legal agreement drawn up, or it is documented to the contrary in the deeds.

Public sewers are generally sewers constructed before 1937, can be of any size and can run across private land, although most run under the public road system.

All public sewers are maintained by the local authority, which acts as agents for the water authority. The local authority may insist that any site or property within 30m/98ft of a public sewer has its foul water drainage system connected to that sewer.

However, the problems experienced by sites located in rural areas and not served by a municipal sewage system can be a major source of worry, expense and difficulty to the property owner.

It is recommended that you endeavour to connect into the main sewerage system. In the long-term it is far cheaper, with less problems likely to occur, and is generally a far cleaner solution.

In fact, the Environment Agencies prefer and have encouraged certain trade and commercial operations to discharge into sewers rather than watercourses, the reasoning being that the municipal treatment plants are more sophisticated and far more able to monitor and balance the overall quality of the effluent.

Sewerage undertakers control all trade waste disposed of into a sewer and are normally a subsidiary of the water companies.

Any form of trade discharge has to have the consent of the sewerage undertaker, who has the right to control:

- The nature of the effluent

- The maximum daily volume allowed

- The maximum rate of flow

- The sewer into which the effluent is discharged

Experience shows that there should not be any difficulties in obtaining permission to discharge into a main sewer.

The good news is that on the whole, the amount and type of discharge produced by even the largest cattery is still relatively small and non-toxic, being primarily clean wash-down, and is of little concern to the sewage companies.

Pumped Sewage System

Ideally, all drainage systems should work by gravity, with the effluent running into the sewer. Often, particularly in rural areas, a public sewer might be available but some distance away, or at a higher level than your site, necessitating the need to pump the effluent under pressure, uphill through small bore pipes.

For most situations, the installation of a packaged pumping station is the most cost-effective. These come in a range of sizes, grades of pump and are highly suitable for most applications. The pumps are generally submersible, electrically operated, and require little maintenance.

Helpful Hints:

- Make a full investigation of suppliers of package systems; these can vary tremendously in price

- Explain fully what the pumps will have to cope with (i.e. the type/amount of solid material)

- Most package systems require a three-phase electricity supply; single-phase pumps are available but are not as robust and capable of dealing with the larger solids. The use of an electrical converter will allow the use of a three-phase pump on a single-phase electricity supply. This is a cost-effective solution for a site that does not have a three-phase supply

- Install hair/grease traps to prevent cat hairs, etc. from entering/blocking up the pumps.

- Try to site the package system close to an access point, as it will require cleaning out periodically.

- Most systems have twin pumps – this is normally referred to as 'duty and stand-by'

Cesspool

A cesspool is an underground, watertight storage reservoir used for domestic purposes, but sized correctly can be used for commercial operations.

The size of the tank should be a minimum of 18,000 litres (18m³)/4,800 gallons for two users, and increased by 6,800 litres (6.8m³)/1,800 gallons for each additional user, but not more than 45,000 litres/12,000 gallons. However, before installing such a tank, carefully establish the volume of liquids entering it, and the costs of pumping it out.

As already mentioned, a medium-sized centre with 30 – 40 kennels and 30 cat units, laundry etc will use on average approximately 4,000 litres/880 gallons per day, seven days a week. With the considerable costs to pump out and remove, this quickly becomes an expensive method of disposal.

Clearly a cattery of 20 – 30 units will not use anything like this volume of water. However it is something that needs consideration.

Every country will have its own regulations on how far away from any dwelling, spring, well or stream used for drinking water it should be placed. (For example building regulations in the UK state that cesspools should be sited at least 15m/50ft away from a dwelling and 18m/60ft away from any spring, well or stream used for drinking water).

The use of cesspools is restricted to areas that do not have mains drainage, and where the subsoil conditions do not allow the use of septic tanks. The reasons for this being: lack of permeability such as clay or dense rock, or being close to areas containing springs, wells and other drinking water supplies.

A modern cesspool is usually constructed of glass reinforced plastic (GRP), although brick, concrete and even steel systems are also used.

Cesspools need to be emptied frequently, usually every 4-6 weeks.

Helpful Hints:

- Ensure that there is good access for the tanker, within approximately 25m/82ft of the tank and should also take into account the depth of the tank

- Ensure that no storm water enters the system, as this would quickly overload the tank and is expensive to have taken away

- Careful management needs to be maintained to ensure that excessive water is not used

Septic/Settlement Tank

If mains sewerage systems are not available, and for financial reasons it is not viable to install a cesspool, then several options remain, the cheapest and simplest being a septic tank or settlement tank. In the USA, these are also referred to as septic tanks. However, in some areas there is a wastewater disposal system called 'Large Capacity Cesspools.' These are similar to septic tanks, but do not provide any form of water treatment; they are simply shallow, bottomless concrete cylinders where wastewater enters and is allowed to slowly filter into the ground. However, these systems are slowly being restricted in their use, due to possible contamination fears of the surrounding land and drinking water supplies. Septic tanks differ from cesspools by having an outlet, which allows the effluent to soak away naturally by the use of surface, subsoil drainage pipes or to flow directly into a stream or river. However, some of the latest building regulations and environment agencies suggest that septic tanks should be used only in conjunction with additional filtration systems, such as drainage mounds or reed beds. For obvious reasons, the use of surface irrigation is not ideal as it sterilises available land and, more importantly, can be a health hazard. The cleaner and preferred method is to lay a series of underground pipes, which are either open-jointed, porous or perforated, and can be laid to either a herringbone or grid system. The consent of the environmental agency is required for all direct discharges from a septic tank (whether into a subsoil system, stream or river).

For a septic tank to function, particularly where a large volume of effluent is produced, requires suitable porous subsoil such as sand, gravel or chalk. The extent of subsoil drainage system will depend on the porosity of the land and therefore, before installing such a system, a site investigation or porosity test should be carried out. A ground engineer or reputable builder will be able to carry out this investigation work for you. Ideally this should be a person who knows the local ground conditions. One consideration to be borne in mind if installing a septic tank, is how to provide adequate soakaway for the final discharge. For larger centres or ground conditions that have poor porosity the total length of the underground pipe system could be over 50m/165ft in length. A septic tank system should be airtight to ensure that anaerobic action takes place. Such a tank does not purify the effluent, but merely breaks down the solids by means of anaerobic bacteria, decomposing the organic matter into methane and carbon dioxide. The heavy sludge then falls to the bottom of the tank whilst the scum floats and settles on the top. A well-balanced tank will have a thick layer of scum on its surface; this will help exclude air and ensure that the system operates to its full efficiency.

One problem with using septic tanks for large-scale cattery developments is the 'loading' factor. Most catteries wash and clean in a relatively short period, but if the wash-down water is allowed to run directly into the tank it could overload it. To prevent this, a common practice is to install an in-line holding tank above the septic tank, which will allow the load to be balanced over a longer period of time. This loading factor is one reason why environment agencies are reluctant to give their consent to septic tanks for animal-related operations. This is also a problem for many older catteries and kennels. Although they can operate at present, any application to upgrade or expand the business will involve the environment agency and will often result in having to upgrade the entire system for the site. This can be expensive. Septic tanks come in a range of construction materials, and older systems used for domestic properties are often brick or concrete. Most modern tanks are glass-reinforced plastic (GRP). All systems work on the same design principle to a lesser or greater degree.

The operation of a modern GRP system is:

- Sewage enters the main chamber of the tank; this is the sludge holding and decomposition section

- From the sludge holding chamber, the effluent rises into smaller chambers where sedimentation of finer solids occurs, thus allowing large sediment to return to the lower chamber

- From this final chamber, the clarified effluent is discharged into the sub-soil drainage system, stream/river or has further treatment

- The solids will need to be removed by suction tanker. This is carried out approximately every 6 – 12 months. A small portion of the solids is left in the bottom of the tank to enable the active bacteria to multiply

Biological Filter or Treatment Plant

Biological filters are normally installed where the environmental agency requires higher discharge consent levels. Most modern biofilters are complete packaged systems, normally manufactured from GRP or polyethylene.

The systems used for animal accommodation are:

Activated sludge

These systems work on the principle of continuously moving or agitating the effluent, either by air or mechanical means. Effluent enters a primary settlement tank, where settlement of the solids takes place, from where the displaced liquid enters the main activation tank.

During this aeration stage, the bacteria or activated sludge multiplies to remove most of the organic pollutants. After the agitation period, the effluent is allowed to settle for a further period, the activated sludge settles at the bottom of the tank and the clarified water is discharged into the drainage system.

Trickling filters

After the effluent has entered and settled in the primary tank, the supernatant liquor enters the main filter unit. The filtration unit makes use of irregular shaped pieces of plastic over which the effluent is allowed to trickle via a rotating system or a shaped disc with holes. Biological treatment takes place in the filter tank by the process of bacteriological oxidation, and the oxidising bacteria collect on the plastic media, and form a jelly-like substance called 'biomass'.

A stage of final settlement is allowed to take place before the effluent is discharged in the watercourse or sub-soil drainage system. The method and means of air entering the system will depend on the manufacturer's specification, with some systems air is forced through the top, while with others air is blown in from the bottom of the filtration tank.

Rotating Biological Filters (RBCs)

These filters operate on a system of rotating discs housed within a packaged unit. They rely upon a colony of micro-organisms becoming established between the discs, which rotate partly submerged through the waste water. The colony is exposed to the air and to the organic material of the effluent. The design of the system to be installed must take into consideration the consent granted for the level of discharge, the volume of effluent and the number of people/animals on your site. The installation might be a combination of two systems (e.g. trickling filter and an activated sludge).

Where current systems are already in place but are not performing to the required discharge consent, then there is a need to install a secondary or tertiary system.

The two main secondary/tertiary systems are:

- Filtration or drainage mound

- Reed bed

Filtration or Drainage Mound

A filtration mound is an extremely efficient way of polishing the final effluent. It is basically a large biological treatment plant and the size and extent of the pipework system will depend on the final level of treatment required to satisfy the Environmental Agency. The mound is normally installed below ground, with a network of perforated pipes being allowed to discharge the treated effluent, usually on a timed and batched process, through a series of layered sands and aggregates. A cut-off drain is installed and all of the polished effluent runs into this and is finally discharged into the watercourse or sub-soil drainage system. This system has given excellent results e.g. one installation reduced the ammonia from 15 mg/L to 3 mg/L. Minimal maintenance is required and the ground above it can be used for lightweight operations (e.g. garden use).

Reed Bed

The use of reed beds is becoming increasingly popular as a method of providing secondary treatment to septic tanks and treatment plants. This system has the benefit of being low maintenance, aesthetic in appearance, is economic and provides extremely high levels of purification.

Like filtration mounds, they require additional land, the size being dictated by the volume of effluent, numbers of people/animals and the consent standard granted. The system works by the reeds' ability to pass oxygen, absorbed by the leaf system, down to their roots. The polluted water passes around the roots and becomes purified by the high concentrations of micro-organisms living there.

There are two main designs of reed bed systems, horizontal flow and vertical flow.

Helpful Hints:

Relevant information
Ensure that all of the relevant information is given to the prospective suppliers, i.e. volume of water used, type and quantity of disinfectant, number of staff/animals on site. The manufacturer or consultant must take full design responsibility for this system, and this must be in writing

Design
Check to see if the system is capable of dealing with cat faeces if applicable; some systems are not suitable

Plan ahead
Take into account possible future expansion of the premises and an increase in the number of staff and animals. Perhaps it will be more cost-effective to look at a slightly larger plant

Laundry
What laundry arrangements have been made? A large commercial machine will use a significant volume of water and detergents

Disinfectants
All biofilters are highly sensitive to disinfectants, soaps, etc. and the micro-organisms can easily be destroyed by the use of too much disinfectant. The wrong type of disinfectant can also be detrimental

Expansion
Allow for possible extensions or secondary treatment to your existing system. The legislation regarding waste is constantly changing and is generally becoming more restrictive. Plan accordingly, and allow for obtaining consent for a higher level of discharge in a few years' time

Monitoring
Monitor the site and be flexible. If there has been a busy period with more visitors than normal, then the current sludge emptying cycle might not be sufficient, and may need to be increased

What to do if the system fails to achieve its discharge consent

The points given below show suggested actions to be taken should the filtration system fail to achieve the standard required for the appropriate consent:

- **Contact the supplier/manufacturer for advice**

- **Ensure that the plant is regularly serviced**

- **Check to see if the circulation fans and pumps are working.**
  Most modern systems have some method to force air into the system

- **Has the plant been regularly desludged?**
  Is the frequency sufficient to ensure that the holding tank is not overflowing into the secondary chamber?

- **Has there been an overdose of chemicals?**
  Most treatment plants will take three/four weeks to re-establish themselves. This is the most common reason for poor performance of septic tanks and sewage treatment plants

- **Do you need to balance the hydraulic loading?**

- **Does the plant need the inclusion of additives**?
  This will help the micro-organisms build up to a sufficient level

- **Temperature**
  Most plants will have a reduction in efficiency during the winter particularly if a severe, and/or prolonged one. At any temperature below 10°C, the metabolism of the bacteria will decrease rapidly

- **Is the filter media becoming waterlogged or clogged?**
  If so, this will require flushing through with fresh water

- **Has the site grown?**
  Is this to the extent that the plant is not capable of reaching the original consent standard?

- **Maintenance**
  Once the system has been installed, remember that like all mechanical items it needs to be maintained and monitored

It is worth having samples of effluent analysed regularly by an accredited company/laboratory to establish if the system is working correctly. This also ensures that there is time to correct any problems found before they become major and the environmental agency becomes involved.

A copy of the analysis should be sent to the agency, even if the system has failed. This proactive approach will demonstrate your commitment to correcting the problem and in the worst case, could prevent you from being prosecuted.

Groundwater Regulations

All consents for commercial discharges are the responsibility of the Environmental Agency (EA) in the UK, Scottish Environment Protection Agency (SEPA) in Scotland and the Environment Protection Agency in America (EPA). These official bodies set the standards for individual sites.

This standard is an individual one for each particular site and takes into account location, type of discharge point (i.e. stream/river or subsoil drainage) the volume of effluent, and the nature of the business.

The area of concern for any official department is the potential pollution to the receiving ground or river.

Once consent has been granted, the system will have to comply with set limits. It is normal for the EA to monitor effluent on a regular basis; this is usually 2–4 times per year. If the plant fails to reach the set standard, the problem must not be ignored; it will not resolve itself and must be corrected.

If the system has failed, then remedial action must be taken.

The UK Groundwater Regulations 1999 (UK discharge consents) help control the discharges of potentially dangerous substances; these are broken down into two categories, these are:

- List I – Substances are the most toxic and must be prevented from entering groundwater. These include pesticides, sheep dip, solvents, hydrocarbons etc

- List II – Substances less dangerous, but if disposed of in large amounts could be harmful. These include heavy metals, ammonia (which is present in sewage effluent)

Clearly the concern for most catteries, particularly the larger developments, is the use of disinfectants, and the potential effects it could have on a treatment plant and ground conditions.

Many of the modern disinfectants such as Trigene, Vircon, Virokill contain List II substances. However, as the daily amount used by most catteries is extremely small, say 0.5 litre/1 pint per day of concentrated disinfectant (of which only a small percentage is active ingredient). For practical purposes, the concentrations of List I and II substances are extremely small, and do not pose a risk either short or long-term, if used correctly.

The use of disinfectants needs to be carefully monitored and managed in order to ensure that this doesn't become an issue for the cattery owner.

On this basis it is unlikely that an authorisation is required under the Groundwater Regulations 1999. However, a Discharge Consent is likely to be required.

Faeces Disposal

The categories fall into five groups for the varying levels of contamination, these groups are as follows:

- A
  1 – soiled surgical dressings, swabs and all other contaminated waste from treatment areas.
  2 – waste materials, where the Control of Substances Hazardous to Health Regulations (COSHH) assessment indicates a risk to staff handling them, for example from infectious disease cases.
  3 – all human tissue, including blood (whether infected or not), animal carcasses and tissues from veterinary centres, hospitals or laboratories and all related swabs and dressings.

- **B** - discarded syringe needles, cartridges, broken glass and other contaminated disposable sharp instruments or items.

- **C** - microbiological cultures and potentially infected waste from pathology departments, clinical or research departments.

- **D** - certain pharmaceutical and chemical waste.

- **E** - used disposable bedpan liners, urine containers and incontinence pads.

Disposal of animal faeces might seem a simple problem to overcome, but from experience it can be expensive, time consuming and very difficult to resolve!

Some companies classify all animal waste, including soiled cat litter as clinical and put it in a Group A. However, some others put the faeces in Group A and the soiled litter in Group E.
Group E waste is not defined as clinical where the risk assessment shows that there is no infection risk and so can go to a licensed land fill site.

The disposal options available are:

- Main sewer

- Biological treatment plant/septic tank

- Landfill

- Incineration

- Composting

We will look at these in detail on the next few pages.

Main Sewer

This is perhaps the preferred option, being the most convenient, hygienic and probably causing the least environmental damage. Most authorities categorise faecal matter under group E, which is suitable for disposal to sewers, particularly for small amounts. As already discussed, any discharges to the sewer require the approval of the sewerage authority; they will set the limits and conditions for the discharge. Due to the relatively small amounts involved, these conditions are generally not too onerous.

However, this still leaves the question of disposal of cat litter.

Cat litter is not generally suitable for disposal into any form of drainage pipe

Biological Plant or Septic Tank

The method of disposal of faecal matter into your treatment plant will depend on several factors, such as whether the plant can handle the type of organic load, and what is the final discharge point.
Will the Environmental Agency allow faecal matter to be disposed of in your area to a watercourse or subsoil drainage system? If so this option is very similar to disposal via the main sewer, being convenient, hygienic and cost-effective.

Landfill

This option normally requires the services of a registered waste carrier. However before entering into an expensive contract, check with the local authority to establish the policy in force for the collection of animal waste.

The collection of soiled animal litter is still somewhat of a 'grey' area. Some local authorities would take this as normal commercial waste, while others classified it as clinical waste. If the local authority or a registered carrier will take away the solid waste as normal commercial waste, this is the cheapest and most convenient option available to the cattery owner.

UK Tip:

The new Hazardous Waste Regulations 2005, are likely to impact the kennel and cattery owner at some stage, and may result in solid waste (special waste) being re-classified as hazardous waste. For areas where solid waste was classified as normal commercial waste, this may no longer be an option, and you may find that it has been re-classified as clinical waste and the cost and legal implications need to be considered.

In July 2005 legislation came into force – The Hazardous Waste (England and Wales) Regulations 2005.
From July 16th 2004, the co-disposal of hazardous waste with non-hazardous waste at the same landfill was banned.
As of 16th July 2005 the Waste Acceptance Criteria (WAC) came into force. This means that producers of hazardous waste will have to make sure that waste to landfill meets the WAC. It is therefore essential that businesses can describe exactly what their waste contains, this will determine what can be done to minimise it, and ensure that it is correctly disposed of.

In essence this has meant that landfill sites that could in the past accept solid/special waste may no longer be able to accept the new Hazardous Waste. The easiest way forward is to use a specialist disposal company, clearly define what type of waste you are disposing of and use the company's knowledge and expertise to ensure that you don't face any legal problems.

Incineration

This is generally the most expensive option available to the cattery owner. The cost will depend on the frequency of collection, the distances involved for collection to the incinerator, and also on the availability of the specialist company.

With this option the standard method is to use either plastic bags or bins, which the specialist carrier/incineration company normally supplies.

It is not uncommon to find rural catteries simply burning soiled litter. Obviously this is only suitable for wood and straw based products. However, open burning may be an offence (e.g. as under the UK Environment Protection Act 1990). It is time consuming, does not create a good business impression, and is likely to upset your neighbours!

Composting

Composting has been around for a long while, and is used extensively in Scandinavia for the disposal of domestic waste from isolated properties and communities. All animal waste will decompose naturally if left in the open air, but the process is slow. The other main obstacle to be overcome is the physical element of handling faecal matter. People often have little interest where all of our waste goes to once it has left our property, so it is difficult to come to terms with the prospect of looking at alternative systems that are just not as convenient.

Decomposition of animal waste requires mixing it with some form of carbonaceous material such as straw, chipbark or newspaper to provide voids through which air can be blown. The amount of air is adjusted to provide the desired temperature for the waste. The optimum temperature is 55°C/131°F for decomposition, and the control of pathogenic bacteria; the end product is suitable for use as a fertiliser on the land.

If you consider this option, then advice should be taken from your local environment agency office as shown below.
For up to date information, please see the following websites:

UK:
- www.environment-agency.gov.uk

- www.sepa.org.uk

- www.defra.gov.uk

- www.hazardouswaste.org.uk

Europe:
- www.eea.eu.int

USA:
- www.epa.gov

Canada:
- www.ec.gc.ca

SURFACE WATER DISPOSAL

The aim is to help minimise the volume of rainwater entering public and foul sewer systems. However, this can overload the capacity of the sewer, and lead to flooding. Depending on the locality, storm water drainage systems may be permitted when combined with the foul sewage system. This is not ideal, as it could also exacerbate the potential flooding issues with foul drainage. Certainly for a new, large development it is highly unlikely that the local authority would allow a combined system.

Modest Developments

For a modest development, the standard soak-away system (either a brick/rubble filled or concrete ring system) will be adequate to dispose of surface water, providing the ground conditions are free-draining and will allow the water to disperse.. Some ground conditions such as clay do not allow this natural seepage.

Larger Developments

For larger developments, it is likely that the local authority and environment agency will want to see a more substantial and engineered method to cope with large volumes of surface water. This is part of the longer-term aims to reduce flooding, by storing the water in underground tanks or large tubes, then releasing it at a controlled rate back into the ground to reduce flooding. This is known as Sustainable Urban Drainage Systems (SUDS).

The SUDS systems are roughly classified into four categories:

1. **Landscaping**
   The inclusion of ponds, construction of wetlands, permeable pavings

2. **Water Recycling**
   Surface water or 'grey-water' is collected in underground tanks and used for non-potable purposes such as washing the cattery, toilet flushing etc

3. **Improve Soakaway Systems**
   The use of cellular plastic units has gained popularity in recent years. These units can be cut and shaped to fit any area. These units are lightweight and have void ratio of approximately 95% as compared with the traditional brick soakaway, which has a typical ratio of around 30%.
   The advantage of these units is their ease of handling compared with the concrete rung structures

4. **Attenuation**
   These are simply tanks or large diameter tubes that store water during a rainfall event, and then through a flow device release it slowly back into the ground at a controlled rate

WATER SUPPLY REGULATIONS

Some water providers are carrying out surveys to establish what type of water fittings, water supplies and cleaning regimes kennels, catteries and stables use. Their concerns are about possible contamination of the main water supply by back-flow or back-siphonage. Even with double-check valves, most supply companies will not accept this as an adequate safeguard to prevent contamination where catteries, kennels and stables are concerned and are asking for non-mechanical means to prevent any possible contamination.

UK Legislation

The UK water authorities have five fluid categories. The main elements of the five categories are:

- **Category 1:**
  Wholesome water supplied by the water undertaker and suitable for drinking

- **Category 2:**
  Water as in Cat 1 except that it has a slight taste, odour, appearance or temperature
  Typical example:
  a.   water that has been softened by salt regeneration,
  b.   Category 1 and 2 water mixed via combination taps

- **Category 3:**
  Fluids presenting a slight health hazard and are not suitable for drinking or other domestic purposes
  Typical example:
  a.   clothes and dishwashing machines,
  b.   hand held garden hoses with flow controlled spray

- **Category 4:**
  Fluids presenting a significant health hazard and not suitable for drinking or other domestic purposes
  Typical example:
  a.   clothes or dishwashing machines other than for domestic use,
  b.   mini irrigation systems

- **Category 5:**
  Fluids presenting a significant health hazard due to the concentrations of pathogenic organisms
  Typical example:
  a.   Grey water re-cycling
  b.   Commercial dishwashing and clothes washing machines

The main distinction between category 4 and 5 is that the level of toxicity or concentrations of substances in category 4 fluids is such that a prolonged period of exposure is generally necessary, before serious harm to health occurs.

To prevent any possible contamination, the water supply authorities require the kennel or cattery owner to install backflow contamination measures. Unfortunately, many businesses are being caught out by this new legislation as most water providers are classifying kennels, catteries and stables as Fluid 5 Category for contamination.

In essence, this means that back flow prevention measures have to be installed to the main cold water supply tank. The systems required for Category 5 fluids are either Type AA or Type AB. Generally with an 'A' gap tank there will be a requirement to install a booster pump in order to meet the minimum pressure required; this is usually a minimum 3 bar. The pump/s will need to be connected.

Inspectors normally visit your premises to establish whether you comply or not. If the premises do not comply, a notice may be issued in which the modification works have to be completed within a stated time (e.g. within 28 days).

If the works are not completed, there are legal and financial implications.

USA Legislation

It is interesting to see that many of the concerns regarding back flow or back-siphonage and the use of cross-connections are very similar to the UK as listed previously. Therefore, before commencing with any installation it would be wise to check with the local water supply company to establish the local rules and regulations for your county.

Laundry

Unfortunately, for many owners water regulations could affect the washing machines installed in your cattery.
Many domestic or older commercial washing machines only have a Category 3 fluid rating. Most local water authorities may insist that all sized washing machines have a Category 5 Fluid Rating. This is applicable to all non-domestic businesses, and operations such as catteries and veterinary surgeries etc.

Hose-pipes

Again, similar issues and concerns about possible backflow relate to the use of hose-pipes in animal accommodation. More importantly, to any tap that can be fitted with a hose-pipe.

The easiest and quickest way to overcome any potential legal issues is to install a storage tank with a suitable capacity for the day, this is then linked to a booster pump. The pump should have a minimum of 3 bar. However, for large organisations which might have several members of staff cleaning at the same time, the bar rating might have to be increased.

17

MAKING IT YOURS

EVERY CATTERY
IS UNIQUE AND
HAS ITS OWN
IMAGE AND
CHARACTERISTICS

MAKING IT YOURS

Now for the fun bit!

One of the biggest factors for making a business/organisation your own is choosing the name and logo. This can be dictated by a house name, location name (village, town, city, county), a theme you like, or you may decide to keep the original name if you are purchasing an existing business.

If you are providing a cat-only facility, this is a BIG selling point. Mention it wherever you can, especially in the USA/Canada where this is more unusual

What you are providing in terms of services, location, construction, size, landscaping, accessories, logo and staff all present an 'image' to your clients. This will come across in your personal communications on the telephone and face-to-face, in your brochures, website and any advertising and marketing you do.

Catteries that are proud of their buildings can easily promote this by using photographs on all cattery-related information. Remember that with a professional, well-designed website showing lots of clear, large photos you will be able to attract customers from further afield, especially if you are providing a building and service that is personal, professional, and one that educates and champions the use of behaviour knowledge for a cat-friendly environment.

Think about what else you can do to provide the right 'feel' to your cattery and give your clients even more reason to talk about what you are doing!

Outside

Initial impact:

- Your logo, stationery and marketing materials such as brochures
- Your website
- Welcoming signage and notices (opening times, logo, phone number, website)
- Landscaping – well kept and interesting!
- Buildings clean and pathways swept
- Provide hanging baskets, well-stocked flower beds, pretty gardens to show off your cattery
- Well placed touches of humour and items with the 'aaaaaah' factor

Incorporating images of cats:

- Topiary
- Sculptures and statues
- Hanging baskets
- Wind chimes
- Weather vanes
- Murals and trompe l'oeil

Inside

- Professional record keeping system
- Cat profiles
- Notes for each cat attached to their unit
- Comfortable area to discuss cats with their owners, take bookings or details
- When obtaining a business phone number, ask the operator to find you an 'easy-to-remember' number
- Once you have decided on your business name, purchase your web name. It would be wise to purchase both the country domain (.co.uk/.us/.ca/.au/.nz/.fr/.ie etc) as well as the dot com (.com) address, as customers may not remember which one you use!
- Boards or signs with helpful information or cat facts (especially for rescues)

On the next few pages we will see a truly unique and stunning garden setting which benefits cats, visitors and staff alike.

CASE STUDY:
JAPANESE FENG SHUI GARDEN

Organisation: Wood Green Animal Shelters
Location: UK, Cambridgeshire
Cattery Type: Semi-outdoor
Cattery Function: Rescue
Number of Units: 4 buildings of 12 units each
Unit Size Sleep: 38 x 30 x 40"/980 x 760 x 102mm
Unit Size Exercise: 89 x 35 x 72"/2.3m x 890mm x 1.8m
Date Built: 2002

www.woodgreen.org.uk

A WORLD RENOWNED RESCUE AND
REHOMING CENTRE CREATED A JAPANESE
AND FENG SHUI GARDEN WITH A RELAXING
ATMOSPHERE, MAKING THEIR CENTRE AN
INVITING AND WELCOMING PLACE TO VISIT
CATS FOR ADOPTION

WOOD GREEN ANIMAL SHELTERS

Wood Green Animal Shelters was founded in 1924 with the aim of alleviating the problems of abandoned and injured animals on the streets after the First World War. The Charity's largest centre and head office is its Godmanchester site near Cambridge, and since opening its doors in 1987, the centre has undergone some dramatic changes.

THE GARDEN

Nigel Mason, Head of Animal Welfare explained:

The buildings are all set in an attractive Japanese feng shui garden. The idea behind feng shui is that it maximises 'chi' (positive energy) in a space, Japanese gardens are symbolic – and both are aimed at relaxation and positively affecting the beings within.

The aim was to build a garden that is good for both cats and people, and also have a little fun with the design.

The Charity wanted something to symbolise the grace and elegance of cats with long, gentle curves to mirror the suppleness of a cat's body – the principles behind both styles certainly achieves that very well. The idea is that the Japanese Feng Shui garden's positive influence will give cats what they need to feel happy and relaxed, while also providing a variety of visual stimuli for them and the visitors.

FUTURE DEVELOPMENT

The Charity is currently constructing a brand new, purpose-built mother and kitten building as part of its long-term development and modernisation plan. In the mid-term, the Charity hopes to demolish the timber buildings and replace them with purpose-built brick accommodation.

This second phase is to consist of a new cat rehoming centre, and a specially designed isolation unit for sick and injured cats and kittens.

Photographs by David Key and Nigel Mason

What are you most pleased with?

Visitors' reactions to the garden – the landscaping gives a home-like garden feel and a relaxing atmosphere in which to view the cats.

What would you do differently?

Larger units to give more internal space for the cats, more storage for staff use and wider corridors to allow easier access for visitors

WOODGREEN
ANIMAL SHELTERS

OTHER SERVICES YOU CAN OFFER

At some point you will be tempted to introduce more units. However, before you do this it would be worth stopping to think before you do so and ask yourself if you really do want to go to all that expense and effort. If you need to increase profit, you can make as much money from selling a few items to your existing clients as you can from boarding their cat for a weekend!

Many welfare organisations now sell retail items such as collars, harnesses, food, litter and toys to increase their funding to care for more cats.

Think in terms of maximising your profit per client and providing a quality service, rather than going to the expense of adding on more units, taking up more land and going through the planning/zoning permission stage.

Consider the possibility that increasing unit numbers may result in your losing the personal and friendly touch, or having to employ more staff.

Ideas of other services to offer:

- Collection and delivery
- Microchipping
- Grooming, nail clipping
- Pet transport and relocation
- Web cameras
- Veterinary services
- Massage
- Hydrotherapy
- Alternative therapies such as acupuncture
- Bach flower remedies
- Clicker training
- Behaviour
- Display arts and crafts from local artisans

And of course, you can always think about retail sales on site or online.

Retail Sales/Store

For larger businesses, or those who have decided to opt for diversity of service rather than just adding more units, a store could be useful to maximise profits from existing customers. This can be useful for both boarding and rescue as a way to increase sales, and can be done on a small basis (eg food and cat litter) or even extend or grow into a larger business selling toys, bedding, bowls, gifts etc).

Ideas for products to sell:

- Cat litter, trays and scoops
- Food – tinned and dry food, treats
- Bedding, cushions, throws, scratching posts, activity centres
- Collars, harnesses
- Toys
- Water fountains
- Gifts, photo frames, mugs, calendars, books etc
- Feline facial pheromone (ask your veterinary surgery which supplier they use)

Keep up-to-date with what is happening in the pet market. This is easy to do online, or at cat shows or trade fairs. This will help you find out what the latest trends are, so you can stock your shop accordingly. One of the biggest areas of change in the pet market food industry is that more spending money on convenience products such as single-serve pouch and gourmet pet foods and products such as age or lifestyle-targeted pet foods (e.g. indoor, mature, cat breed, dental, diet, activity levels etc).

Another option is to use affiliate programs to sell items from other online pet stores, and gain commission by placing links on your website to cat-related products, and gaining 2%-15% commission whenever a sale is made. This would allow you to 'sell' items on your website, without having the cost of paying for stock. This may be especially useful for you if you are just starting up and have no budget for store products as yet, but would like to provide more interest on your website.

YOUR WEBSITE

In the course of researching this book, we used the internet to source interesting cattery buildings, welfare improvement ideas and photos from around the world. Finding a website of quality was rare!

So, to help us while we were working on the book and to look purely from the pet owner's point of view, we asked a pet-owning friend involved with breed rescues to try and track down interesting and noteworthy websites from existing catteries on the internet. After the first day of research, Sue came back to us quite disappointed and downhearted. Even though we had forewarned her that it would be time-consuming, she was still shocked (her words) at what she had seen.

Estimating that something like 1 in a 100 websites had anything of quality or good ideas to show, she also confirmed that in direct contrast to this, over 90% had the word 'luxury' to describe their cattery, no matter what the quality of building. **However, when she did come across a website of note, she was relieved and delighted – these catteries really stood out and encouraged her to spend more time there!**

Discouraging findings of our tester were:

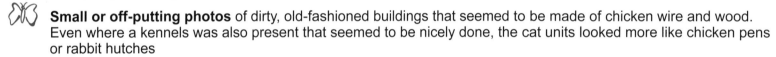 **Small or off-putting photos** of dirty, old-fashioned buildings that seemed to be made of chicken wire and wood. Even where a kennels was also present that seemed to be nicely done, the cat units looked more like chicken pens or rabbit hutches

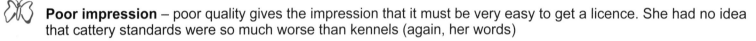 **Poor impression** – poor quality gives the impression that it must be very easy to get a licence. She had no idea that cattery standards were so much worse than kennels (again, her words)

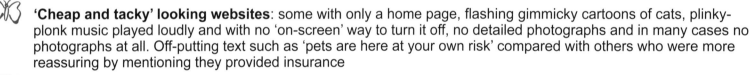 **'Cheap and tacky' looking websites**: some with only a home page, flashing gimmicky cartoons of cats, plinky-plonk music played loudly and with no 'on-screen' way to turn it off, no detailed photographs and in many cases no photographs at all. Off-putting text such as 'pets are here at your own risk' compared with others who were more reassuring by mentioning they provided insurance

Inappropriate photos or images of cats that were obviously either frightened or bored. She found that no photos at all, or flashing cartoons only, made her feel highly suspicious of the organisation

Lack of welfare implies lack of interest. No photographs or mention of grass or catnip being offered was found. Many had bare units with no toys or alternative bedding (to provide a choice of places to rest)

Good ideas found by our tester were:

Web cams - where you can log in and see what your cat is doing

Virtual tours (clear, large or close-up photos, movies)

Printable, online **brochure**

Fees shown clearly

Catteries where thought was given to **cat welfare** and amusement stood out a mile

As the vast majority of units were timber (UK) or small cages (USA) any construction other than these stood out

A good photograph speaks a thousand words!

There are some very basic rules to creating a **good** website.

A website is the 'clicks and mortar' representation of a business – and it is available to everyone. If a poor quality cattery has nothing to shout about, then you wouldn't expect to see big photos and lots of descriptive text – but a good quality cattery should have a website that reflects this by providing plenty of photographs (preferably ones that can be enlarged for a better view) and lots of descriptive text to give you a feeling for the cattery and care available.

Appeal to your audience and provide lots of photos

Your cattery and website **must** appeal to your clients, visitors or 'audience'… in this case of course – cat owners.

So, ask yourself, what do cat owners love about their cats? This will give you an understanding of what will appeal to them. Cat lovers are seduced by the cat's beauty, elegance, enigmatic, mysterious, intangible, intelligent, captivating, agile, clean, fastidious nature and keen senses. Aim for a website that is well designed, attractive, elegant, gentle, understated, interesting, full of photographs and with obvious links such as contact, tour, about your cattery, fees, terms and conditions, special needs catered for and descriptions that help visitors understand quickly what your business is about.

Make it easy to use

Have a simple, easy-to-navigate layout with the logo in the top left corner and the navigation links/buttons in the same place on every page (either at the side or at the top). Have short pages with anything of importance highlighted. Visitors should 'get' your site without having to think about it – people 'scan' web pages, they don't read them! Purchase the .com web name (domain name) as well as the country-based one. That way, if clients cannot remember which version you use it won't matter, as you can automatically direct one to the other. Once you've captured your visitor's imagination, they will relax and look at your website properly.

Visitors are always in a hurry and will want to be able to find out about whether your business is worth further investigation quickly, so:

- **Use soft or appealing colours**

- **Make links stand out** (use larger text or buttons) so they're easy to find

- Have **navigation** links/buttons to obvious things like fees, tour, terms, contact, photos, questions

- **Include photos of your cattery**, not just pictures of your pets or cartoons

- **Keep the layout as simple as possible** – busy pages put people off

- **Keep the pages short** – if you can avoid scroll bars altogether, great! At the very least keep away from 'miles-and-miles-and-miles-of-text-all-on-a-single-page'

- **Text should be in very short paragraphs and have titles** to help people 'scan' to find what they want

- Ask friends to test drive the website for you, they will always come up with good suggestions and ways to improve it

- **Provide an online brochure** by providing a PDF document from your existing marketing material (anyone, anywhere can read a PDF using the free Adobe Reader). You can then place this on your website, or send it by email (recording clients' email addresses is a fast way to send out updates).
  You can even convert your documents online for free by going to www.adobe.com

Next we will look at how a software booking system can ensure a professional, caring image, and help keep you organised with your administration.

BOOKINGS AND SOFTWARE

Chris Wye, PetAdmin

WORK SMARTER, NOT HARDER

As you may already know, or are certainly about to find out, the amount of paperwork that even a small business generates is quite surprising! It is in your best interests to spend as much time with the cats in your care and their owners as possible, and the less time you spend on paperwork, the easier this is to do, and is obviously much better for you too! **It is a good idea to think about how you will handle the bookings and run your business at this early stage**. In fact, we would recommend that you download a free trial of a booking software program very early on. Not only will this help you familiarise yourself with how you want your business to run (so you can include this in your cattery design), but it can also help you 'picture' in your mind what it will be like to manage the business.

A revamped hotel computer program is not the answer! You are not just dealing with allocating 'rooms' but the need to record a great deal of information about cats, owners and requirements

---

The sort of information you will need to record is very varied. This can include everything from photographs, behavioural issues, likes and dislikes to important health, medication and veterinary requirements. Owner home/away details, emergency contacts and the cats' usual vets will need to be kept documented to help provide a personal and professional service.

PAPER, ROCK, SCISSORS

The advantage of a computer program over paper records or a diary are considerable. When you produce a new brochure or leaflet, change things on your website, or want to rekindle your existing customers' interest - you should be able to do it at the touch of a button, not have to trawl through umpteen record cards stapled together! Further advantages of a computerised system are the **impression this gives to your customers**, that you can make your licensing officer's life easier, and that you can find anything immediately as all the information is to hand. You should be able to search for any part of the customers' or cats' details, which could be handy when someone doesn't leave their telephone number, but expects you to know exactly who Fluffy belongs to!

Of course, your bookings and management software should be extremely easy to use and intuitive. This alone is a good reason to start trying out software early - after all, you will be using it every single day for as long as you are running your cattery. If you have some experience with computers this will probably already be obvious, but it is essential if you have not used computers in business before. **Your software should look attractive, be easy to use** and preferably provide easy-view charts or graphs to show you what you need to know quickly. It should be fully integrated with your operating system (e.g.Windows) and have a 'Help' or 'Tutorial' section to help get you started. However, with a good system, you should be given pointers on screen that are intuitive and allow you to start using it straight away.

TAILOR-MADE TO YOUR CATTERY

While you are at the stage of thinking about designing your cattery, try out a bookings program on **the sort of services that you want to set up** (e.g. boarding/rescue, grooming, microchipping, food or toy sales, medication etc) and you can use this to help you visualise your whole service, and set up your fees and contacts. This is where you will find out how customisable the software is - can you categorise units (kitten, senior, diabetic, nervous, isolated or active cats) or give your cat unit names, colours or fun themes rather than just numbers? Can you select breeds, categories, what customers have purchased, colour schemes, special needs areas? Can it work out discounts for multiple cats? You might decide to start selling a special new line of cat collars, books, or china with specific cat breeds on and want to select relevant clients to inform them.

Think about how you will use your booking system, and remember that flexibility for now and the future is important. You will probably want to be able to use it both in the cattery reception and in your home (as most of our customers do). During the evening, availability can be checked and bookings taken/modified via your home computer in response to telephone calls for bookings from clients. You may want to expand the business in the future. The way to do this is to have your system fully network-able and as your business grows you can add more computers if required. Perhaps you will take on a groomer, receptionist or office/shop staff, trainee, rescue/fostering work?

WHAT TO CONSIDER

The following will provide a good idea of the kind of things you will need your booking system to be able to handle:

Bookings and Diary/Schedule:

- Capable of handling an unlimited number of customers, cats and bookings and highlight 'no-show' customers
- Link family cats to the same owner
- Booking confirmation letters, contracts and history
- Booking arrivals and departures
- Occupancy for the month ahead
- Handle all your contacts via an address book
- Control your workload with a diarised task schedule

Health:

- Cat details for the unit or vet
- Vet, insurance and vaccination details including warnings for expired inoculations
- Daily reports (e.g. feed and medication schedules, exercise/welfare schedules, collection/delivery
- Dietary or medical requirements

Finance and Accounts:

- Customer invoices, outstanding debts
- Sales reports to assist with sales tax returns
- Sales forecasts by detail or summarised by period
- Payments received between specified dates
- Payments received by payment type (e.g.cash, cheque)
- Handle dual sales taxes such as VAT, HST, GST, PST

Marketing:

- Customer lists (select specific customers for mailings, special offers, Christmas cards, announcements etc)
- Ability to include your logo and contact details
- Ability to design your own letters, contracts, cards, invoices etc to cut down on stationery costs

Ease of Use:

- Easy view of cat/owner details and photos to re-familiarise yourself with customers
- Easy 'point & click' assignment of cats to units
- Easily manage cats that require isolation
- Easy view of categorised runs and availability
- Easily produce a 'stand-by' list - e.g. take details for bookings turned away, and this list is searched when you cancel another booking, notifying you of matches, helping you to maximise your occupancy and turnover
- Easily export data to other applications (e.g.accounts)

PETADMIN

PetAdmin is the software management package designed to meet the requirements of any business where where animals require boarding and associated services.

Our customers are worldwide (from the UK, Eire, Spain, South Africa, Australia and the USA), successfully using PetAdmin to save themselves costs, time and effort and to enhance the image of their business to customers.

Download a trial copy of PetAdmin from our website or contact us to be sent a trial CD to try out at home!

We can assist and advise you on most aspects of IT and your other technology requirements including web or site cameras. A Network IP Camera is a stand-alone device which simply connects to your existing PC network and allows live, full motion video on your computer network, or over the Internet. These versatile devices can be used as webcams to feed images to your website, or for replacing traditional CCTV systems.

Please download a trial copy of PetAdmin from our website, and contact Chris Wye to discuss requirements for your own cattery bookings program.

PetAdmin, Woodhouse Technology Ltd, Woodhouse, Woodhouse Lane, Little Waltham, Chelmsford, Essex, CM3 3PW, UK. Tel: +44 (0)1245 362211

www.petadmin.com

CASE STUDY:
READY TO GO!

PRESTON HILLS CAT HOTEL

This impressive English Grade II Listed barn has been converted to a cattery and is just at the stage where the owners are piecing together all the information and photographs to start marketing their brand new business.

Owners Natalie and Nick Cross have already had experience running successful small businesses (Natalie runs two livery stables and Nick runs a landscaping and property maintenance business) and have always been very animal oriented. When they found their beautiful farm (which has stables and two of these impressive barns) in this quiet country location, they knew it would be an ideal place to concentrate on cats!

MAPS, DIRECTION AND SIGNS

With so much beautiful countryside around them, the map and directions to the business will need to be very clear to help customers along the winding country lanes. Natalie has started work on the signage for the property, which is at the end of a long, private lane – and have even been offered space for several advertising signs on a large roundabout with several exits (one leading to a major airport) at a very reasonable rate by the local authority.

UP AND RUNNING

With the UPVC cat units just having been installed by Pedigree Pens, they are starting to take bookings and get the business up and running in earnest. Every cat pen is double-sized, and there are even innovative 'removable' panels (which you can see in the photograph below right) so that 2 double units can be joined together to make a super-sized pen, which provides flexibility for a cat family or very active cats.

SO MUCH TO DO!

There is so much to do when you first start up – Natalie is focusing on getting the website built, and the marketing brochures and material ready. A welcoming answer phone message needs to be written and recorded, and they have already taken out radio advertising and given leaflets to the local veterinary surgeries, which is how they got their first bookings! It is extremely important to the couple to provide a highly personal, caring service which is extremely professional, and so their next step is to purchase a booking software programme to help them achieve this.

We wish them great luck in their exciting new cattery venture!

Organisation:	Preston Hills Cat Hotel
Location:	UK, Hertfordshire
Cattery Type:	Semi-outdoor
Cattery Function:	Boarding
Number of Units:	10
Unit Size Sleep:	1220 x 1220mm (4ft x 4ft)
Unit Size Exercise:	1220 x 1830mm (4ft x 6ft)
Date Built:	2006

www.prestonhillscathotel.co.uk

WE WISH THIS BRAND NEW, SMALL BOARDING CATTERY BUSINESS GREAT SUCCESS AND MET THE OWNERS JUST AS THEY WERE STARTING TO PUT TOGETHER ALL THEIR MARKETING, BROCHURES AND WEBSITE

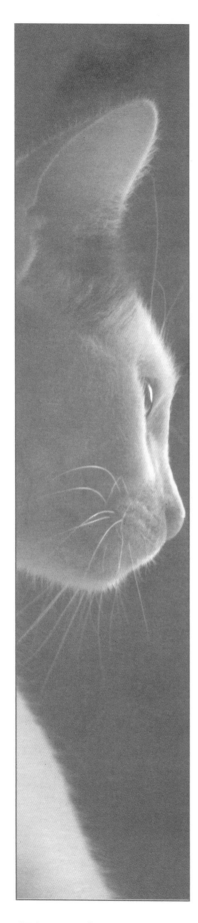

CASE STUDIES

REFERENCES

ORGANISATIONS

Feline Advisory Bureau	www.fabcats.org
Cats Protection UK	www.cats.org.uk
Humane Society of the United States	www.hsus.org
Association of Pet Behaviour Counsellors	www.apbc.org.uk
International Fund for Animal Welfare	www.ifaw.org
Universities Fund for Animal Welfare	www.ufaw.org.uk
Governing Council of the Cat Fancy UK	www.gccfcats.org
The Cat Fanciers' Association, Inc USA	www.cfa.org
The International Cat Association	www.tica.org
American Cat Fanciers' Association	www.acfacats.com
Cat Fanciers' Federation	www.cffinc.org

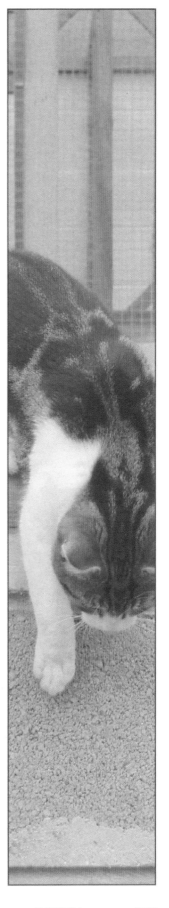

BOOKS

Cat Confidential	Vicky Halls
Cat Detective	Vicky Halls
What is my Cat Thinking?	Gwen Bailey
Boarding Cattery Manual	Claire Bessant
Rescue Cattery Manual	Anne Haughie
The Emotional Life of Cats	Nadine Gourkow BCSPCA
The Welfare of Cats	Irene Rochlitz
The Domestic Cat	Dennis C Turner & Patrick Bateson
The Behaviour of the Domestic Cat	John Bradshaw

QUOTATIONS

My

other

cat

is

a

Jaguar!

Anonymous

YOU ARE ALWAYS WELCOME TO VISIT US FOR MORE INSPIRATION @ WWW.CATTERYDESIGN.COM